THE NEW CROCHET
STITCH DICTIONARY

STACKPOLE BOOKS

An imprint of The Globe Pequot Publishing Group, Inc.
64 South Main Street
Essex, CT 06426
www.globepequot.com

Distributed by NATIONAL BOOK NETWORK
800-462-6420

The original German edition was published as *Häkelmuster*.
Copyright © 2018 frechverlag GmbH, Stuttgart, Germany (www.topp-kreativ.de)
This edition is published by arrangement with Claudia Böhme Rights & Literary Agency, Hannover, Germany (www.agency-boehme.com)

THANK YOU!
We would like to thank company MEZ gmbh (www.mezcrafts.com) for providing yarn support for this book.
PHOTOS: frechverlag gmbh, 70499 Stuttgart; lichtpunkt, Michael Ruder, Stuttgart
PRODUCT MANAGEMENT: Mareike Upheber, Franziska Schmidt
EDITING: Regina Sidabras, Berlin
GRAPHIC DESIGN: Petra Theilfarth
TRANSLATION: Katharina Sokiran

British Library Cataloguing in Publication Information available

Library of Congress Cataloging-in-Publication Data available

Names: Braas, Nele, author. | Hetty-Burkart, Eveline, author.
Title: The new crochet stitch dictionary : 440 patterns for textures,
    shells, bobbles, lace, cables, chevrons, edgings, granny squares, and
    more / Nele Braas, Eveline Hetty-Burkart.
Other titles: Häkelmuster. English.
Description: First edition. | Lanham, MD : Stackpole Books, an imprint of
    The Rowman & Littlefield Publishing Group, [2021] | "The original German
    edition was published as Häkelmuster"— title page verso. | Summary:
    "This is the ultimate collection of crochet stitch inspiration! 440
    stitches are presented, each with a sample swatch of the fabric and
    charted instructions. Divided into ten chapters, this collection boast a
    great variety of stitches, well organized and presented in an
    easy-to-use fashion"— Provided by publisher.
Identifiers: LCCN 2020010349 (print) | LCCN 2020010350 (ebook) | ISBN
    9780811738699 (paperback) | ISBN 9780811768672 (epub)
Subjects: LCSH: Knitting—Patterns. | Crocheting—Patterns.
Classification: LCC TT820 .B71813 2021 (print) | LCC TT820 (ebook) | DDC
    746.43/4041—dc23
LC record available at https://lccn.loc.gov/2020010349
LC ebook record available at https://lccn.loc.gov/2020010350

♾™ The paper used in this publication meets the minimum requirements of American National Standard for Information Sciences—Permanence of Paper for Printed Library Materials, ANSI/NISO Z39.48-1992.

First Edition

NELE BRAAS · EVELINE HETTY-BURKART

THE NEW CROCHET
STITCH DICTIONARY

If you have been drawn in by the allure of crocheting, you've chosen just the right book! Using only a few basic stitches, a multitude of fascinating stitch patterns have been compiled for you, waiting to be turned into awesome crochet projects fueled by your imagination.

This collection contains 440 stitch patterns, providing wonderful pattern suggestions for simple crochet projects, as well as challenging and sophisticated ideas for master crocheters.

The book is divided into eleven chapters—ten stitch pattern chapters and one chapter with crochet basics for reference when working with this book.

To classify the different stitch pattern types, and make orientation within the book easier, every stitch pattern chapter is presented in its own color scheme.

Well-known classics and traditional crochet stitches are supplemented by many newly created stitch patterns. Feel inspired by this indispensable reference work. Plan your upcoming projects and create your very own crochet design.

CONTENTS

BASIC STITCH PATTERNS

Variations with Basic Stitches

001 SLIP STITCH RIDGES

+1 → [any st ct + 1 beg-ch]

Work in rows, following the chart. Work Rows 1–4 once, and then repeat Rows 3 and 4 for pattern.

Chart Key

○ Chain 1

● 1 slip stitch into the slip stitch of the previous row, which is tilted toward the back

♣ 1 slip stitch through the back loop of the beginning chains only

002 V-RIDGE LOOK

+1 → [any st ct + 1 beg-ch]

Work in rows, following the chart. Work Rows 1–3 once, and then repeat Rows 2 and 3 for pattern.

Chart Key

○ Chain 1

♣ 1 slip stitch through the back loop of the beginning chains only, and from Row 2 on, through the back loop of the slip stitches of the previous row only, which are tilted toward the back and pointing upward

003 KNIT-LOOK GARTER STITCH

+1 → [any st ct + 1 beg-ch]

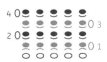

Work in rows, following the chart. Work Rows 1–4 once, and then repeat Rows 3 and 4 for pattern.

Chart Key

○ Chain 1

♣ 1 slip stitch through the back loop of the beginning chains only

● 1 slip stitch through the front loop only, which is located directly at the edge of the crocheted piece and pointing upward

004 CORD-LOOK TEXTURE

+1 [any st ct + beg-ch]

Work in rows, following the chart. Work Rows 1–4 once, and then repeat Rows 3 and 4 for pattern.

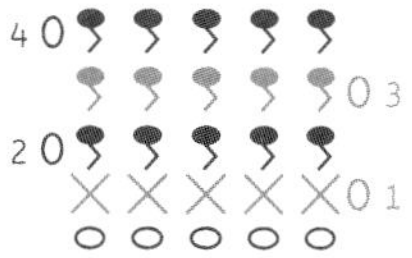

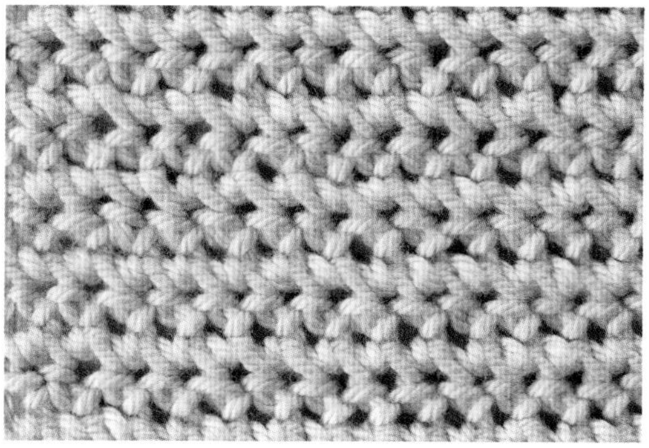

Chart Key

- Chain 1
- 1 single crochet
- 1 twisted slip stitch: Insert hook from back to front underneath the back and front loops, with working yarn located behind the crochet hook. Draw the working yarn through and immediately pull it through the loop on the hook. The stitch will turn out twisted.

005 FLAT SINGLE CROCHETS

+1 [any st ct + 2 beg-ch]

Work in rows, following the chart. Work Rows 1–3 once, and then repeat Rows 2 and 3 for pattern.

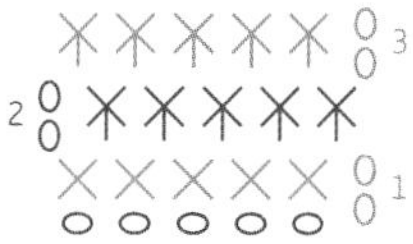

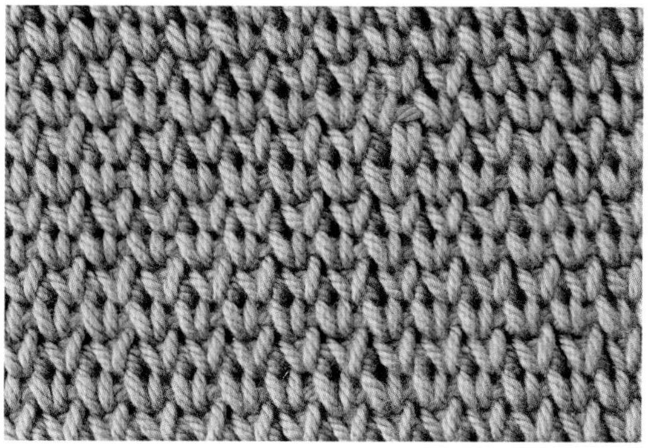

Chart Key

- Chain 1
- 1 single crochet
- 1 flat single crochet: Insert the hook into the body of the single crochet of the previous row, directly underneath the horizontal loop located under the loop of the stitch—this spot is between 2 strands of the stitch that are converging like the legs of an upside-down V. Draw the working yarn through the two loops on the hook to finish working the single crochet.

006 BROAD SLIP STITCH RIDGES

+1 [any st ct + 1 beg-ch]

Work in rows, following the chart. Row 1 is a WS row. Work Rows 1–4 once, and then repeat Rows 3 and 4 for pattern.

The more loosely the slip stitches are worked, the easier it will be to insert the hook into the stitch. For Row 1 with single crochets, use a smaller hook size to prevent the edge from stretching.

In the final row of the crocheted piece, work regular slip stitches.

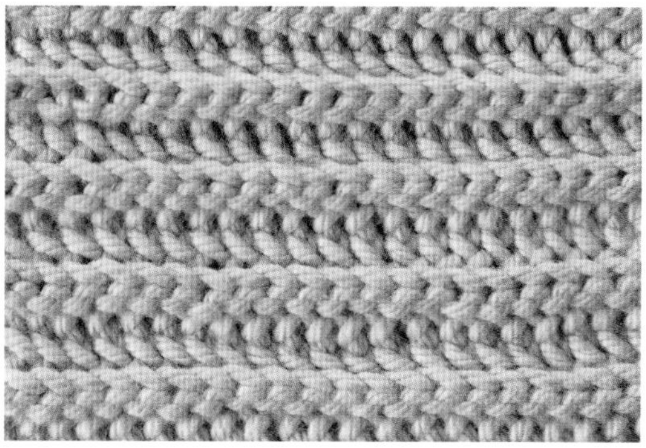

Chart Key

- Chain 1
- 1 single crochet
- 1 twisted slip stitch through the back loop only: Insert hook from back to front under the back loop, with working yarn located behind the crochet hook. (Tip: First grasp the back loop with the tip of the hook from below, and then insert the hook all the way through to the front.) Draw the working yarn through and immediately pull it through the loop on the hook. The stitch will turn out twisted.

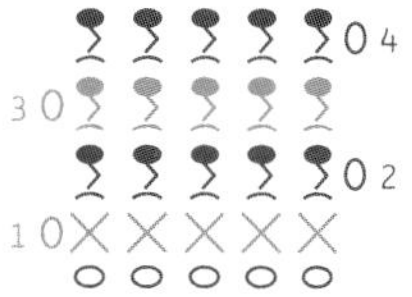

007 RIDGED LINES
[any st ct + 1 beg-ch]

Work in rows, following the chart. Work Rows 1–3 once, and then repeat Rows 2 and 3 for pattern.

Chart Key

○ Chain 1

✕ 1 single crochet

✕ Flo-sc: 1 single crochet through the front loop only

✕ Blo-sc: 1 single crochet through the back loop only

008 CURLY STRIPES
[odd st ct + 1 beg-ch]

Work in rows, following the chart. Work Rows 1–3 once, and then repeat Rows 2 and 3 for pattern.

Chart Key

○ Chain 1

✕ 1 single crochet

✕ Flo-sc: 1 single crochet through the front loop only

✕ Blo-sc: 1 single crochet through the back loop only

009 SINGLE CROCHET RIDGES
[any st ct + 1 beg-ch]

Work in rows, following the chart. Work Rows 1–3 once, and then repeat Rows 2 and 3 for pattern.

Chart Key

○ Chain 1

✕ 1 single crochet

✕ Blo-sc: 1 single crochet through the back loop only

010 HORIZONTAL V-STITCH RIDGES

[any st ct + 1 beg-ch]

Work in rows, following the chart. Work Rows 1–4 once, and then repeat Rows 3 and 4 for pattern.

Chart Key

o   Chain 1   ✕   1 single crochet

✕   1 single crochet, inserting the hook the following way: On the right side of the fabric, insert the hook through the horizontal loop underneath the front loop of the stitch with the crochet hook from the bottom to the top, draw the working yarn through, and then finish working the single crochet.

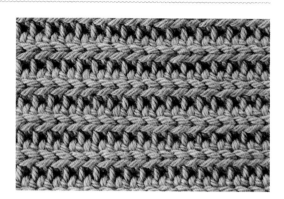

011 STAGGERED HALF DOUBLE CROCHETS

[any st ct + 2 beg-ch]

Work in rows, following the chart. Work Rows 1–3 once, and then repeat Rows 2 and 3 for pattern.

    From Row 2 on, half double crochets are worked in the space between half double crochets of the previous row; the last half double crochet of every row is worked between the half double crochet and the turning chain.

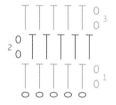

Chart Key

o   Chain 1

╥   1 half double crochet

012 RIDGES WITH HALF DOUBLE CROCHETS

[any st ct + 2 beg-ch]

Work in rows, following the chart. Work Rows 1–4 once, and then repeat Rows 3 and 4 for pattern.

Chart Key

o   Chain 1

╥   1 half double crochet

╥   1 half double crochet, inserting the hook the following way: Yarn over hook once, on the right side of the fabric, insert the hook through the horizontal loop underneath the front loop of the stitch from the bottom to the top, draw the working yarn through, and then finish working the half double crochet.

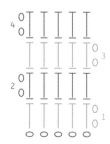

013 COMBINED STRIPES [any st ct + 3 beg-ch]

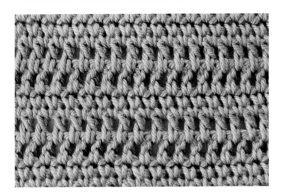

Work in rows, following the chart; Row 1 is a WS row. Work Rows 1–6 once, and then repeat Rows 3–6 for pattern.

In Rows 2 and 6, work the double crochets from the space between the double crochets of the previous row.

Chart Key

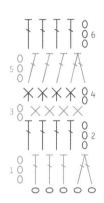

○ Chain 1   ✕ 1 single crochet

✕ 1 flat single crochet: Insert the hook into the body of the single crochet of the previous row, directly underneath the horizontal loop located under the loop of the stitch—this spot is between 2 strands of the stitch that are converging like the legs of an upside-down V. Draw the working yarn through, and then finish working the single crochet.

┃ 1 double crochet   ⋀ Dc2tog: Double crochet 2 stitches together

014 KNOT STITCH IN ROWS [any st ct + 1 beg-ch]

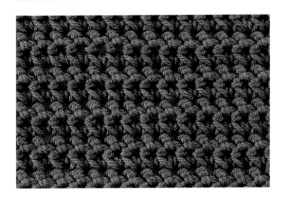

Work in rows, following the chart. Work Rows 1–4 once, and then repeat Rows 3 and 4 for pattern.

To make a knot stitch, crochet 2 adjoining single crochets together. For every subsequent knot stitch, insert the hook first into the second insertion point of the previous knot stitch. From Row 2 on, always work the single crochet at the end of the row into the second insertion point of the last knot stitch.

Chart Key

○ Chain 1
✕ 1 single crochet
⋀ Sc2tog: Single crochet two stitches together

015 KNOTTED DOUBLE CROCHET [any st ct + 2 beg-ch]

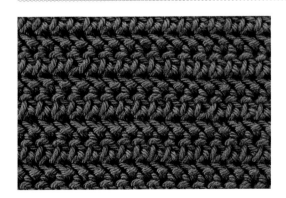

Work in rows, following the chart. Work Rows 1–3 once, and then repeat Rows 2 and 3 for pattern.

Since knotted double crochet has less height than regular double crochet, 2 turning chains (beginning chains) are sufficient.

Chart Key

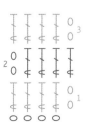

○ Chain 1

┃ 1 knotted double crochet: Yarn over hook once, insert hook, draw the working yarn through, and, directly afterward, pull it through the first loop on the hook, too. Now, crochet the 2 loops on the hook off together.

016 KNOTTED HALF DOUBLE CROCHET

[any st ct + 1 beg-ch]

Work in rows, following the chart. Work Rows 1–3 once, and then repeat Rows 2 and 3 for pattern.

Since knotted half double crochet has less height than regular half double crochet, 1 turning chain (beg-ch) is sufficient.

Chart Key

○ Chain 1 ⨯ 1 single crochet

⊤⫠ 1 knotted half double crochet: Yarn over hook once, insert hook through stitch and draw the working yarn through all 3 loops on hook

017 TWISTED SINGLE CROCHET

[any st ct + 1 beg-ch]

Work in rows, following the chart. Work Rows 1–3 once, and then repeat Rows 2 and 3 for pattern.

Chart Key

○ Chain 1 ⨯ 1 single crochet

⊗ 1 twisted single crochet: Insert the hook from the back to the front into the stitch (i.e., the hook goes through under both loops, with the working yarn behind the hook). Draw the working yarn through, and then pull it out to the height of the working loop. Crochet the 2 loops on the hook off together as for a regular single crochet.

018 TWISTED SINGLE CROCHET, MODIFICATION

[any st ct + 1 beg-ch]

Work in rows, following the chart. Work Rows 1–3 once, and then repeat Rows 2 and 3 for pattern.

Chart Key

○ Chain 1 ⨯ 1 single crochet

⨉⟩ 1 twisted single crochet: Bring the hook behind the working yarn. Now, insert the hook into the stitch from back to front (i.e., the hook goes through under both loops, with the working yarn in front of the hook). Draw the working yarn through, and then pull it out to the height of the working loop. Crochet the 2 loops on the hook off together as for a regular single crochet.

019 TWISTED HALF DOUBLE CROCHET

[any st ct + 2 beg-ch]

Work in rows, following the chart. Work Rows 1–3 once, and then repeat Rows 2 and 3 for pattern.

Chart Key

○ Chain 1

T 1 half double crochet

1 twisted half double crochet: Yarn over hook once, insert the hook into the stitch from back to front (i.e., the hook goes through under both loops, with working yarn located behind the hook). Draw the working yarn through. Draw the working yarn through once more, pulling it through all 3 loops on the hook at once.

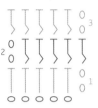

020 GRITTY ALLOVER PATTERN

[odd st ct + 1 beg-ch]

Work in rows, following the chart. Work Rows 1–5 once, and then repeat Rows 2–5 for pattern.

Chart Key

○ Chain 1   ✕ 1 single crochet

1 twice extended single crochet: Insert the hook into the stitch, draw the working yarn through. * Draw the working yarn through once more, pulling it through the first loop on the hook; repeat from * once. Draw the working yarn through again, pulling it through the 2 loops on the hook. As soon as the next single crochet has been completed, the resulting chain of stitches will fold over forward.

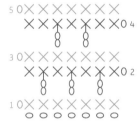

021 ZIGZAG PATTERN

[any st ct + 2 beg-ch]

Work in rows, following the chart. Work Rows 1–3 once, and then repeat Rows 2 and 3 for pattern.

In Row 2, the elongated single crochets are always worked into the body of the previous row stitch. For this, insert the hook directly underneath the horizontal loop located under the top loop of the stitch. The last stitch of the row is worked between the last elongated single crochet of the previous row and the turning chain.

In Row 3, the elongated single crochets are worked into the stitch of the previous row.

Chart Key

○ Chain 1

1 elongated single crochet: Insert the hook into the stitch, draw the working yarn through. Draw the working yarn through once more, pulling it through the first loop on the hook. Draw the working yarn through both loops on the hook.

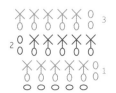

022 STAGGERED MESH PATTERN

[odd st ct + 2 beg-ch]

Work in rows, following the chart. Work Rows 1–3 once, and then repeat Rows 2 and 3 for pattern.

In Rows 2 and 3, always work the elongated single crochet in the chain space of the previous row, around the chain.

Chart Key

○ Chain 1

✗ 1 elongated single crochet: Insert the hook into the stitch, draw the working yarn through. Yarn over, draw through the first loop on the hook; yarn over, pull it through both loops on the hook.

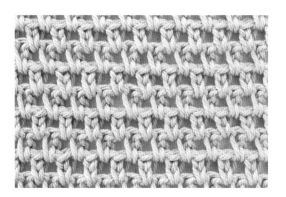

023 HERRINGBONE PATTERN

[any st ct + 2 beg-ch]

Work in rows, following the chart. Work Rows 1–3 once, and then repeat Rows 2 and 3 for pattern.

For this stitch type, an elongated single crochet is combined with a yarn over hook once, which will drape itself around the base of the stitch when crocheted off. At the end of the row, work the combined stitch around the turning chain.

Chart Key

○ Chain 1

✗ 1 combined stitch: Yarn over hook once, insert the hook into the stitch, draw the working yarn through, and directly afterward pull it through the first loop on the hook, too. Yarn over the hook; pull it through the first loop on the hook. Yarn over the hook, and now, pull it through both loops on the hook.

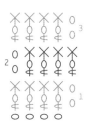

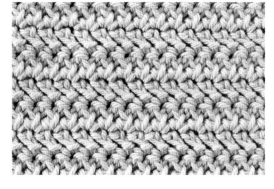

024 SWIRL PATTERN

[odd st ct + 1 beg-ch]

Work in rows, following the chart. Begin every row with the stitches before the pattern repeat, repeat the marked pattern repeat (2 stitches wide) widthwise, and end with the stitches after the pattern repeat. Work Rows 1–3 once, and then repeat Rows 2 and 3 for pattern.

Chart Key

○ Chain 1

✗ 1 single crochet

✗ Flo-sc: 1 single crochet through the front loop only

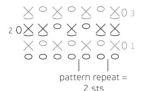

pattern repeat = 2 sts

025 PEARL EYELETS [odd st ct + 1 beg-ch]

Work in rows, following the chart. Work Rows 1–3 once, and then repeat Rows 2 and 3 for pattern.

Chart Key

○ Chain 1

✕ 1 single crochet

≍ Work 1 single crochet into the chain, inserting the hook under the back loop of the chain and the horizontal ridge

026 ALLOVER TEXTURE [odd st ct + 3 beg-ch]

Work in rows, following the chart. Begin every row with the stitches before the pattern repeat, repeat the marked pattern repeat (2 sts wide) widthwise, and end with the stitches after the pattern repeat. Work Rows 1–3 once, and then repeat Rows 2 and 3 for pattern.

Chart Key

○ Chain 1

● 1 slip stitch

| 1 double crochet

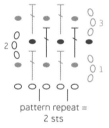

pattern repeat = 2 sts

027 LITTLE COMBS [odd st ct + 1 beg-ch]

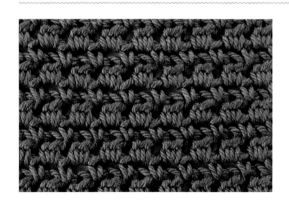

Work in rows, following the chart. Begin every row with the stitches before the pattern repeat, repeat the marked pattern repeat (2 sts wide) widthwise, and end with the stitches after the pattern repeat. Work Rows 1–3 once, and then repeat Rows 2 and 3 for pattern.

In Row 2, always work 2 half double crochets in the chain space of the previous row, around the chain. In Row 3, work the single crochets between pairs of half double crochet.

Chart Key

○ Chain 1

✕ 1 single crochet

| 1 half double crochet

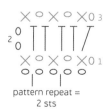

pattern repeat = 2 sts

028 BLOCK MESH

[multiple of 3 + 1 beg-ch]

Work in rows, following the chart. Begin every row with the stitches before the pattern repeat, repeat the marked pattern repeat (3 sts wide) widthwise, and end with the stitches after the pattern repeat. Work Rows 1–4 once, and then repeat Rows 3 and 4 for pattern. In Row 3, always work 3 single crochets in the chain space of the previous row, around the chain. In Row 4, work the single crochet into the first and last single crochet of the group of 3.

Chart Key

○ Chain 1

✕ 1 single crochet

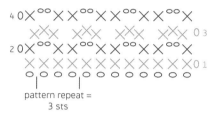

pattern repeat =
3 sts

029 STAGGERED BLOCK MESH

[multiple of 3 + 1 beg-ch]

Work in rows, following the chart. Begin every row with the stitches before the pattern repeat, repeat the marked pattern repeat (3 sts wide) widthwise, and end with the stitches after the pattern repeat. Work Rows 1–3 once, and then repeat Rows 2 and 3 for pattern. In Rows 2 and 3, always work 2 single crochets in the chain space of the previous row, around the chain.

Chart Key

○ Chain 1

✕ 1 single crochet

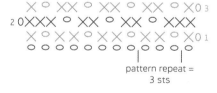

pattern repeat =
3 sts

030 RIDGES AND BANDS

[multiple of 6 + 3 beg-ch]

Work in rows, following the chart. Begin every row with the stitches before the pattern repeat, repeat the marked pattern repeat (6 sts wide) widthwise, and end with the stitches after the pattern repeat. Work Rows 1–3 once, and then repeat Rows 2 and 3 for pattern.

Chart Key

○ Chain 1

● Blo-sl st: 1 slip stitch through the back loop only

| 1 double crochet

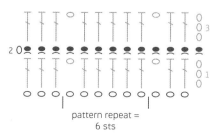

pattern repeat =
6 sts

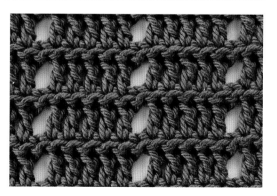

031 WAVES AND FURROWS

[odd st ct + 2 beg-ch]

Work in rows, following the chart. Begin every row with the stitches before the pattern repeat, repeat the marked pattern repeat (2 sts wide) widthwise, and end with the stitches after the pattern repeat. Work Rows 1–3 once, and then repeat Rows 2 and 3 for pattern.

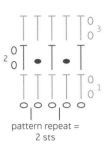

pattern repeat = 2 sts

Chart Key

○ Chain 1
● 1 slip stitch
⊤ 1 half double crochet

032 SIMPLE TEXTURED PATTERN

[even st ct + 1 beg-ch]

Work in rows, following the chart. Begin every row with the stitches before the pattern repeat, repeat the marked pattern repeat (2 sts wide) widthwise, and end with the stitches after the pattern repeat. Work Rows 1–3 once, and then repeat Rows 2 and 3 for pattern.

Chart Key

○ Chain 1
✕ 1 single crochet
⊤ 1 double crochet

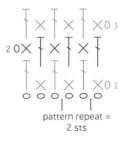

pattern repeat = 2 sts

033 DOUBLE CROCHET TRIO

[multiple of 4 + 1 ch + 1 beg-ch]

Work in rows, following the chart. Begin every row with the stitches before the pattern repeat, repeat the marked pattern repeat (4 sts wide) widthwise, and end with the stitches after the pattern repeat. Work Rows 1–3 once, and then repeat Rows 2 and 3 for pattern.

Chart Key

○ Chain 1
✕ 1 single crochet
⊤ 1 half double crochet
 [1 half double crochet, 1 double crochet, 1 half double crochet] into the same stitch
 [1 half double crochet, 1 double crochet] into the same stitch

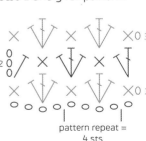

pattern repeat = 4 sts

034 STAGGERED PAIRED STITCHES

[multiple of 4 + 3 ch + 1 beg-ch]

Work in rows, following the chart. Begin every row with the stitches before the pattern repeat, repeat the marked pattern repeat (4 sts wide) widthwise, and end with the stitches after the pattern repeat. Work Rows 1–3 once, and then repeat Rows 2 and 3 for pattern.

From Row 2 on, always work single crochets between pairs of double crochets, always work double crochets into the first single crochet of a single crochet pair.

Chart Key

o   Chain 1

✗   1 single crochet

\2/   Sc2-in-1: 2 single crochets into the same stitch

V   Dc2-in-1: 2 double crochets into the same stitch

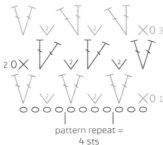

pattern repeat =
4 sts

035 FISH SCALE PATTERN

[even st ct + 1 beg-ch]

Work in rows, following the chart. Begin every row with the stitches before the pattern repeat, repeat the marked pattern repeat (2 sts wide) widthwise, and end with the stitches after the pattern repeat. Work Rows 1–3 once, and then repeat Rows 2 and 3 for pattern.

The treble crochets worked in WS rows will bulge out toward the back, which makes them pop out on the right side of the fabric.

Chart Key

o   Chain 1

●   1 slip stitch

✗   1 single crochet

\2/   Sc2-in-1: 2 single crochets into the same stitch

┬   1 treble crochet

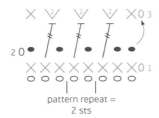

pattern repeat =
2 sts

036 SHALLOW NUPP PATTERN

[multiple of 4 + 3 ch + 1 beg-ch]

Work in rows, following the chart. Begin every row with the stitches before the pattern repeat, repeat the marked pattern repeat (4 sts wide) widthwise, and end with the stitches after the pattern repeat. Work Rows 1–5 once, and then repeat Rows 2–5 for pattern. In Rows 3 and 5, only 1 single crochet is worked atop the sequence of [1 single crochet, 1 double crochet, 1 single crochet]; it is always worked into the single crochet after the double crochet.

Chart Key

○   Chain 1

✕   1 single crochet

↓   Group of stitches: [1 single crochet, 1 double crochet, 1 single crochet] into the same stitch

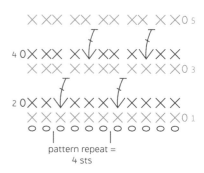

pattern repeat = 4 sts

037 STAGGERED TRIPLETS

[multiple of 3 + 1 ch + 1 beg-ch]

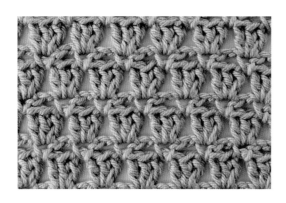

Work in rows, following the chart; Row 1 is a WS row. Begin every row with the stitches before the pattern repeat, repeat the marked pattern repeat (3 sts wide) widthwise, and end with the stitches after the pattern repeat. Work Rows 1–5 once, and then repeat Rows 2–5 for pattern.

In Rows 3 and 5, the single crochet is worked between groups of double crochets.

Chart Key

○   Chain 1

✕   1 single crochet

†   1 double crochet

⋁   Dc2-in-1: 2 double crochets into the same stitch

⋁   Dc3-in-1: 3 double crochets into the same stitch

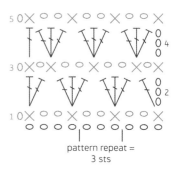

pattern repeat = 3 sts

038 LITTLE LATTICE
[odd st ct + 1 beg-ch]

Work in rows, following the chart. Work Rows 1–3 once, and then repeat Rows 2 and 3 for pattern.

Chart Key

o Chain 1
X 1 single crochet

039 ZIGZAG ROWS
[odd st ct + 3 beg-ch]

Work in rows, following the chart. Work Rows 1–3 once, and then repeat Rows 2 and 3 for pattern.

Chart Key

o Chain 1

ꞁ 1 double crochet

Ʌ Dc2tog: Double crochet 2 stitches together

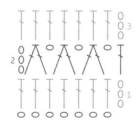

040 BROAD HORIZONTAL RIDGES
[any st ct + 2 beg-ch]

Work in rows, following the chart. Work Rows 1–3 once, and then repeat Rows 2 and 3 for pattern.

Chart Key

o Chain 1

• Blo-sl st: 1 slip stitch through the back loop only

ꞁ 1 half double crochet

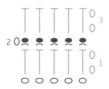

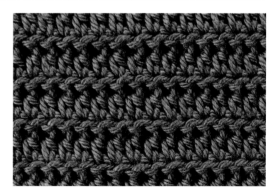

041 BUD PATTERN

[even or odd st ct + 1 beg-ch]

Work in rows, following Crochet Chart 1 (or 2). Work Rows 1–3 once, and then repeat Rows 2 and 3 for pattern.

Always work both the single crochet and the double crochet together into 1 chain of the beginning chain, and from Row 2 on, work into every double crochet of the previous row.

Working the stitch pattern from Crochet Chart 1 (odd stitch count) results in wavy side edges. Working from Crochet Chart 2 (even stitch count) will give you straight side edges.

Chart Key

o Chain 1

✕ 1 single crochet

丅 1 double crochet

⅄ Dc2tog: Double crochet 2 stitches together

Crochet Chart 1   Crochet Chart 2

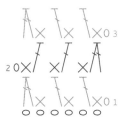

042 SLING RIDGES

[any st ct + 1 beg-ch]

Work in rows, following the chart. Work Rows 1–4 once, and then repeat Rows 3 and 4 for pattern.

From Row 2 on, 1 half double crochet and 1 single crochet are always crocheted together. The entry point for each half double crochet will be the last point of entry of the single crochet of the stitch before.

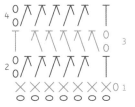

Chart Key

o Chain 1

✕ 1 single crochet

丅 1 half double crochet

⅄ 1 half double crochet and 1 single crochet crocheted together: Yarn over hook once, insert the hook into the stitch of the previous row, and pull a loop through; during the next stitch, pull another loop through, then yarn over and pull it through all 4 loops on the hook at once.

043 HORIZONTAL RIDGES WITH EYELETS [odd st ct + 3 beg-ch]

Work in rows, following the chart. Work Rows 1–5 once, and then repeat Rows 2–5 for pattern.

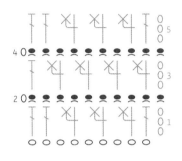

Chart Key

○   Chain 1

   Blo-sl st: 1 slip stitch through the back loop only

   1 double crochet

   1 double crochet with attached single crochet: Work 1 double crochet, and then work 1 single crochet into the middle of the double crochet. To make the single crochet, insert the hook into the diagonal loop and the vertical strand of the stitch at the bottom left of the double crochet, pull the working yarn through, and crochet the two loops on the hook off together.

044 JOINED DOUBLE CROCHETS [odd st ct + 3 beg-ch]

Work in rows, following the chart. Work Rows 1–3 once, and then repeat Rows 2 and 3 for pattern.

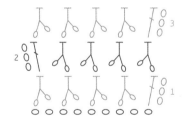

Chart Key

○   Chain 1

   1 double crochet

   1 joined double crochet: With the crochet hook, insert the hook into the vertical strand of the stitch at the bottom left of the previously worked double crochet, pull the working yarn through, and then chain 1. In subsequent stitches in the first row, insert the hook, the second time skipping 1 chain of the beginning chain, pull the working yarn through, and then chain 1. Draw the working yarn through all 3 loops on the hook at once.

     In Rows 2 and 3, after the first double crochet, continue to work 1 joined double crochet into each double crochet of the previous row.

045 SEPARATED BOXES

[multiple of 4 + 1 ch + 2 beg-ch]

Work in rows, following the chart; Row 1 is a WS row. Begin every row with the stitches before the pattern repeat, repeat the marked pattern repeat (4 sts wide) widthwise; end with the stitches after the pattern repeat. Work Rows 1–3 once, and then repeat Rows 2 and 3 for pattern.

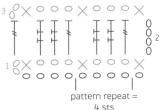

pattern repeat =
4 sts

Chart Key

○ Chain 1

✕ 1 single crochet

╎ 1 treble crochet

1 joined treble crochet: Insert hook into the upper, diagonal loop of the previous treble crochet, and then pull the working yarn through. Insert hook into the diagonal loop at the bottom of the treble crochet, and then pull the working yarn through again. Insert hook into the next chain of the previous row, and then pull the working yarn through. There are 4 loops on the hook now. Grasping the working yarn and pulling it through every time, crochet 2 loops off together, 3 times in all. The first joined treble crochet has been completed. For the second joined treble crochet, work into the top and bottom horizontal loops of the preceding one.

046 TEXTURED LATTICE

[even st ct + 1 beg-ch]

Front of work

Back of work

Work in rows, following the chart; Row 1 is a WS row. Work Rows 1–3 once, and then repeat Rows 2 and 3 for pattern.

In the back of the work, the vertical strands of the stitch are visible, which gives the pattern a linear structure.

Chart Key

○ Chain 1

✕ 1 single crochet

Sc2tog-ext: 2 single crochets crocheted together plus extension: Pull the loops from 2 stitches of the previous row through, and then draw the working yarn through 2 loops on the hook; then, to add the extension, draw the working yarn through the remaining 2 loops to finish.

1 elongated single crochet: Insert hook into the stitch, draw the working yarn through. Draw the working yarn through the first loop on the hook. Draw the working yarn through both loops on the hook.

047 BOW PATTERN

[odd st ct + 1 beg-ch]

Work in rows, following the chart. Work Rows 1–3 once, and then repeat Rows 2 and 3 for pattern.

Chart Key

o   Chain 1

✕   1 single crochet

⋀   3 single crochets crocheted together: Insert the hook and draw the working yarn through 3 stitches of the previous row, and then draw the working yarn through all 4 loops on the hook at once.

048 SLING ROOFTOPS

[odd st ct + 1 beg-ch]

Work in rows, following the chart; Row 1 is a WS row. Work Rows 1–4 once, and then repeat Rows 3 and 4 for pattern.

Chart Key

o   Chain 1

✕   1 single crochet

⋀   Sc3tog: Single crochet 3 stitches together: Insert the hook and draw the working yarn through 3 stitches of the previous row, and then draw the working yarn through all 4 loops on the hook at once. Pull the loops a little to elongate them until they've reached the same height.

T   1 half double crochet

049 STAGGERED PAIRED DOUBLE CROCHETS

[odd st ct + 3 beg-ch]

Work in rows, following the chart. Work Rows 1–3 once, and then repeat Rows 2 and 3 for pattern.

Always insert the hook under the front and back loop of the chain (or the shared top loop of the pair of double crochets of the previous row).

The side edges of this stitch pattern will be wavy.

Chart Key

o   Chain 1

| 1 double crochet

⋀   Dc2tog: Double crochet 2 stitches together

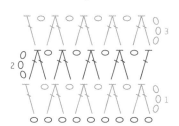

050 KNOT PATTERN

[odd st ct + 2 beg-ch]

Work in rows, following the chart. Work Rows 1–3 once, and then repeat Rows 2 and 3 for pattern.

In Rows 2 and 3, to work the single crochet decreases, always insert the hook before and after a pair of single crochets.

Chart Key

○ Chain 1

✕ 1 single crochet

⋀ Sc2tog: single crochet 2 stitches together into 1 stitch

051 DOUBLE CROCHET DUO

[odd st ct + 3 beg-ch]

Work in rows, following the chart. Work Rows 1–3 once, and then repeat Rows 2 and 3 for pattern.

Chart Key

○ Chain 1

| 1 double crochet

⋀ Dc2tog: Double crochet 2 stitches together

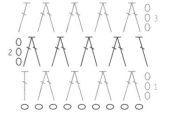

052 ZIGZAG LINES

[odd st ct + 2 beg-ch]

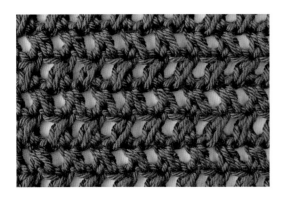

Work in rows, following the chart. Work Rows 1–3 once, and then repeat Rows 2 and 3 for pattern.

Chart Key

○ Chain 1

| 1 half double crochet

⋀ Hdc2tog: Half double crochet 2 stitches together

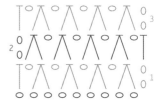

053 LITTLE TREE PATTERN

[odd st ct + 3 beg-ch]

Work in rows, following the chart. Work Rows 1–3 once, and then repeat Rows 2 and 3 for pattern.

Chart Key

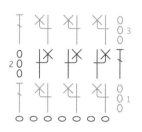

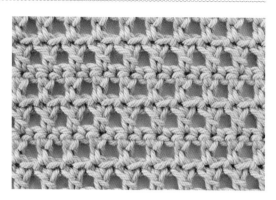

○ Chain 1

T 1 double crochet

1 double crochet with attached single crochet: Work 1 double crochet, and then work 1 single crochet in the middle of the double crochet. To make the single crochet, insert the hook into the diagonal loop and the vertical strand of the stitch at the bottom left of the double crochet with the crochet hook, and pull the working yarn through; then draw the working yarn through again, crocheting the two loops on the hook off together.

054 WAVY LINES

[multiple of 6 + 2 ch + 1 beg-ch]

Work in rows, following the chart. Begin every row with the stitches before the pattern repeat, repeat the marked pattern repeat (6 sts wide) widthwise, and end with the stitches after the pattern repeat. Work Rows 1–6 once, and then repeat Rows 3–6 for pattern.

The pronounced wavy lines on the right side of the crocheted fabric are receding into the background on the wrong side of work, creating a dimensional effect with oval shapes.

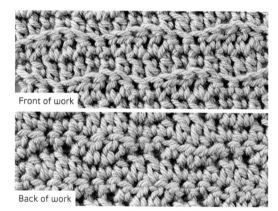

Front of work

Back of work

Chart Key

○ Chain 1

✕ 1 single crochet

✕ Blo-sc: 1 single crochet through the back loop only

T 1 half double crochet

T Blo-hdc: 1 half double crochet through the back loop only

T 1 double crochet

T Blo-dc: 1 double crochet through the back loop only

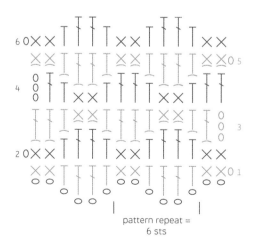

pattern repeat = 6 sts

055 SMALL TRIANGLE PATTERN

[even st ct + 1 beg-ch]

Work in rows, following the chart; Row 1 is a WS row. Work Rows 1–3 once, and then repeat Rows 2 and 3 for pattern.

In Row 3, always work the single crochets in the chain space of the previous row, around the chain.

Chart Key

○   Chain 1

✕   1 single crochet

$\top$ 1 half double crochet

$\wedge$ Hdc2tog: Half double crochet 2 stitches together

056 LITTLE BELLS

[even st ct + 1 beg-ch]

Work in rows, following the chart. Work Rows 1–3 once, and then repeat Rows 2 and 3 for pattern.

In Row 2, crochet together 1 single crochet and 1 half double crochet into single crochets of the previous row. In Row 3, work the single crochet in the chain space of the previous row, around the chain.

Chart Key

○   Chain 1

✕   1 single crochet

$\top$ 1 half double crochet

$\wedge$ 1 single crochet and 1 half double crochet crocheted together: Insert hook into the stitch of the previous row, and pull a loop through. Yarn over hook once, insert hook into the next stitch, and pull a loop through; then yarn over and pull it through all 4 loops on the hook at once.

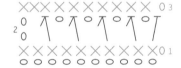

057 DOUBLE CROCHET VS

[multiple of 3 + 1 ch + 3 beg-ch]

Work in rows, following the chart. Begin every row with the stitches before the pattern repeat, repeat the marked pattern repeat (3 sts wide) widthwise, and end with the stitches after the pattern repeat. Work Rows 1–3 once, and then repeat Rows 2 and 3 for pattern. In Rows 2 and 3, work the pairs of double crochets between the two double crochets of the pairs of double crochets of the previous row.

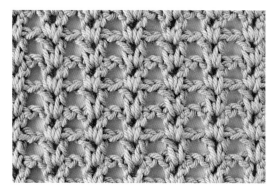

Chart Key

o   Chain 1

†   1 double crochet

V   Dc2-in-1: 2 double crochets into the same stitch

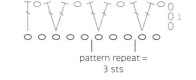

pattern repeat =
3 sts

058 STAGGERED DOUBLE CROCHET VS

[multiple of 2 + 3 beg-ch]

Work in rows, following the chart. Begin every row with the stitches before the pattern repeat, repeat the marked pattern repeat (2 sts wide) widthwise, and end with the stitches after the pattern repeat. Work Rows 1–3 once, and then repeat Rows 2 and 3 for pattern.

In Rows 2 and 3, work the pairs of double crochets between the pairs of double crochets of the previous row so that they end up staggered.

Chart Key

o   Chain 1

†   1 double crochet

V   Dc2-in-1: 2 double crochets into the same stitch

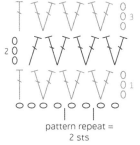

pattern repeat =
2 sts

059 THREE AND THREE STAGGERED

[multiple of 3 + 1 ch + 3 beg-ch]

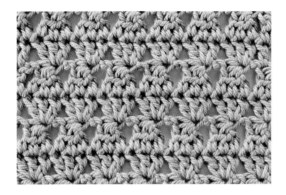

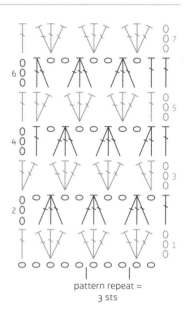

Chart Key

○	Chain 1
⊤	1 double crochet
V	Dc2-in-1: 2 double crochets into the same stitch
⋏	Dc2tog: Double crochet 2 stitches together
W	Dc3-in-1: 3 double crochets into the same stitch
⋏	Dc3tog: double crochet 3 stitches together into 1 stitch

Work in rows, following the chart. Begin every row with the stitches before the pattern repeat, repeat the marked pattern repeat (3 sts wide) widthwise, and end with the stitches after the pattern repeat. Work Rows 1–7 once, and then repeat Rows 2–7 for pattern.

pattern repeat = 3 sts

060 COMPACT TRIANGLES

[multiple of 4 + 1 ch + 4 beg-ch]

Work in rows, following the chart. Begin every row with the stitches before the pattern repeat, repeat the marked pattern repeat (4 sts wide) widthwise, and end with the stitches after the pattern repeat. Work Rows 1–4 once, and then repeat Rows 3 and 4 for pattern.

Chart Key

○	Chain 1
✕	1 single crochet
⊤	1 half double crochet
⊤	1 double crochet
⊤	1 treble crochet

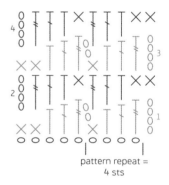

pattern repeat = 4 sts

Stitch Patterns in the **Round**

061 SINGLE CROCHETS

➡ [any st ct]

Work in rounds, following the chart. Join the beginning chain into the round by working 1 slip stitch into the first chain of the beginning chain. Work Rounds 1 and 2 once, and then repeat Round 2 for pattern. Since the hook is always inserted to the right of the body of the stitch, single crochets will end up slightly shifted to the right with every round worked.

Chart Key

○ Chain 1

● 1 slip stitch

✕ 1 single crochet

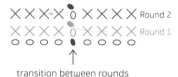

transition between rounds

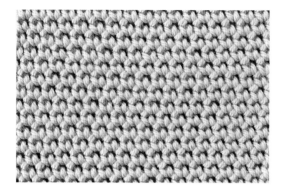

062 NARROW TEXTURED RIDGES

➡ [any st ct]

Work in rounds, following the chart. Join the beginning chain into the round by working 1 slip stitch into the first chain of the beginning chain. Work Rounds 1 and 2 once, and then repeat Round 2 for pattern.

Chart Key

○ Chain 1

● 1 slip stitch

✕ 1 single crochet

⋉ Blo-sc: 1 single crochet through the back loop only

transition between rounds

063 BOSNIAN CROCHET STITCH

➡ [any st ct]

Work from the chart in spiral rounds (i.e., do not join the end of the round to the beginning). The first stitch of the new round is worked immediately into the first stitch of the previous round, which results in a spiral course of the round. Work Rounds 1 and 2 once, and then repeat Round 2 for pattern. With every new round worked, stitches will slightly slant to the right.

Chart Key

○ Chain 1

● In Round 1, 1 slip stitch through the back loop only of the beginning chain; in Round 2, 1 slip stitch through the back loop only of the slip stitch of the previous round

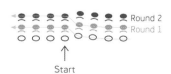

Start

064 KNOT STITCH IN THE ROUND
➡ [any st ct]

Work in rounds, following the chart. Join the beginning chain into the round by working 1 slip stitch into the first chain of the beginning chain. Work Rounds 1 and 2 once, and then repeat Round 2 for pattern.

Chart Key

○ Chain 1   ● 1 slip stitch

∧ 1 knot stitch: In Round 1, pull a loop through each of the next 2 stitches. Draw the working yarn through all 3 loops on the hook at once (= 2 single crochets crocheted off together). * For the next knot stitch, first insert the hook into the second insertion point of the preceding knot stitch, and pull 1 loop through; then insert the hook into the next chain, pull 1 loop through, and pull the working yarn through all 3 loops on the hook at once. Repeat from * throughout pattern. In Round 2, work the knot stitches into the stitches of the previous round; for the first knot stitch, pull the first loop through the same insertion point as the slip stitch.

Round 2
Round 1

transition between rounds

065 SMALL HERRINGBONE PATTERN
➡ [any st ct]

Work in rounds, following the chart. Join the beginning chain into the round by working 1 slip stitch into the first chain of the beginning chain. Work Rounds 1 and 2 once, and then repeat Round 2 for pattern.

Since knotted stitches have less height than regular double crochets, 2 beginning chains at the transition between rounds are sufficient.

Round 2

Round 1

transition between rounds

Chart Key

○ Chain 1
● 1 slip stitch

T‡ 1 knotted double crochet: Yarn over hook once, insert hook, draw the working yarn through, and then pull it through the first loop on the hook, too. Now, crochet the 2 loops on the hook off together.

066 MESH TREE PATTERN
➡ [multiple of 3]

Work in rounds, following the chart. Join the beginning chain into the round by working 1 slip stitch into the first chain of the beginning chain. In every round, first work the stitches before the pattern repeat, repeat the marked pattern repeat (3 sts wide) widthwise, and end with the stitches after the pattern repeat. Work Rounds 1 and 2 once, and then repeat Round 2 for pattern.

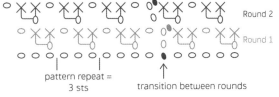

Round 2

Round 1

pattern repeat = 3 sts

transition between rounds

Chart Key

○ Chain 1   ● 1 slip stitch

✕✕ 1 elongated single crochet with attached single crochet: Insert the hook into the stitch, draw the working yarn through. Draw the working yarn through the first loop on the hook. Now, yarn over and pull it through both loops on the hook. Finally, work 1 single crochet into the first loop of the previously crocheted elongated single crochet.

067 KNIT-LOOK STOCKINETTE

+1 ➡ [any st ct]

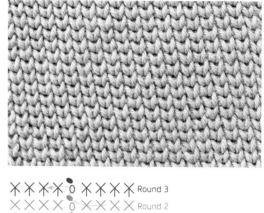

Work in rounds, following the chart. Join the beginning chain into the round by working 1 slip stitch into the first chain of the beginning chain. Work Rounds 1 and 2 once, and then repeat Round 2 for pattern.

The single crochets will slightly slant to the left with every round worked.

Chart Key

○ Chain 1

● 1 slip stitch

✕ 1 single crochet

⋏ 1 flat single crochet: Insert hook into the body of the single crochet of the previous round, directly underneath the top loop—this spot is located between 2 strands of the stitch diverging like the two legs of the letter V. Draw the working yarn through, forming a loop, and then finish working the single crochet.

transition between rounds

068 PLAIT STITCH

➡ [any st ct]

Work in rounds, following the chart. Join the beginning chain into the round by working 1 slip stitch into the first chain of the beginning chain. Work Rounds 1 and 2 once, and then repeat Round 2 for pattern.

The single crochets will slightly slant to the left with every round worked.

Chart Key

○ Chain 1

● 1 slip stitch

✕ 1 single crochet

⋏ 1 single crochet, inserting the hook the following way: On the right side of the fabric, insert the hook through the horizontal loop underneath the front loop of the stitch from the bottom to the top, pull through a loop, and then finish working the single crochet.

transition between rounds

069 PIXEL PATTERN

➡ [even st ct]

Work in rounds, following the chart. Join the beginning chain into the round by working 1 slip stitch into the first chain of the beginning chain. Work Rounds 1–3 once, and then repeat Round 3 for pattern. The stitches will slightly slant to the left with every round worked, creating a fine textured line.

Chart Key

○ Chain 1

● 1 slip stitch

✕ 1 single crochet

⋎2 Sc2-in-1: 2 single crochets into the same stitch

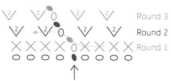

transition between rounds

SHELL AND FAN PATTERNS

070 BROKEN SHELL-AND-FAN PATTERN

[multiple of 10 + 1 ch + 1 beg-ch]

Work in rows, following the chart. Begin every row with the stitches before the pattern repeat, repeat the marked pattern repeat (10 sts wide) widthwise, and end with the stitches after the pattern repeat. Work Rows 1–5 once, and then repeat Rows 2–5 for pattern.

From Row 2 on, always work the double crochets or half double crochets from the groups of [3 double crochets, chain 1, 3 double crochets] or [1 half double crochet, chain 1, 1 half double crochet] in the chain space of the chain or chain arc of the previous row; single crochets are always worked into the chain of the previous row.

Chart Key

○ Chain 1

✕ 1 single crochet

 1 half double crochet

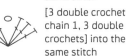 2 half double crochets into the same stitch

Dc3-in-1: 3 double crochets into the same stitch

[3 double crochets, chain 1, 3 double crochets] into the same stitch

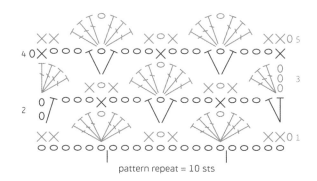

pattern repeat = 10 sts

071 SHELLS AND ARCS

[multiple of 8 + 5 ch + 1 beg-ch]

Work in rows, following the chart; Row 1 is a WS row. Begin every row with the stitches before the pattern repeat, repeat the marked pattern repeat (8 sts wide) widthwise, and end with the stitches after the pattern repeat. Work Rows 1–6 once, and then repeat Rows 3–6 for pattern.

In Rows 3 and 5, always work the groups of 4 double crochets in the chain space of the previous row, around the chain.

Chart Key

○ Chain 1

✕ 1 single crochet

T 1 double crochet

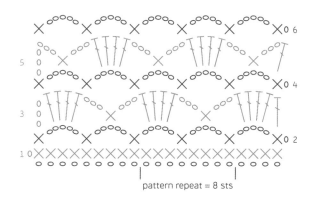

pattern repeat = 8 sts

072 SHELLS AND TRELLIS

[multiple of 12 + 1 ch + 3 beg-ch]

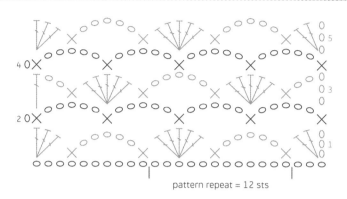

pattern repeat = 12 sts

Chart Key

○ Chain 1

╳ 1 single crochet

1 double crochet

V Dc2-in-1: 2 double crochets into the same stitch

Dc3-in-1: 3 double crochets into the same stitch

Dc5-in-1: 5 double crochets into the same stitch

Work in rows, following the chart. Begin every row with the stitches before the pattern repeat, repeat the marked pattern repeat (12 sts wide) widthwise, and end with the stitches after the pattern repeat. Work Rows 1–5 once, and then repeat Rows 2–5 for pattern.

073 LATTICE TIARA

[multiple of 12 + 1 ch + 1 beg-ch]

Work in rows, following the chart; Row 1 is a WS row. Begin every row with the stitches before the pattern repeat, repeat the marked pattern repeat (12 sts wide) widthwise, and end with the stitches after the pattern repeat. Work Rows 1–3 once, and then repeat Rows 2 and 3 for pattern.

In Row 2, always work the groups of 7 double crochets in the chain space of the previous row, around the chain. In Row 2, always work the single crochet into the middle chain of the chain-arc.

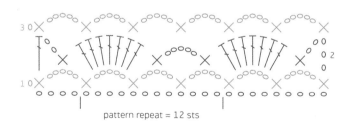

pattern repeat = 12 sts

Chart Key

○ Chain 1

╳ 1 single crochet

1 double crochet

074 PEACOCK TAIL FAN

[multiple of 10 + 1 ch + 1 beg-ch]

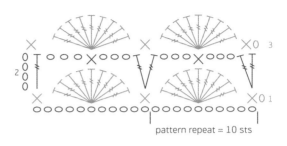

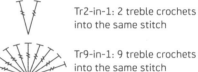

pattern repeat = 10 sts

Work in rows, following the chart. Begin every row with the stitches before the pattern repeat, repeat the marked pattern repeat (10 sts wide) widthwise, and end with the stitches after the pattern repeat. Work Rows 1–3 once, and then repeat Rows 2 and 3 for pattern.

Chart Key

○   Chain 1

✕   1 single crochet

⊺   1 treble crochet

V   Tr2-in-1: 2 treble crochets into the same stitch

    Tr9-in-1: 9 treble crochets into the same stitch

075 SHELL GRID

[multiple of 10 + 2 beg-ch]

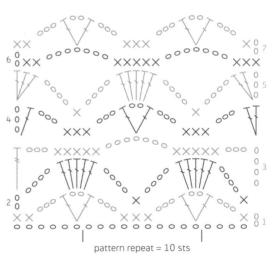

pattern repeat = 10 sts

Work in rows, following the chart. Begin every row with the stitches before the pattern repeat, repeat the marked pattern repeat (10 sts wide) widthwise, and end with the stitches after the pattern repeat. Work Rows 1–7 once, and then repeat Rows 2–7 for pattern. In Rows 2 and 5, always work the groups of 5 double crochet in the chain space of the previous row, around the chain.

Chart Key

○   Chain 1

✕   1 single crochet

⊺   1 double crochet   ⊺   1 treble crochet

V   Dc2-in-1: 2 double crochets into the same stitch   V   Dc3-in-1: 3 double crochets into the same stitch

   Dc5-in-1: 5 double crochets into the same stitch   [1 double crochet, chain 2, 1 double crochet] into the same stitch

076 SHELLS AND RIBBONS

[multiple of 10 + 3 ch + 1 beg-ch]

Work in rows, following the chart. Begin every row with the stitches before the pattern repeat, repeat the marked pattern repeat (10 sts wide) widthwise, and end with the stitches after the pattern repeat. Work Rows 1–4 once, and then repeat Rows 3 and 4 for pattern. In Rows 3 and 4, always work the groups of 5 double crochet into the last double crochet of the group in the previous row.

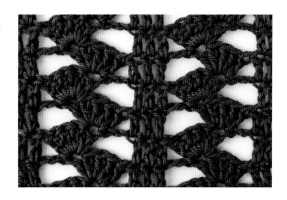

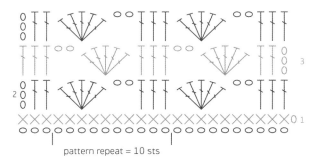

pattern repeat = 10 sts

Chart Key

○ Chain 1   ✕ 1 single crochet

⊤ 1 double crochet   Dc5-in-1: 5 double crochets into the same stitch

077 ARCHWAYS

[multiple of 7 + 1 ch + 1 beg-ch]

Work in rows, following the chart. Begin every row with the stitches before the pattern repeat, repeat the marked pattern repeat (7 sts wide) widthwise, and end with the stitches after the pattern repeat. Work Rows 1–6 once, and then repeat Rows 3–6 for pattern.

In Rows 2, 4, and 6, always work the single crochet and the group of 9 double crochet in the chain space of the previous row, around the chain.

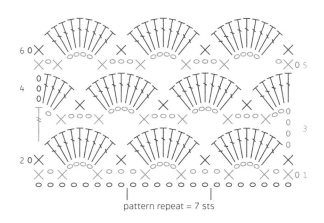

pattern repeat = 7 sts

Chart Key

○ Chain 1   ✕ 1 single crochet

⊤ 1 double crochet   1 treble crochet

078 TIARA PATTERN

[multiple of 5 + 1 ch + 3 beg-ch]

Work in rows, following the chart. Begin every row with the stitches before the pattern repeat, repeat the marked pattern repeat (5 sts wide) widthwise, and end with the stitches after the pattern repeat. Work Rows 1–3 once, and then repeat Rows 2 and 3 for pattern.

In Row 2, work the groups of 7 double crochet in the chain space of the previous row, around the chain.

Chart Key

o   Chain 1

     1 double crochet

    1 double crochet, chain 3, 1 double crochet into the same stitch

    Dc7-in-1: 7 double crochets into the same stitch

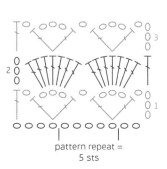

pattern repeat = 5 sts

079 TUFTS OF GRASS

[multiple of 4 + 1 ch + 1 beg-ch]

Work in rows, following the chart. Begin every row with the stitches before the pattern repeat, repeat the marked pattern repeat (4 sts wide) widthwise, and end with the stitches after the pattern repeat. Work Rows 1–5 once, and then repeat Rows 2–5 for pattern.

Chart Key

o   Chain 1

X   1 single crochet

     1 double crochet

V   Dc2-in-1: 2 double crochets into the same stitch

    [1 double crochet, chain 1, 1 double crochet] into the same stitch

    Dc3-in-1: 3 double crochets into the same stitch

    Dc2tog: Double crochet 2 stitches together

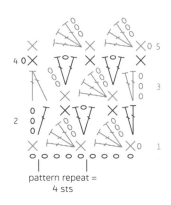

pattern repeat = 4 sts

080 SPLIT SHELLS

[multiple of 6 + 1 ch + 3 beg-ch]

Work in rows, following the chart. Begin every row with the stitches before the pattern repeat, repeat the marked pattern repeat (6 sts wide) widthwise, and end with the stitches after the pattern repeat. Work Rows 1–4 once, and then repeat Rows 3 and 4 for pattern. Always work the double crochet from the sequence of [3 double crochets, chain 2, 3 double crochets] in the chain space of the previous row, around the chain. In Row 2, also work the individual double crochets between the groups in the chain space of the previous row.

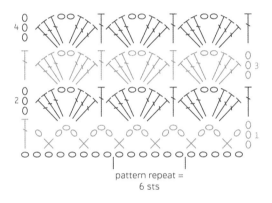

pattern repeat =
6 sts

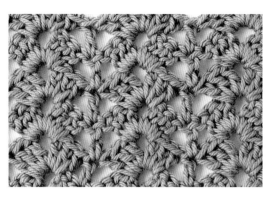

Chart Key

○ Chain 1

✕ 1 single crochet

† 1 double crochet

081 SHELLS IN FILET SQUARES

[multiple of 8 + 2 ch + 3 beg-ch]

Work in rows, following the chart. Begin every row with the stitches before the pattern repeat, repeat the marked pattern repeat (8 sts wide) widthwise, and end with the stitches after the pattern repeat. Work Rows 1–3 once, and then repeat Rows 2 and 3 for pattern.

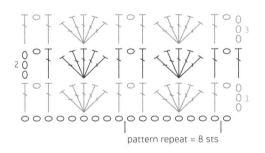

pattern repeat = 8 sts

Chart Key

○ Chain 1

† 1 double crochet

 Dc5-in-1: 5 double crochets into the same stitch

082 WHOLE SHELLS

[multiple of 10 + 1 ch + 1 beg-ch]

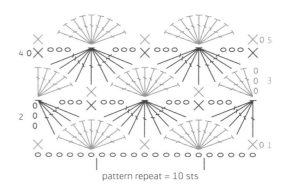

pattern repeat = 10 sts

Work in rows, following the chart. Begin every row with the stitches before the pattern repeat, repeat the marked pattern repeat (10 sts wide) widthwise, and end with the stitches after the pattern repeat. Work Rows 1–5 once, and then repeat Rows 2–5 for pattern.

Chart Key

o   Chain 1

✕   1 single crochet

┬   1 double crochet

 Dc4-in-1: 4 double crochets into the same stitch

Dc4tog: Double crochet 4 stitches together

 Dc5-in-1: 5 double crochets into the same stitch

Dc5tog: 5 double crochets crocheted together

 Dc9-in-1: 9 double crochets into the same stitch

9 double crochets crocheted together into 1 stitch

083 ARCED SHELLS

[multiple of 6 + 1 beg-ch]

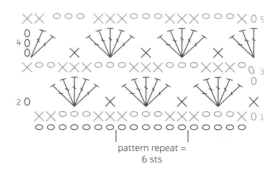

pattern repeat = 6 sts

Work in rows, following the chart. Begin every row with the stitches before the pattern repeat, repeat the marked pattern repeat (6 sts wide) widthwise, and end with the stitches after the pattern repeat. Work Rows 1–5 once, and then repeat Rows 2–5 for pattern.

Chart Key

o   Chain 1

✕   1 single crochet

┬   1 double crochet

 Dc2-in-1: 2 double crochets into the same stitch

 Dc3-in-1: 3 double crochets into the same stitch

 Dc5-in-1: 5 double crochets into the same stitch

084 SHELL-AND-FAN LACE

[multiple of 7 + 1 ch + 2 beg-ch]

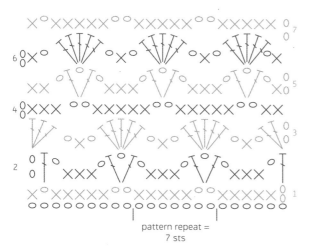

pattern repeat = 7 sts

Chart Key

○ Chain 1

✕ 1 single crochet

† 1 double crochet

Dc2-in-1: 2 double crochets into the same stitch

Dc3-in-1: 3 double crochets into the same stitch

Dc5-in-1: 5 double crochets into the same stitch

Work in rows, following the chart. Begin every row with the stitches before the pattern repeat, repeat the marked pattern repeat (7 sts wide) widthwise, and end with the stitches after the pattern repeat. Work Rows 1–7 once, and then repeat Rows 2–7 for pattern.

From Row 2 on, always work the double crochet from the sequence of [1 double crochet, chain 1, 1 double crochet] in the chain space of the previous row, and always work the groups of 5 double crochet in the chain space of the previous row, around the chain.

085 ENTANGLED SHELLS

[multiple of 10 + 2 ch + 3 beg-ch]

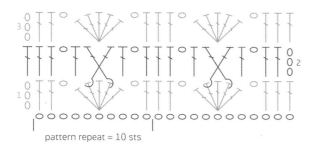

pattern repeat = 10 sts

Chart Key

○ Chain 1

† 1 double crochet

Dc5-in-1: 5 double crochets into the same stitch

 2 crossed front post double crochets: Work the first front post double crochet around the fourth double crochet of the previous row, the second front post double crochet going back into the second double crochet of the shell of the previous row.

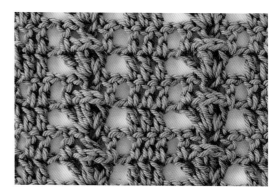

Work in rows, following the chart; Row 1 is a WS row. Begin every row with the stitches before the pattern repeat, repeat the marked pattern repeat (10 sts wide) widthwise, and end with the stitches after the pattern repeat. Work Rows 1–3 once, and then repeat Rows 2 and 3 for pattern.

In Row 3, work the groups of 5 double crochet between the crossed raised double crochet of the previous row.

086 PALMETTES

[multiple of 3 + 1 beg-ch]

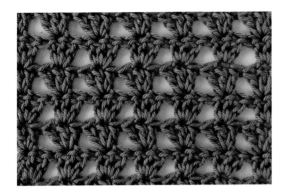

Work in rows, following the chart. Begin every row with the stitches before the pattern repeat, repeat the marked pattern repeat (3 sts wide) widthwise, and end with the stitches after the pattern repeat. Work Rows 1–3 once, and then repeat Rows 2 and 3 for pattern.

Chart Key

o	Chain 1
	Dc3-in-1: 3 double crochets into the same stitch

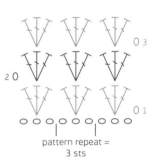

pattern repeat = 3 sts

087 DIAGONAL SHELLS

[multiple of 4 + 1 ch + 1 beg-ch]

Work in rows, following the chart. Begin every row with the stitches before the pattern repeat, repeat the marked pattern repeat (4 sts wide) widthwise, and end with the stitches after the pattern repeat. Work Rows 1–3 once, and then repeat Rows 2 and 3 for pattern.

Chart Key

o	Chain 1
X	1 single crochet
	Dc2tog: Double crochet 2 stitches together
	Dc4-in-1: 4 double crochets into the same stitch

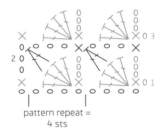

pattern repeat = 4 sts

088 SHELLS ON CHAINS

[multiple of 5 + 1 ch + 3 beg-ch]

Work in rows, following the chart. Begin every row with the stitches before the pattern repeat, repeat the marked pattern repeat (5 sts wide) widthwise, and end with the stitches after the pattern repeat. Work Rows 1–3 once, and then repeat Rows 2 and 3 for pattern.

    In Row 2, always work the single crochets between chain arcs and between the shells of the previous row.

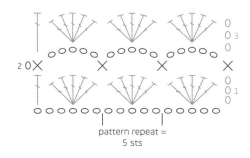

pattern repeat =
5 sts

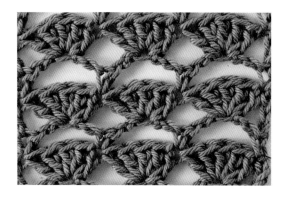

Chart Key

o   Chain 1

✕   1 single crochet

†   1 double crochet

   Dc5-in-1: 5 double crochets into the same stitch

089 BREEZY FANS

[multiple of 8 + 1 ch + 3 beg-ch]

Work in rows, following the chart. Begin every row with the stitches before the pattern repeat, repeat the marked pattern repeat (8 sts wide) widthwise, and end with the stitches after the pattern repeat. Work Rows 1–3 once, and then repeat Rows 2 and 3 for pattern.

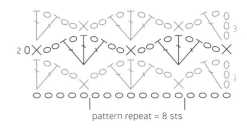

pattern repeat = 8 sts

Chart Key

o   Chain 1

✕   1 single crochet

   [1 double crochet, chain 1, 1 double crochet] into the same stitch

†   1 double crochet

   [1 double crochet, chain 1, 1 double crochet, chain 1, 1 double crochet] into the same stitch

48

090 BLOCKS AND TRELLISES

[multiple of 5 + 1 ch + 1 beg-ch]

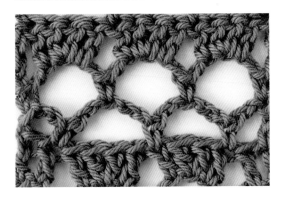

Chart Key

o   Chain 1

✕   1 single crochet

†   1 double crochet

V   Dc2-in-1: 2 double crochets into the same stitch

†   1 treble crochet

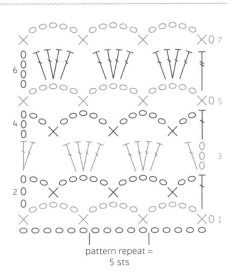

pattern repeat =
5 sts

Work in rows, following the chart. Begin every row with the stitches before the pattern repeat, repeat the marked pattern repeat (5 sts wide) widthwise, and end with the stitches after the pattern repeat.

Work Rows 1–7 once, and then repeat Rows 2–7 for pattern.

091 SHELL-AND-LACE PATTERN

[multiple of 4 + 1 ch + 2 beg-ch]

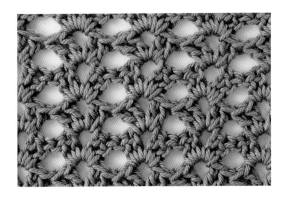

Work in rows, following the chart. Begin every row with the stitches before the pattern repeat, repeat the marked pattern repeat (4 sts wide) widthwise, and end with the stitches after the pattern repeat. Work Rows 1–3 once, and then repeat Rows 2 and 3 for pattern.

From Row 2 on, work the double crochets from the groups of [2 double crochets, chain 2, 2 double crochets] in the chain space of the previous row, around the chain.

Chart Key

o   Chain 1

✕   1 single crochet

V   Dc2-in-1: 2 double crochets into the same stitch

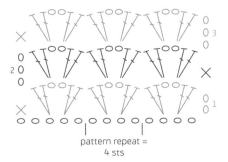

pattern repeat =
4 sts

092 FANS ON STICKS

[multiple of 8 + 3 ch + 1 beg-ch]

Work in rows, following the chart. Begin every row with the stitches before the pattern repeat, repeat the marked pattern repeat (8 sts wide) widthwise, and end with the stitches after the pattern repeat. Work Rows 1–5 once, and then repeat Rows 2–5 for pattern.

In Rows 2 and 4, always work the individual double treble crochets in the chain space of the chain or chain arc of the previous row; always work the stitches at the end of the row into the top chain of the turning chain of the previous row.

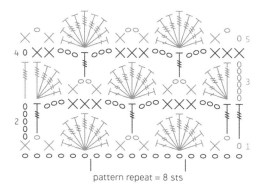

pattern repeat = 8 sts

Chart Key

○   Chain 1

✕   1 single crochet

⟊   1 double treble crochet

⟊   1 triple treble crochet

   [1 double crochet, 1 treble crochet, 2 double treble crochets, 1 triple treble crochet] into the same stitch

   [1 triple treble crochet, 2 double treble crochets, 1 treble crochet, 1 double crochet] into the same stitch

   [1 double crochet, 1 treble crochet, 2 double treble crochets, 1 triple treble crochet, 2 double treble crochets, 1 treble crochet, 1 double crochet] into the same stitch

093 PICOTS IN ARCS

[multiple of 6 + 1 ch + 1 beg-ch]

Work in rows, following the chart; Row 1 is a WS row. Begin every row with the stitches before the pattern repeat, repeat the marked pattern repeat (6 sts wide) widthwise, and end with the stitches after the pattern repeat. Work Rows 1–5 once, and then repeat Rows 2–5 for pattern.

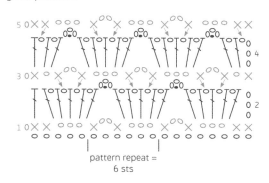

pattern repeat = 6 sts

Chart Key

○   Chain 1

✕   1 single crochet

⟊   1 double crochet

 1 picot of 3: Chain 3, and then join with 1 slip stitch back into the first chain

094 EMBELLISHED ARCHWAYS

[multiple of 11 + 3 ch + 1 beg-ch]

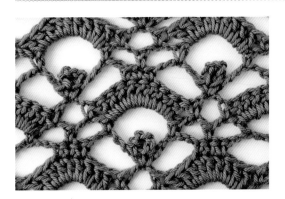

Work in rows, following the chart. Begin every row with the stitches before the pattern repeat, repeat the marked pattern repeat (11 sts wide) widthwise, and end with the stitches after the pattern repeat. Work Rows 1–7 once, and then repeat Rows 2–7 for pattern.

In Rows 2 and 5, always work the groups of 9 or 4 double crochet in the chain space of the previous row, around the chain. In Rows 4 and 7, always work the single crochet into the second chain of the chain of 4.

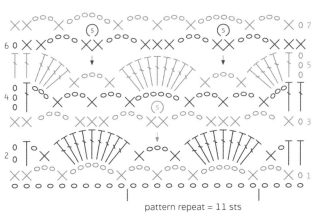

pattern repeat = 11 sts

Chart Key

o   Chain 1

✕   1 single crochet

⑤✕✕   1 single crochet, chain arc of 5 chains, 1 single crochet into the same space

T   1 half double crochet

†   1 double crochet

095 LACY FANS

[multiple of 12 + 1 ch + 3 beg-ch]

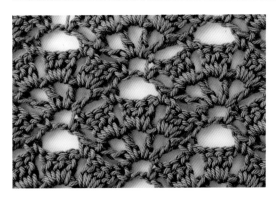

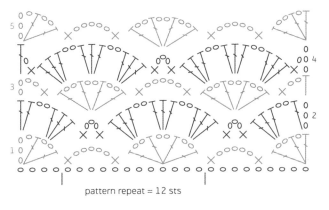

pattern repeat = 12 sts

Chart Key

o   Chain 1

✕   1 single crochet

†   1 double crochet

 [1 double crochet, chain 2, 1 double crochet] into the same stitch

[1 double crochet, chain 2, 1 double crochet, chain 1, 1 double crochet] into the same stitch

 [1 double crochet, chain 2, 1 double crochet, chain 2, 1 double crochet, chain 2, 1 double crochet] into the same stitch

Work in rows, following the chart; Row 1 is a WS row. Begin every row with the stitches before the pattern repeat, repeat the marked pattern repeat (12 sts wide) widthwise, and end with the stitches after the pattern repeat. Work Rows 1–5 once, and then repeat Rows 2–5 for pattern. From Row 2 on, always work the groups of double crochet in the chain space of the previous row, around the chain.

096 BIG TREE PATTERN

[multiple of 8 + 1 ch + 3 beg-ch]

Work in rows, following the chart. Begin every row with the stitches before the pattern repeat, repeat the marked pattern repeat (8 sts wide) widthwise, and end with the stitches after the pattern repeat. Work Rows 1–9 once, and then repeat Rows 2–9 for pattern.

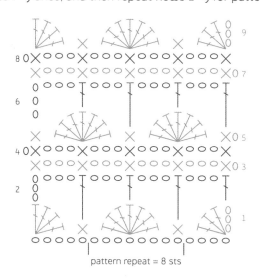

pattern repeat = 8 sts

Chart Key

○	Chain 1		Dc4-in-1: 4 double crochets into the same stitch
✕	1 single crochet		Dc7-in-1: 7 double crochets into the same stitch
	1 double crochet		
	Dc3-in-1: 3 double crochets into the same stitch		

097 JOINED SHELLS

[multiple of 6 + 4 ch + 3 beg-ch]

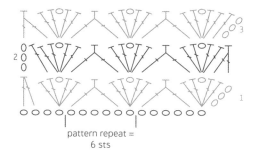

pattern repeat = 6 sts

Chart Key

○   Chain 1

1 double crochet

Dc2tog: Double crochet 2 stitches together

[2 double crochets, chain 1, 2 double crochets] into the same stitch

Dc2tog-skip3: Double crochet 2 stitches together, while skipping 3 stitches of the previous row when working the second double crochet

Dc2tog-skip1: Double crochet 2 stitches together, while skipping 1 double crochet of the previous row when working the second double crochet

Dc2tog-skip2: Double crochet 2 stitches together, while skipping 2 double crochets of the previous row when working the second double crochet

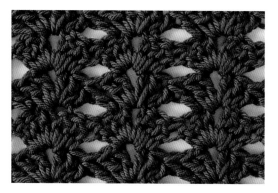

Work in rows, following the chart. Begin every row with the stitches before the pattern repeat, repeat the marked pattern repeat (6 sts wide) widthwise, and end with the stitches after the pattern repeat. Work Rows 1–3 once, and then repeat Rows 2 and 3 for pattern.

From Row 2 on, work the double crochets from the groups of [2 double crochets, chain 1, 2 double crochets] in the chain space of the previous row.

098 V-STITCH PATTERN [multiple of 3 + 3 beg-ch]

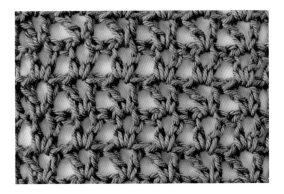

Work in rows, following the chart. Begin every row with the stitches before the pattern repeat, repeat the marked pattern repeat (3 sts wide) widthwise, and end with the stitches after the pattern repeat. Work Rows 1–3 once, and then repeat Rows 2 and 3 for pattern. From Row 2 on, work the double crochets from the groups of [1 double crochet, chain 1, 1 double crochet] in the chain space of the previous row, around the chain.

Chart Key

o Chain 1

† 1 double crochet

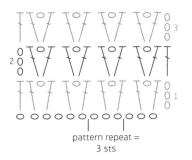

pattern repeat =
3 sts

099 IRIS [multiple of 4 + 3 ch + 3 beg-ch]

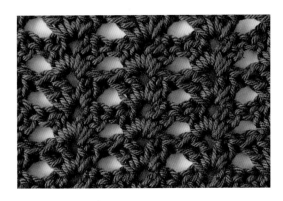

Work in rows, following the chart. Begin every row with the beg-ch before the pattern repeat, and then repeat the marked pattern repeat (4 sts wide) widthwise, and end with the stitches after the pattern repeat. Work Rows 1–3 once, and then repeat Rows 2 and 3 for pattern.

From Row 2 on, work the double crochets from the groups of [2 double crochets, chain 1, 2 double crochets] in the chain space of the previous row, around the chain.

Chart Key

o Chain 1

† 1 double crochet

 [2 double crochets, chain 1, 2 double crochets] into the same stitch

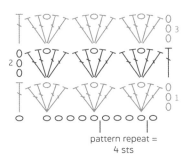

pattern repeat =
4 sts

100 FANS WITH PICOTS

[multiple of 12 + 1 ch + 1 beg-ch]

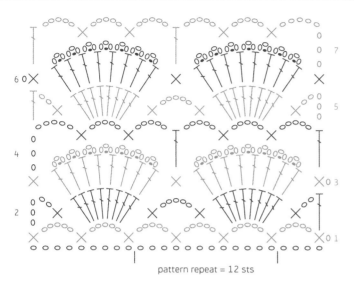

pattern repeat = 12 sts

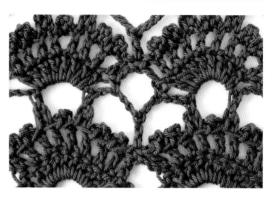

Chart Key

○ Chain 1

✕ 1 single crochet

T 1 double crochet

○•○ 1 picot of 3: Chain 3, and join with 1 slip stitch back into the first chain

Work in rows, following the chart. Begin every row with the stitches before the pattern repeat, repeat the marked pattern repeat (12 sts wide) widthwise, and end with the stitches after the pattern repeat. Work Rows 1–7 once, and then repeat Rows 2–7 for pattern.

In Rows 2, 3, 5, and 6, always work the single crochet into the middle chain of the chain arc. In Rows 4 and 7, always work the single crochet around the picots.

101 ROUND ARCS WITH MULLION AND TRANSOM

[multiple of 8 + 1 beg-ch]

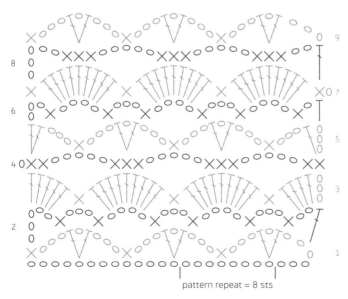

pattern repeat = 8 sts

Chart Key

○ Chain 1

✕ 1 single crochet

T 1 half double crochet

T 1 double crochet

V Dc2-in-1: 2 double crochets into the same stitch

V [1 double crochet, chain 1, 1 double crochet] into the same stitch

Work in rows, following the chart. Begin every row with the stitches before the pattern repeat, repeat the marked pattern repeat (8 sts wide) widthwise, and end with the stitches after the pattern repeat. Work Rows 1–9 once, and then repeat Rows 2–9 for pattern.

In Rows 3 and 7, always work the groups of 9, 5, or 4 double crochet in the chain space of the previous row, around the chain.

102 SHELL-AND-FAN BOXES [multiple of 5 + 1 ch + 3 beg-ch]

Work in rows, following the chart. Begin every row with the stitches before the pattern repeat, repeat the marked pattern repeat (5 sts wide) widthwise, and end with the stitches after the pattern repeat. Work Rows 1–3 once, and then repeat Rows 2 and 3 for pattern.

Chart Key

○ Chain 1

| 1 double crochet

⋀ Dc5-in-1: 5 double crochets into the same stitch

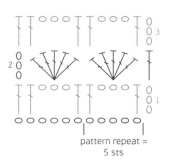

pattern repeat = 5 sts

103 STAGGERED HALF SHELLS [multiple of 5 + 1 ch + 3 beg-ch]

Work in rows, following the chart. Begin every row with the stitches before the pattern repeat, repeat the marked pattern repeat (5 sts wide) widthwise, and end with the stitches after the pattern repeat. Work Rows 1–3 once, and then repeat Rows 2 and 3 for pattern.

Chart Key

○ Chain 1

| 1 double crochet

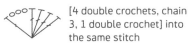 [4 double crochets, chain 3, 1 double crochet] into the same stitch

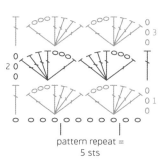

pattern repeat = 5 sts

104 RIGHT-LEFT SHELLS [multiple of 4 + 1 ch + 3 beg-ch]

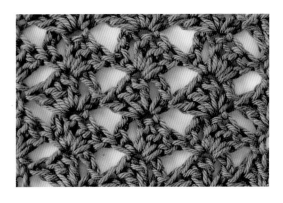

Work in rows, following the chart. Begin every row with the stitches before the pattern repeat, repeat the marked pattern repeat (4 sts wide) widthwise, and end with the stitches after the pattern repeat. Work Rows 1–3 once, and then repeat Rows 2 and 3 for pattern.

Chart Key

○ Chain 1

✕ 1 single crochet

  Dc3-in-1: 3 double crochets into the same stitch

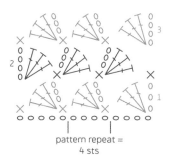

pattern repeat = 4 sts

105 CAPITALS AND WINDOWS

[multiple of 7 + 3 ch + 3 beg-ch]

Work in rows, following the chart. Begin every row with the stitches before the pattern repeat, repeat the marked pattern repeat (7 sts wide) widthwise, and end with the stitches after the pattern repeat. Work Rows 1–5 once, and then repeat Rows 2–5 for pattern.

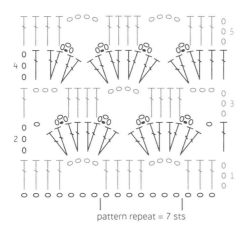

pattern repeat = 7 sts

Chart Key

○ Chain 1

 1 picot of 3: Chain 3, and join with 1 slip stitch back into the first chain

┃ 1 double crochet

V Dc2-in-1: 2 double crochets into the same stitch

106 DIAMOND RAYS

[multiple of 8 + 1 ch + 1 beg-ch]

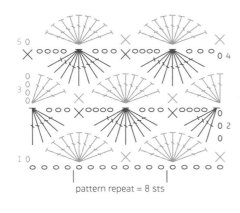

pattern repeat = 8 sts

Chart Key

○ Chain 1

✕ 1 single crochet

┃ 1 double crochet

 Dc4-in-1: 4 double crochets into the same stitch

Dc4tog: Double crochet 4 stitches together

Dc5-in-1: 5 double crochets into the same stitch

Dc5tog: Double crochet 5 stitches together

 Dc9-in-1: 9 double crochets into the same stitch

Dc9tog: Double crochet 9 stitches together

Work in rows, following the chart; Row 1 is a WS row. Begin every row with the stitches before the pattern repeat, repeat the marked pattern repeat (8 sts wide) widthwise, and end with the stitches after the pattern repeat. Work Rows 1–5 once, and then repeat Rows 2–5 for pattern.

107 SHELLS IN ZIGZAG NETTING

[multiple of 9 + 2 ch + 1 beg-ch]

Work in rows, following the chart. Begin every row with the stitches before the pattern repeat, repeat the marked pattern repeat (9 sts wide) widthwise, and end with the stitches after the pattern repeat. Work Rows 1–5 once, and then repeat Rows 2–5 for pattern.

From Row 2 on, always work the double crochets in the chain space of the previous row, around the chain.

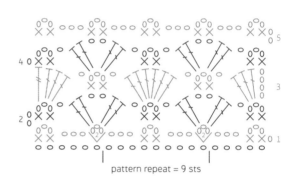

pattern repeat = 9 sts

Chart Key

- ○ Chain 1
- ✕ 1 single crochet
- ⊺ 1 treble crochet
- ⊤ 1 double crochet
- [1 single crochet, chain 3, 1 single crochet] into the same stitch

108 DOUBLE CROCHET LACE

[multiple of 8 + 5 ch + 3 beg-ch]

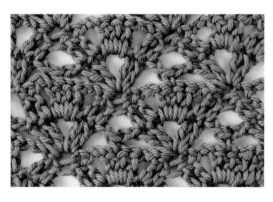

Work in rows, following the chart; Row 1 is a WS row. Begin every row with the stitches before the pattern repeat, repeat the marked pattern repeat (8 sts wide) widthwise, and end with the stitches after the pattern repeat. Work Rows 1–5 once, and then repeat Rows 2–5 for pattern.

In Rows 2 and 4, always work the middle 3 double crochets in the groups of [2 double crochets, chain 2, 3 double crochets, chain 2, 2 double crochets] in the chain space of the previous row, around the chain.

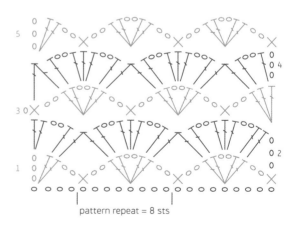

pattern repeat = 8 sts

Chart Key

- ○ Chain 1
- ✕ 1 single crochet
- ⊤ 1 double crochet
- ⋀ Dc2tog: Double crochet 2 stitches together
- ⋁ Dc2-in-1: 2 double crochets into the same stitch
- [2 double crochets, chain 2, 2 double crochets] into the same stitch

109 STRIPES AND ZIGZAGS

[multiple of 6 + 4 ch + 3 beg-ch]

Work in rows, following the chart. Begin every row with the stitches before the pattern repeat, repeat the marked pattern repeat (6 sts wide) widthwise, and end with the stitches after the pattern repeat. Work Rows 1–3 once, and then repeat Rows 2 and 3 for pattern.

In Rows 2 and 3, always work the groups of 3 double crochet into the chain next to the single crochet.

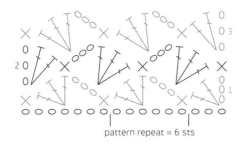

pattern repeat = 6 sts

Chart Key

o	Chain 1	V	Dc2-in-1: 2 double crochets into the same stitch
✕	1 single crochet		
┃	1 double crochet	⋎	Dc3-in-1: 3 double crochets into the same stitch

110 SHELLS AND CROSSES

[multiple of 8 + 1 ch + 1 beg-ch]

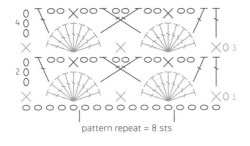

pattern repeat = 8 sts

Chart Key

o	Chain 1
✕	1 single crochet
┃	1 double crochet

 Cross 2 double crochets with 2 chains in between: Work the first double crochet into the second double crochet of the next shell of the previous row, chain 2, work the second double crochet, going back behind the first double crochet into the next-to-last double crochet of the previous shell of the previous row

Dc9-in-1: 9 double crochets into the same stitch

Work in rows, following the chart. Begin every row with the stitches before the pattern repeat, repeat the marked pattern repeat (8 sts wide) widthwise, and end with the stitches after the pattern repeat. Work Rows 1–4 once, and then repeat Rows 3 and 4 for pattern.

111 ORNAMENTAL

[multiple of 6 + 1 ch + 3 beg-ch]

Work in rows, following the chart. Begin every row with the stitches before the pattern repeat, repeat the marked pattern repeat (6 sts wide) widthwise, and end with the stitches after the pattern repeat. Work Rows 1–5 once, and then repeat Rows 2–5 for pattern.

From Row 2 on, always work the double crochets from the groups of [3 double crochets, chain 3, 3 double crochets], as well as the groups of 5 double crochet, in the chain space of the previous row, around the chain.

Chart Key

○ Chain 1

| 1 double crochet

‡ 1 treble crochet

 Dc2-in-1: 2 double crochets into the same stitch

Dc3-in-1: 3 double crochets into the same stitch

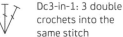 Dc5-in-1: 5 double crochets into the same stitch

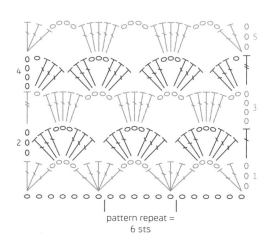

pattern repeat = 6 sts

112 ASCENDING SHELLS

[multiple of 8 + 1 ch + 3 beg-ch]

Work in rows, following the chart. Begin every row with the stitches before the pattern repeat, repeat the marked pattern repeat (8 sts wide) widthwise, and end with the stitches after the pattern repeat. Work Rows 1–5 once, and then repeat Rows 2–5 for pattern.

From Row 2 on, always work the double crochets in the chain space of the previous row; only the double crochets at the beginning and end of the row are worked into the last double crochet of the previous row or in the top chain of the turning chain.

Chart Key

○ Chain 1

| 1 double crochet

 Dc2-in-1: 2 double crochets into the same stitch

[1 double crochet, chain 1, 1 double crochet] into the same stitch

[2 double crochets, chain 1, 2 double crochets, chain 1, 2 double crochets] into the same stitch

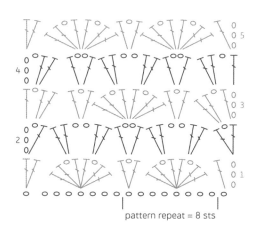

pattern repeat = 8 sts

113 TRUSSES

[multiple of 8 + 3 ch + 1 beg-ch]

Work in rows, following the chart; Row 1 is a WS row. Begin every row with the stitches before the pattern repeat, repeat the marked pattern repeat (8 sts wide) widthwise, and end with the stitches after the pattern repeat. Work Rows 1–6 once, and then repeat Rows 3–6 for pattern.

From Row 2 on, always work the double crochets in the chain space of the previous row, around the chain.

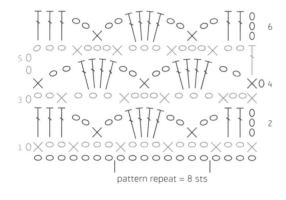

pattern repeat = 8 sts

Chart Key

○ Chain 1

✕ 1 single crochet

│ 1 double crochet

114 OVERLAPPING ARCHWAYS

[multiple of 7 + 1 ch + 1 beg-ch]

Work in rows, following the chart; Row 1 is a WS row. Begin every row with the stitches before the pattern repeat, repeat the marked pattern repeat (7 sts wide) widthwise, and end with the stitches after the pattern repeat. Work Rows 1–8 once, and then repeat Rows 3–8 for pattern.

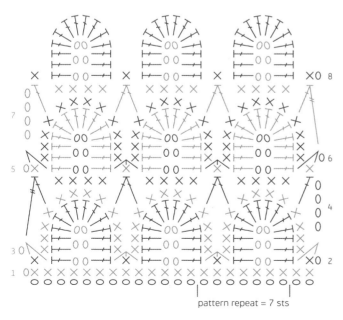

pattern repeat = 7 sts

Chart Key

○ Chain 1

✕ 1 single crochet

│ 1 double crochet

∧ Sc2tog: Single crochet 2 stitches together

⋀ Sc3tog: Single crochet 3 stitches together

Ⱥ Dc2tog: Double crochet 2 stitches together

⋀ 1 double crochet and 1 treble crochet crocheted together

115 CROWN PATTERN

[multiple of 12 + 1 ch + 1 beg-ch]

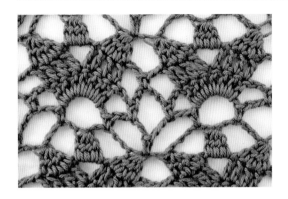

Work in rows, following the chart; Row 1 is a WS row. Begin every row with the stitches before the pattern repeat, repeat the marked pattern repeat (12 sts wide) widthwise, and end with the stitches after the pattern repeat. Work Rows 1–5 once, and then repeat Rows 2–5 for pattern.

In Row 2, always work the groups of 7 double crochets, and in Row 4, the middle 4 double crochets, which are crocheted off together, in the chain space of the previous row, around the chain.

Chart Key

○	Chain 1	✕	1 single crochet
⊤	1 double crochet	‡	1 treble crochet
⋀	Dc4tog: Double crochet 4 stitches together	⌄○○○⌄	1 double crochet, chain 3, 1 double crochet into the same stitch

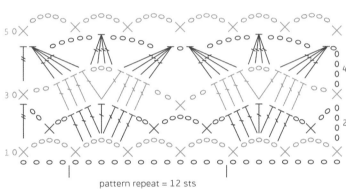

pattern repeat = 12 sts

116 SHELLS AND SWITCHED BOXES

[multiple of 12 + 1 ch + 3 beg-ch]

Work in rows, following the chart. Begin every row with the stitches before the pattern repeat, repeat the marked pattern repeat (12 sts wide) widthwise, and end with the stitches after the pattern repeat. Work Rows 1–7 once, and then repeat Rows 2–7 for pattern.

From Row 2 on, always work the groups of [3 double crochets, chain 1, 3 double crochets] in the chain space of the previous row.

Chart Key

○	Chain 1	⋁	Dc3-in-1: 3 double crochets into the same stitch
✕	1 single crochet		
⋁	Dc2-in-1: 2 double crochets into the same stitch	⋁○⋁	[3 double crochets, chain 1, 3 double crochets] into the same stitch

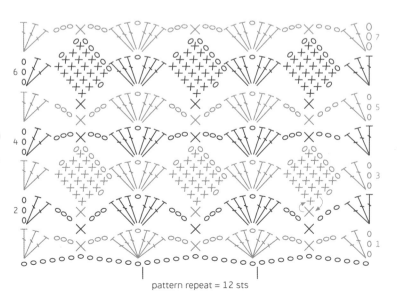

pattern repeat = 12 sts

117 OPEN SHELL-AND-FAN PATTERN

[multiple of 8 + 1 ch + 3 beg-ch]

Work in rows, following the chart. Begin every row with the stitches before the pattern repeat, repeat the marked pattern repeat (8 sts wide) widthwise, and end with the stitches after the pattern repeat. Work Rows 1–3 once, and then repeat Rows 2 and 3 for pattern.

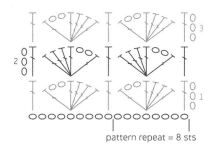

pattern repeat = 8 sts

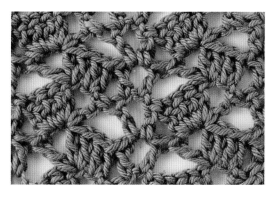

Chart Key

○ Chain 1

⊤ 1 double crochet

[4 double crochets, chain 2, 1 double crochet] into the same stitch

118 DIAMOND PATTERN

[multiple of 7 + 1 ch + 3 beg-ch]

Work in rows, following the chart; Row 1 is a WS row. Begin every row with the stitches before the pattern repeat, repeat the marked pattern repeat (7 sts wide) widthwise, and end with the stitches after the pattern repeat. Work Rows 1–3 once, and then repeat Rows 2 and 3 for pattern.

Chart Key

 ○ Chain 1

 Dc2-in-1: 2 double crochets into the same stitch

Dc3-in-1: 3 double crochets into the same stitch

 Dc5-in-1: 5 double crochets into the same stitch

Dc5tog: Double crochet 5 stitches together

 2 front post double crochets crocheted together

 2 front post double crochets, 1 double crochet crocheted together

 5 front post double crochets crocheted together

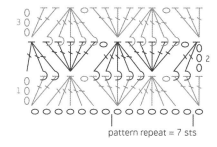

pattern repeat = 7 sts

CLUSTERS,
POPCORNS,
BOBBLES,
PUFFS, AND
NUPPS

Patterns with **Groups of Stitches**

119 PAIRED DOUBLE CROCHETS

[any st ct + 3 beg-ch]

Start with a loosely worked beginning chain. Work in rows, following the chart. Work Rows 1–3 once, and then repeat Rows 2 and 3 for pattern.

Chart Key

○   Chain 1

│   1 double crochet

   Dc2tog-in-1: 2 double crochets worked into the same stitch and crocheted together

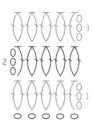

120 PENNY RIDGES

[multiple of 2 + 3 beg-ch]

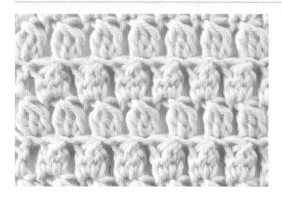

Work in rows, following the chart. Begin every row with the stitches before the pattern repeat, repeat the marked pattern repeat (2 sts wide) widthwise, and end with the stitches after the pattern repeat. Work Rows 1–3 once, and then repeat Rows 2 and 3 for pattern.

Chart Key

○   Chain 1

│   1 double crochet

   Dc2tog-in-1: 2 double crochets into the same stitch and crocheted together

   Dc3tog-in-1: 3 double crochets into the same stitch and crocheted together

   Blo-dc3tog-in-1: 3 double crochets into the same stitch, working only into the back loop of the stitch of the previous row, and crocheted off together

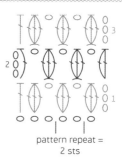

pattern repeat = 2 sts

121 DOUBLE CROCHET QUARTETS

[multiple of 3 + 3 beg-ch]

Work in rows, following the chart. Begin with the stitches before the pattern repeat, repeat the marked pattern repeat (3 sts wide) widthwise, and end with the stitches after the pattern repeat. Work Rows 1–3 once, and then repeat Rows 2 and 3 for pattern.

From Row 2 on, always work the dc2tog or dc4tog in the chain space of the previous row, around the chain.

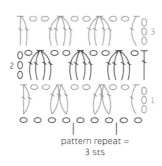

pattern repeat =
3 sts

Chart Key

○   Chain 1

╿   1 double crochet

⋔   Dc2tog: double crochet 2 stitches together

⋔   Dc2tog-in-1: 2 double crochets into the same stitch and crocheted together

⋔   Dc4tog: double crochet 4 stitches together

⋔   2 pairs of 2 double crochets each crocheted together: 4 double crochets in 2 (adjacent) chains and crocheted off together—work the first and second double crochet together into the same chain, the third and fourth double crochet together into the next chain

122 ACORN CLUSTERS

[odd st ct + 1 beg-ch]

Chart Key

○   Chain 1

✕   1 single crochet

   [1 single crochet, chain 2, 1 single crochet] into the same chain of the beginning chain or in the chain space of the previous row

╿   1 double crochet

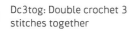   Dc2tog: Double crochet 2 stitches together

⋔   Dc3tog: Double crochet 3 stitches together

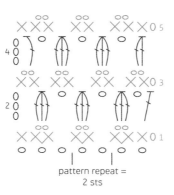

pattern repeat =
2 sts

Work in rows, following the chart. Begin every row with the stitches before the pattern repeat, repeat the marked pattern repeat (2 sts wide) widthwise, and end with the stitches after the pattern repeat. Work Rows 1–5 once, and then repeat Rows 2–5 for pattern.

Always work the cluster of either 3 or 2 double crochets, which are crocheted off together, in the chain space of the previous row.

From Row 3 on, always work the groups of [1 single crochet, chain 2, 1 single crochet] in the chain space of the previous row, around the chain; at the end of the row, work it between the cluster of 3 double crochets and the turning chain.

123 TRIANGLE SLIVERS [multiple of 4 + 3 beg-ch]

Work in rows, following the chart. Begin with the stitches before the pattern repeat, repeat the marked pattern repeat (4 sts wide) width-wise, and end with the stitches after the pattern repeat. Work Rows 1–5 once, and then repeat Rows 2–5 for pattern.

In Rows 3 and 5, always work the individual double crochets into the joined tops or in the chain space of the previous row, around the chain.

Chart Key

o   Chain 1

†   1 double crochet

⋏   Dc2tog: Double crochet 2 stitches together

⋀   Dc3tog: Double crochet 3 stitches together

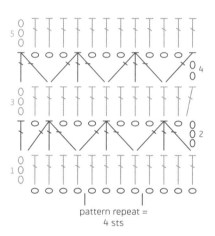

pattern repeat = 4 sts

124 LATTICE WITH LITTLE BELLS [multiple of 8 + 1 ch + 1 beg-ch]

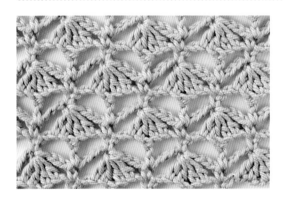

Work in rows, following the chart. Begin with the stitches before the pattern repeat, repeat the marked pattern repeat (8 sts wide) width-wise, and end with the stitches after the pattern repeat. Work Rows 1–5 once, and then repeat Rows 2–5 for pattern.

In Rows 3 and 5, work the cluster of double crochets, which are crocheted off together, directly into the chains of the previous row. In Rows 2 and 4, work the single crochets into the chain that had been worked immediately after the group of double crochets; this chain stitch gathers all loops of the double crochets together into a cluster.

Chart Key

o   Chain 1

✕   1 single crochet

†   1 double crochet

⋀   Dc2tog: Double crochet 2 stitches together

⋀   Dc3tog: Double crochet 3 stitches together

⋀   Dc4tog: Double crochet 4 stitches together

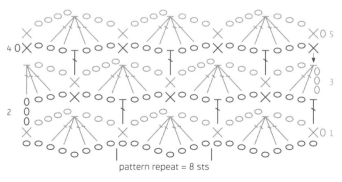

pattern repeat = 8 sts

125 FILLED DIAMOND GRID

[multiple of 9 + 7 ch + 1 beg-ch]

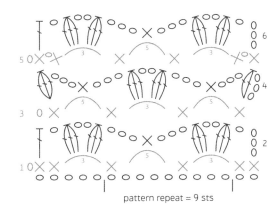

pattern repeat = 9 sts

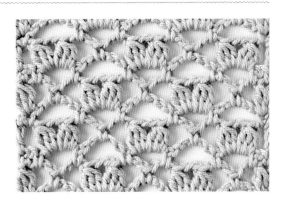

Work in rows, following the chart; Row 1 is a WS row. Begin with the stitches before the pattern repeat, repeat the marked pattern repeat (9 sts wide) widthwise, and end with the stitches after the pattern repeat. Work Rows 1–6 once, and then repeat Rows 3–6 for pattern.

From Row 2 on, always work the single crochets and the clusters of double crochets in the chain space of the chain or chain-arc of the previous row.

Chart Key

o Chain 1

X 1 single crochet

T 1 double crochet

Dc2tog-in-1: 2 double crochets into the same stitch and crocheted together

Dc3tog-in-1: 3 double crochets into the same stitch and crocheted together

Dc3tog: Double crochet 3 stitches together

3 Chain arc of 3 chains

5 Chain arc of 5 chains

126 LOZENGE GRID

[multiple of 5 + 1 ch + 3 beg-ch]

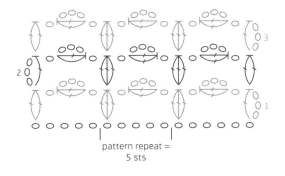

pattern repeat = 5 sts

Work in rows, following the chart. Begin with the stitches before the pattern repeat, repeat the marked pattern repeat (5 sts wide) widthwise, and end with the stitches after the pattern repeat. Work Rows 1–3 once, and then repeat Rows 2 and 3 for pattern.

Chart Key

o Chain 1

T 1 double crochet

Dc2tog-in-1: 2 double crochets into the same stitch and crocheted together

Dc3tog-in-1: 3 double crochets into the same stitch and crocheted together

1 horizontal popcorn: Chain 3, 2 double crochets into the first chain and crocheted off together

127 FLOWERS ON A MESH GROUND

[multiple of 16 + 8 ch + 3 beg-ch]

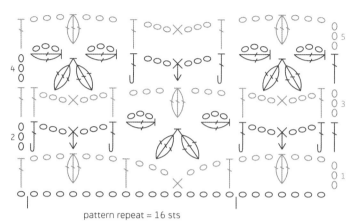

pattern repeat = 16 sts

Work in rows, following the chart. Begin with the stitches before the pattern repeat, repeat the marked pattern repeat (16 sts wide) width-wise, and end with the stitches after the pattern repeat. Work Rows 1–5 once, and then repeat Rows 2–5 for pattern.

In Rows 3 and 5, for the 3 double crochets that are crocheted off together, to complete the flower motif, insert the hook into the center of the group from the previous row, below 2 horizontal loops.

Chart Key

○   Chain 1

✕   1 single crochet

⊤   1 double crochet

    1 single crochet from the front around the group of double crochets: Insert the hook before the group of double crochets, move the hook toward the back, around the group of double crochets to the front again; from there, draw the working yarn through and finish the single crochet

⊔   1 double crochet in the chain space of the previous row

    Dc3tog-in-1: 3 double crochets into the same stitch and crocheted together

    1 horizontal popcorn: Chain 3, work 2 double crochets into the horizontal ridge of the first chain of the group on the back of the work, and finish them off together

    1 double bobble from two sets of 3 double crochets: * Work a popcorn of 3 double crochets into the same stitch and crocheted together as follows. Work the double crochets into the middle chain of the previous row, inserting through both the back loop of the stitch and the horizontal loop. Work 3 double crochets into the same stitch, pulling the working yarn each time through 2 loops, and then draw the working yarn through 3 loops, leaving 2 loops on the hook; repeat from * once for the next chain arc; finally, pull the yarn through the remaining 3 loops together.

128 COMB GRID

[multiple of 5 + 1 ch + 4 beg-ch]

Work in rows, following the chart. Begin with the stitches before the pattern repeat, repeat the marked pattern repeat (5 sts wide) widthwise, and end with the stitches after the pattern repeat. Work Rows 1–3 once, and then repeat Rows 2 and 3 for pattern.

Always work the cluster of 4 double crochets, which are crocheted off together, around the just-worked treble crochet.

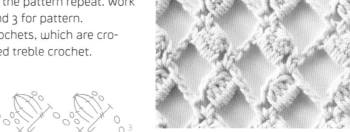

Chart Key

o	Chain 1
✕	1 single crochet
⊤	1 double crochet
⊤ (treble)	1 treble crochet
⊤ (around chain)	1 treble crochet around the chain from the group of stitches of the previous row
⋀	Dc4tog: Double crochet 4 stitches together

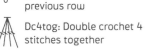

pattern repeat = 5 sts

129 MAPLE FANS

[multiple of 4 + 1 ch + 1 beg-ch]

Work in rows, following the chart. Begin with the stitches before the pattern repeat, repeat the marked pattern repeat (4 sts wide) widthwise, and end with the stitches after the pattern repeat. Work Rows 1–4 once, and then repeat Rows 3 and 4 for pattern.

Chart Key

o	Chain 1
✕	1 single crochet
⊤	1 treble crochet
⋀ (Tr2tog)	Tr2tog-in-1: 2 treble crochets into the same stitch and crocheted together

2 pairs of 2 treble crochets crocheted together. Work [2 treble crochets into the same stitch] twice: In the first row, space 3 single crochets of the previous row between them; for every subsequent group of treble crochets within the same row, the insertion point for the first and second treble crochet is the same as the one for the third and fourth treble crochets of the previous group. In Rows 3 and 4, for the treble crochet, always insert the hook in the spot of the previous row where the loops of the joined treble crochets and the working loop converge (i.e., before the group).

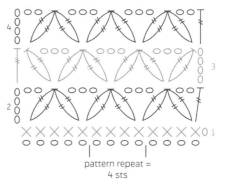

pattern repeat = 4 sts

130 TRIANGLE TRACKS

[multiple of 6 + 1 ch + 4 beg-ch]

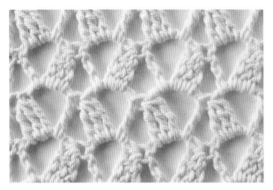

Work in rows, following the chart. Begin with the stitches before the pattern repeat, repeat the marked pattern repeat (6 sts wide) widthwise, and end with the stitches after the pattern repeat. Work Rows 1–3 once, and then repeat Rows 2 and 3 for pattern.

From Row 2 on, always work the individual treble crochets, as well as the treble crochets that are crocheted off together, in the chain space of the previous row, around the chain.

Chart Key

○ Chain 1

 1 treble crochet

Tr3tog: cluster of 3 treble crochets crocheted together

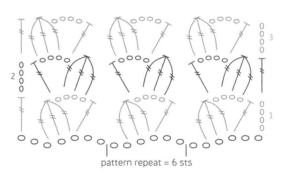

pattern repeat = 6 sts

131 EYELET ROWS WITH TRIANGLES

[multiple of 2 + 1 ch + 3 beg-ch]

Work in rows, following the chart. Begin every row with the stitches before the pattern repeat, repeat the marked pattern repeat (2 sts wide) widthwise, and end with the stitches after the pattern repeat. Work Rows 1–3 once, and then repeat Rows 2 and 3 for pattern.

In Row 2, work the double crochets in the chain space of the previous row, around the chain.

Chart Key

○ Chain 1

1 double crochet

Dc3tog: Double crochet 3 stitches together

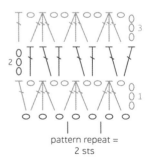

pattern repeat = 2 sts

132 ZIGZAG BANDS

[multiple of 4 + 2 ch + 3 beg-ch]

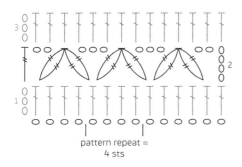

pattern repeat =
4 sts

Chart Key

○   Chain 1   1 treble crochet

2 pairs of 2 treble crochets each crocheted together: Working [2 treble crochets into the same stitch] twice, space 3 double crochets of the previous row between them. The insertion point for the first and second treble crochet is the same as the one for the third and fourth treble crochets of the previous group.

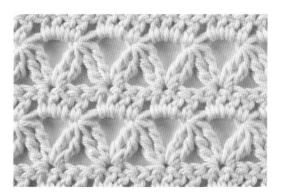

Work in rows, following the chart; Row 1 is a WS row. Begin with the stitches before the pattern repeat, repeat the marked pattern repeat (4 sts wide) widthwise, and end with the stitches after the pattern repeat. Work Rows 1–3 once, and then repeat Rows 2 and 3 for pattern.

133 TALL TRIANGLES

[multiple of 4 + 1 ch + 1 beg-ch]

Work in rows, following the chart. Begin with the stitches before the pattern repeat, repeat the marked pattern repeat (4 sts wide) widthwise, and end with the stitches after the pattern repeat. Work Rows 1–4 once, and then repeat Rows 3 and 4 for pattern.

Chart Key

○   Chain 1

     1 single crochet   1 treble crochet

2 pairs of 2 treble crochets each crocheted together: Working [2 treble crochets into the same stitch] twice, space 3 single crochets of the previous row between them. The insertion point for the first and second treble crochet is the same as the one for the third and fourth treble crochets of the previous group.

1 cluster of paired treble crochets: 4 treble crochets crocheted off together, working the first and second treble crochet into the same chain before a group of the previous row, and the third and fourth treble crochet after a group. For every subsequent group of treble crochets within the same row, the insertion point for the first and second treble crochet is located directly next to the one for the previous group of treble crochets.

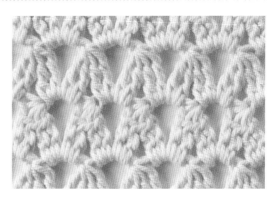

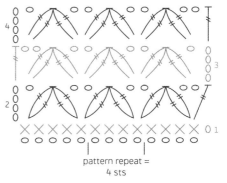

pattern repeat =
4 sts

134 SIDEWAYS POPCORN OVALS

[multiple of 4 + 1 ch + 1 beg-ch]

Work in rows, following the chart. Begin with the stitches before the pattern repeat, repeat the marked pattern repeat (4 sts wide) widthwise, and end with the stitches after the pattern repeat. Work Rows 1–6 once, and then repeat Rows 3–6 for pattern.

In Rows 4 and 6, work the single crochets between the groups of stitches.

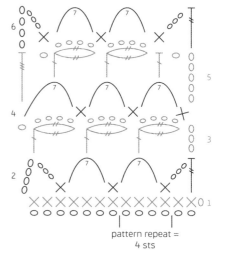

Chart Key

○	Chain 1
⌒7	Chain arc of 7 chains
✕	1 single crochet
╤	1 double crochet

╤	1 treble crochet
╤	1 double treble crochet

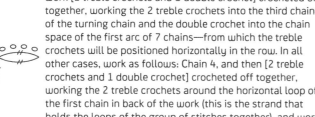 1 sideways popcorn: At the beginning of the row (in Row 3), work [2 treble crochets and 1 double crochet] crocheted off together, working the 2 treble crochets into the third chain of the turning chain and the double crochet into the chain space of the first arc of 7 chains—from which the treble crochets will be positioned horizontally in the row. In all other cases, work as follows: Chain 4, and then [2 treble crochets and 1 double crochet] crocheted off together, working the 2 treble crochets around the horizontal loop of the first chain in back of the work (this is the strand that holds the loops of the group of stitches together), and work the double crochet in the chain space of the next chain arc of the previous row.

pattern repeat =
4 sts

Cluster and Puff Stitch Patterns

135 SIMPLE MESH PATTERN

[multiple of 2 + 1 beg-ch]

Work in rows, following the chart; Row 1 is a WS row. Begin with the stitches before the pattern repeat, repeat the marked pattern repeat (2 sts wide) widthwise, and end with the stitches after the pattern repeat. Work Rows 1–4 once, and then repeat Rows 3 and 4 for pattern.

Chart Key

○ Chain 1

✕ 1 single crochet

T 1 double crochet

Half double crochet twins: [Yarn over hook once, insert hook, pull the working yarn through] twice, slightly lengthen the loops, draw the working yarn through 4 loops at once. Draw the working yarn through once more, crocheting the remaining 2 loops off together.

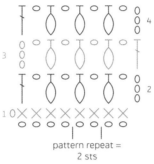

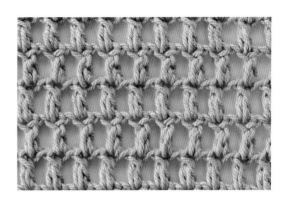

pattern repeat = 2 sts

136 MACRAMÉ-LOOK STITCH

[multiple of 2 + 1 beg-ch]

Work in rows, following the chart; Row 1 is a WS row. Begin with the stitches before the pattern repeat, repeat the marked pattern repeat (2 sts wide) widthwise, and end with the stitches after the pattern repeat. Work Rows 1–5 once, and then repeat Rows 2–5 for pattern.

In Rows 3 and 5, work the single crochet in the chain space of the previous row, around the chain.

Chart Key

○ Chain 1

✕ 1 single crochet

T 1 half double crochet

2 half double crochets into the same stitch and crocheted together: [Yarn over hook once, insert hook, pull the working yarn through] twice, slightly lengthen the loops, draw the working yarn through, pulling it through all 5 loops on the hook at once.

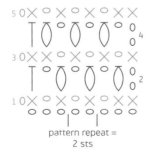

pattern repeat = 2 sts

137 TWISTER

[multiple of 4 + 1 ch + 1 beg-ch]

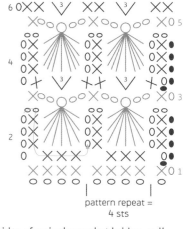

Chart Key

 Chain 1

● 1 slip stitch

✕ 1 single crochet

⌄3 Sc3-in-1: 3 single crochets into the same stitch

pattern repeat = 4 sts

 9-loop-cluster: Between 2 vertical sides of a single crochet bridge, pull through a total of 9 loops from different insertion points, inserting the hook as follows, and pulling the working yarn through: 3 times into the beginning chains of the bridge, 3 times into the single crochets of the horizontal base row, 3 times into the single crochets of the next bridge, pulling the loops somewhat longer, especially the ones atop the horizontally placed stitches. Finally, yarn over and draw the working yarn through all 9 loops on the hook and through the working loop at once. Chain 1, which will fasten the converging loops.

11-loop-cluster: Between 2 vertical sides of a single crochet bridge, pull through a total of 11 loops from different insertion points, inserting the hook as follows, and pulling the working yarn through: 3 times into the beginning chains of the bridge, 5 times into the single crochets of the horizontal base row, 3 times into the single crochets of the next bridge, pulling the loops somewhat longer, especially the ones atop the horizontally placed stitches. Finally, draw the working yarn through all 11 loops on the hook and through the working loop at once. Chain 1, which will fasten the converging loops.

Work in rows, following the chart. Begin with the stitches before the pattern repeat, repeat the marked pattern repeat (4 sts wide) widthwise, and end with the stitches after the pattern repeat. Work Rows 1–5 once, and then repeat Rows 4 and 5 for pattern. Finish by adding Row 6 as the final row.

In Rows 2 and 4, vertical bridges made of single crochets are added at short intervals; the spaces between them will be filled with clusters of 9 or 11 loops in the following row. Onto the last bridge of every row, work 4 slip stitches to travel to the beginning of the next row.

138 WRAP-AROUND LOOK

[multiple of 2 + 1 ch + 1 beg-ch]

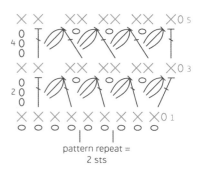

Chart Key

○ Chain 1

✕ 1 single crochet

⊤ 1 double crochet

 1 puff from 3 half double crochets, worked around the previously worked double crochets from the group of stitches, and crocheted together

pattern repeat = 2 sts

1 group of stitches: 1 puff and 1 double crochet crocheted together: [Yarn over hook once, insert hook around the previously worked double crochet, and draw the working yarn through 3 times, and then slightly lengthen the loops. Now, to work a double crochet, yarn over hook once, skip 1 single crochet and insert the hook into the next single crochet of the previous row, draw the working yarn through, and then pull the yarn through 2 loops on the hook. After this, draw the working yarn through all 8 loops on the hook at once. The chain worked after this will hold all loops from the group of stitches together.

Work in rows, following the chart. Begin with the stitches before the pattern repeat, repeat the marked pattern repeat (2 sts wide) widthwise, and end with the stitches after the pattern repeat. Work Rows 1–4 once, and then repeat Rows 3 and 4 for pattern, ending with Row 5 (single crochet).

Within Rows 3 and 5, always work the 2 single crochets between the puffs of the previous row (i.e., around a joined top).

139 PUFFS STAGGERED ON A CHECKERBOARD [multiple of 5 + 3 beg-ch]

Chart Key

o   Chain 1 | 1 double crochet

 1 puff stitch around the double crochet worked last: [Yarn over hook once, insert the hook around the last double crochet worked, and pull the working yarn through] 3 times, slightly lengthen the loops, draw the working yarn through again, pulling it through all 7 loops on the hook at once.

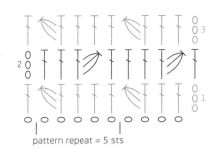

pattern repeat = 5 sts

Work in rows, following the chart. Begin with the stitches before the pattern repeat, repeat the marked pattern repeat (5 sts wide) widthwise, and end with the stitches after the pattern repeat. Work Rows 1–3 once, and then repeat Rows 2 and 3 for pattern.

140 SNAPDRAGONS [multiple of 5 + 4 beg-ch]

Work in rows, following the chart; Row 1 is a WS row. Begin with the stitches before the pattern repeat, repeat the marked pattern repeat (5 sts wide) widthwise, and end with the stitches after the pattern repeat. Work Rows 1–6 once, and then repeat Rows 3–6 for pattern.

In Rows 2, 4, and 6, always work the single crochet in the chain space of the single chain between the treble crochets. In Rows 3 and 5, to work the sequence of [2 treble crochets, chain 1, 2 treble crochets], insert the hook into the cluster of the previous row in the spot where the loops of the cluster stitches converge.

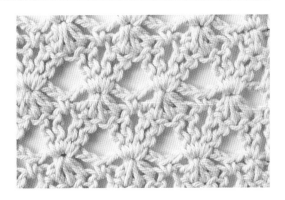

Chart Key

o   Chain 1   ✕   1 single crochet | 1 half double crochet

| 1 double crochet   ╪   1 treble crochet   V   2 treble crochets into the same stitch

 [2 treble crochets, chain 1, 2 treble crochets] into the same stitch

1 cluster from 4 treble crochets: Work [yarn over hook once, insert hook, pull the working yarn through] 4 times total, one after another, in 4 treble crochets of the previous row; slightly lengthen the loops, and then draw the working yarn through and pull it through all loops on the hook at once (except for the working loop). After this, crochet the remaining 2 loops off together.

 1 cluster from 2 treble crochets: Work [yarn over hook once, insert hook, pull the working yarn through] twice, one after another, in 2 treble crochets of the previous row; then draw working yarn through 4 loops once, and, after this, crochet the remaining 2 loops off together.

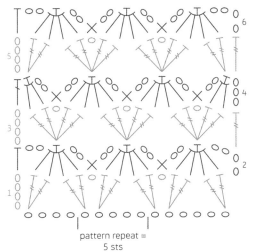

pattern repeat = 5 sts

141 PUFFS ON A ZIGZAG PATH
[multiple of 3 + 2 beg-ch]

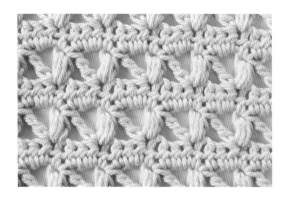

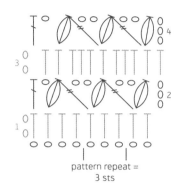

Chart Key

o — Chain 1

⊤ — 1 half double crochet

⊤ — 1 double crochet

◊ — Half double crochet—puff stitch: 3 half double crochets worked into the same insertion point and crocheted off together.

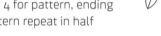

pattern repeat = 3 sts

Work in rows, following the chart; Row 1 is a WS row. Begin with the stitches before the pattern repeat, repeat the marked pattern repeat (3 sts wide) widthwise, and end with the stitches after the pattern repeat. Work Rows 1–4 once, and then repeat Rows 3 and 4 for pattern, ending with a Row 3 of the pattern repeat in half double crochet.

During Row 3, work the half double crochets directly into the stitch located where the loops of the group of stitches converge, and in between work into the chain space of the previous row.

1 group of stitches: 1 treble crochet and 1 half double crochet—puff stitch crocheted off together, inserting the hook into two different insertion points. Work the treble crochet into the same insertion point as the previously worked half double crochet—puff stitch, and pull the working yarn through all loops on the hook except for the last 2. In Row 2, work the half double crochet—puff stitch into the following third half double crochet of the previous row; in Row 4, skip 3 instead of 2 stitches, by working [yarn over hook once, insert hook, pull the working yarn through] 3 times, slightly lengthen the loops, draw the working yarn through, and pull it through all 9 loops on the hook at once (the following chain will hold all loops from the group of stitches together).

142 PUFF GRID
[multiple of 4 + 2 ch + 4 beg-ch]

pattern repeat = 4 sts

Work in rows, following the chart. Begin with the stitches before the pattern repeat, repeat the marked pattern repeat (4 sts wide) widthwise, and end with the stitches after the pattern repeat. Work Rows 1–3 once, and then repeat Rows 2 and 3 for pattern.

From Row 2 on, work the vertically placed half double crochet—puffs of 4 into the joined top of the vertically placed half double crochet—puffs of the previous row.

Chart Key

o — Chain 1   ⊤ — 1 treble crochet

◊ — Half double crochet—puff of 3: [Yarn over hook once, insert hook, pull the working yarn through] 3 times, slightly lengthen the loops, draw the working yarn through, pulling it through all loops on the hook at once (except for the working loop). Draw the working yarn through once more, crocheting the remaining 2 loops off together.

— 1 horizontal puff: Chain 3, work a half double crochet—puff of 3 into the horizontal ridge on the back of the work of the first chain.

◊ — Half double crochet—puff of 4: [Yarn over hook once, insert hook, pull the working yarn through] 4 times, slightly lengthen the loops, draw the working yarn through, pulling it through all loops on the hook at once (except for the working loop). Draw the working yarn through once more, crocheting the remaining 2 loops off together.

143 LINED-UP PUFFS

[multiple of 2 + 1 beg-ch]

Work in rows, following the chart; Row 1 is a WS row. Begin with the stitches before the pattern repeat, repeat the marked pattern repeat (2 sts wide) widthwise, and end with the stitches after the pattern repeat. Work Rows 1–4 once, and then repeat Rows 3 and 4 for pattern.

From Row 3 on, always work the half double crochet–puffs in the chain space of the previous row.

Chart Key

o   Chain 1

✕   1 single crochet

⊤   1 double crochet

Half double crochet–puff: [Yarn over hook once, insert hook, pull the working yarn through] 4 times, slightly lengthen the loops, draw the working yarn through all the loops on the hook at once (except for the working loop). Draw the working yarn through once more, crocheting the remaining 2 loops off together.

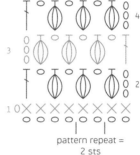

pattern repeat =
2 sts

144 PLAITED LOOK

[multiple of 2 + 1 beg-ch]

Work in rows, following the chart. Begin with the stitches before the pattern repeat, repeat the marked pattern repeat (2 sts wide) widthwise, and end with the stitches after the pattern repeat. Work Rows 1–4 once, and then repeat Rows 3 and 4 for pattern.

Chart Key

o   Chain 1

✕   1 single crochet

⊤   1 double crochet

1 group of stitches worked into the same stitch: Begin with 1 single crochet, and then work [yarn over hook once, insert hook, pull the working yarn through] 3 times, slightly lengthen the loops, draw the working yarn through, and pull it through all loops on the hook at once (except for the working loop). Draw the working yarn through once more, crocheting the remaining 2 loops off together.

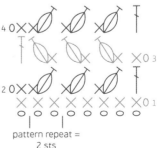

pattern repeat =
2 sts

145 PAIRED CLUSTERS

[multiple of 6 + 4 ch + 3 beg-ch]

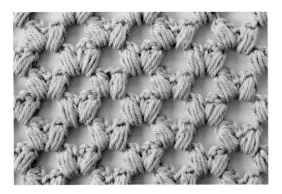

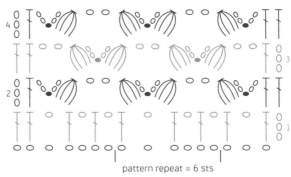

pattern repeat = 6 sts

Work in rows, following the chart. Begin with the stitches before the pattern repeat, repeat the marked pattern repeat (6 sts wide) width-wise, and end with the stitches after the pattern repeat. Work Rows 1–4 once, and then repeat Rows 3 and 4 for pattern.

Chart Key

○ Chain 1

● 1 slip stitch

⊤ 1 double crochet

⋔ Work 1 cluster in the chain space around the chain: [Yarn over hook once, insert hook, pull the working yarn through] 4 times, slightly lengthen the loops, yarn over hook once, and pull it through all 9 loops on the hook at once. The chain worked after this will hold the converging loops together.

146 SLANTED CLUSTERS

[multiple of 10 + 1 ch + 3 beg-ch]

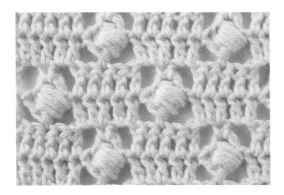

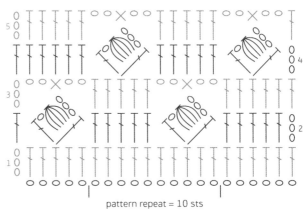

pattern repeat = 10 sts

Work in rows, following the chart; Row 1 is a WS row. Begin with the stitches before the pattern repeat, repeat the marked pattern repeat (10 sts wide) widthwise, and end with the stitches after the pattern repeat. Work Rows 1–5 once, and then repeat Rows 2–5 for pattern.

In Rows 3 and 5, always work the single crochet in the chain space of the group of stitches, around the chain.

Chart Key

○ Chain 1

✕ 1 single crochet

⊤ 1 double crochet

1 group of stitches: Work 1 double crochet in the following third stitch, chain 3, work 1 cluster around the diagonally placed double crochet by working [yarn over hook once, insert hook before the double crochet, and pull the working yarn through] 5 times, lengthen the loops to the height of the 3 chains, draw the working yarn through, and pull it through all 11 loops on the hook at once; chain 1 to secure the loops that were crocheted together and complete the group by working a final double crochet after the cluster.

147 RAISED PUFF STITCH COLUMNS

[multiple of 4 + 1 ch + 3 beg-ch]

Work in rows, following the chart. Begin with the stitches before the pattern repeat, repeat the marked pattern repeat (4 sts wide) widthwise, and end with the stitches after the pattern repeat. Work Rows 1–3 once, and then repeat Rows 2 and 3 for pattern.

From Row 2 on, work the pairs of double crochets between two double crochets of the previous row.

Chart Key

○   Chain 1   ┬   1 double crochet   V   Dc2-in-1: 2 double crochets into the same stitch

1 puff into the same stitch: Work [yarn over hook once, insert hook, pull the working yarn through] 3 times, slightly lengthen the loops, draw the working yarn through, and pull it through all 7 loops on the hook at once. Finally, chain 1 to secure the converging loops.

1 raised puff from the back around the top part of the puff of the previous row: Work 1 puff into the same stitch as above, inserting hook from the back under the joined top and in front of the converging loops, passing the hook in front of the loops, and then again toward the back. The puff from the previous row will bulge out to the back on the hook.

1 raised puff from the front around the top part of the puff of the previous row: Work 1 puff into the same stitch as above, inserting hook from the front under the joined top and in front of the converging loops, passing the hook behind the loops, and then again toward the front. The puff from the previous row will bulge out to the front on the hook.

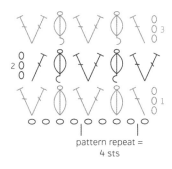

pattern repeat = 4 sts

148 PUFF-AND-DOUBLE-CROCHET COLUMNS

[multiple of 10 + 3 beg-ch]

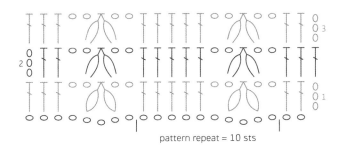

pattern repeat = 10 sts

Chart Key

○   Chain 1   ┬   1 double crochet

1 pair of puff stitches worked around the chain: * [Yarn over hook once, insert hook into the first insertion point, and then pull the working yarn through] twice, slightly lengthen the loops, draw the working yarn through, pulling it through 4 loops on the hook; repeat from * once in the second insertion point. Finally, draw the working yarn through and pull it through the 3 loops together at once.

1 pair of puff stitches worked as before, but always worked into 1 chain of the beginning chain, while skipping 1 chain of the beginning chain

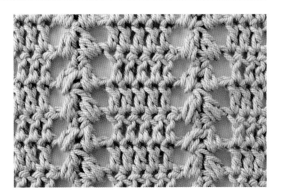

Work in rows, following the chart. Begin with the stitches before the pattern repeat, repeat the marked pattern repeat (10 sts wide) widthwise, and end with the stitches after the pattern repeat. Work Rows 1–3 once, and then repeat Rows 2 and 3 for pattern.

149 PUFFS IN WINDOWS

[multiple of 6 + 1 ch + 1 beg-ch]

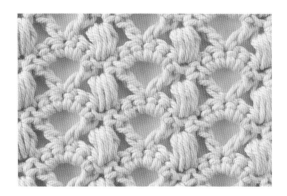

Work in rows, following the chart; Row 1 is a WS row. Begin with the stitches before the pattern repeat, repeat the marked pattern repeat (6 sts wide) widthwise, and end with the stitches after the pattern repeat. Work Rows 1–3 once, and then repeat Rows 2 and 3 for pattern.

In Row 3, at the beginning and at the end of the row, work 3 single crochets into each chain space, and within the row, always work 5 single crochets into the chain space, 1 single crochet into each half double crochet—puff directly underneath the spot where the loops converge.

pattern repeat = 6 sts

Chart Key

○ Chain 1

✕ 1 single crochet

⊤ 1 double crochet

 [1 double crochet, chain 2, 1 treble crochet] into the same stitch

[1 double crochet, chain 3, 1 double crochet] into the same stitch

1 half double crochet—puff into the same stitch: [Yarn over hook once, insert hook, pull the working yarn through] 4 times, lengthen the loops to the height of the double crochets, draw the working yarn through, and pull it through all 9 loops on the hook at once. Finally, chain 1 to secure the converging loops.

150 PUFFS IN DIAMOND MESH

[multiple of 6 + 1 ch + 1 beg-ch]

Work in rows, following the chart. Begin with the stitches before the pattern repeat, repeat the marked pattern repeat (6 sts wide) widthwise, and end with the stitches after the pattern repeat. Work Rows 1–3 once, and then repeat Rows 2 and 3 for pattern.

pattern repeat = 6 sts

Chart Key

○ Chain 1

✕ 1 single crochet

⊤ 1 double crochet

1 half double crochet—puff into the same stitch: Work [yarn over hook once, insert hook, pull the working yarn through] 3 times, slightly lengthen the loops, draw the working yarn through all loops on the hook at once (except for the working loop). Draw the working yarn through once more, crocheting the remaining 2 loops off together.

151 TWISTED CLUSTERS
[multiple of 2 + 1 ch + 1 beg-ch]

Work in rows, following the chart; Row 1 is a WS row. Begin with the stitches before the pattern repeat, repeat the marked pattern repeat (2 sts wide) widthwise, and end with the stitches after the pattern repeat. Work Rows 1–4 once, and then repeat Rows 3 and 4 for pattern. Row 5 shown in the chart is the final row.

In Rows 3 and 5, work the single crochet exactly in the spot of the cluster where the loops from crocheting together converge.

Chart Key

o   Chain 1

✕   1 single crochet

⊤   1 double crochet

1 twisted cluster: Pull a total of 6 loops from two different insertion points through by working [insert hook in first spot, pull the working yarn through, insert hook in second spot, pull the working yarn through] 3 times (i.e., draw the loops through, alternating between the first and second spots, around the chain of the previous row, and slightly lengthen the loops). Yarn over hook and draw the working yarn through all 7 loops on the hook at once. This way, the loops end up crossed over each other. The chain worked after this will hold the converging loops together. In subsequent repeats, the first insertion point of a cluster will always coincide with the preceding cluster.

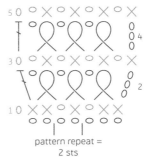

pattern repeat =
2 sts

152 PUFFS IN A DOUBLE CROCHET GRID
[multiple of 6 + 4 ch + 3 beg-ch]

Work in rows, following the chart. Begin with the stitches before the pattern repeat, repeat the marked pattern repeat (6 sts wide) widthwise, and end with the stitches after the pattern repeat. Work Rows 1–3 once, and then repeat Rows 2 and 3 for pattern.

From Row 2 on, when working the sequence of [1 double crochet, chain 2, 1 double crochet] into the cluster, insert the hook directly underneath the top of the cluster where the loops converge.

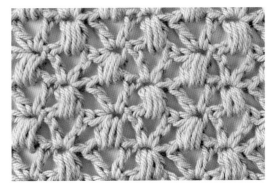

Chart Key

o   Chain 1

⊤   1 double crochet

 [1 double crochet, chain 2, 1 double crochet] into the same stitch

1 cluster in the chain space of the 2 chains between double crochets: [Yarn over hook once, insert hook, pull the working yarn through] 4 times, slightly lengthen the loops, draw the working yarn through all 9 loops on the hook at once. Finally, chain 1 to secure the converging loops.

1 puff worked into 1 chain of the beginning chain: [Yarn over hook once, insert hook, pull the working yarn through] 4 times, slightly lengthen the loops, draw the working yarn through all 9 loops on the hook at once. Finally, chain 1 to secure the converging loops.

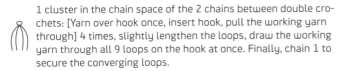

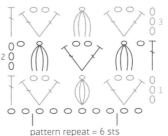

pattern repeat = 6 sts

153 PUFFS WITH FANS

[multiple of 8 + 5 ch + 3 beg-ch]

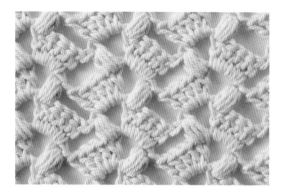

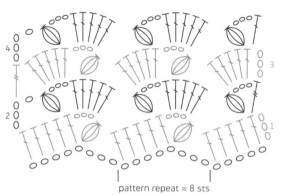

pattern repeat = 8 sts

Work in rows, following the chart. Begin with the stitches before the pattern repeat, repeat the marked pattern repeat (8 sts wide) width-wise, and end with the stitches after the pattern repeat. Work Rows 1–3 once, and then repeat Rows 2 and 3 for pattern.

From Row 2 on, work the 5 double crochets in the chain space of the previous row and always work the half double crochet—puffs into the fifth double crochet of the previous row. When the desired height has been reached, at the end of the final row, work a double crochet instead of the treble crochet.

Chart Key

○ Chain 1

┬ 1 double crochet

┬ 1 treble crochet

1 half double crochet—puff into the same stitch: [Yarn over hook once, insert hook, pull the working yarn through] 4 times, lengthen the loops to the height of the double crochets, draw the working yarn through all 9 loops on the hook at once. The chain worked next in the pattern will secure the converging loops.

154 ALLOVER 3-LOOP STARS [multiple of 2 + 1 beg-ch]

Chart Key

○ Chain 1   ✕ 1 single crochet

⌐ 3-loop-star: Pull the first loop through around the horizontal strand of the chain on the back of the work (from the second star on, this will be the strand that holds the loops of the star together). For the second loop, insert the hook from the back into the last loop of the previously worked star, and then pull the working yarn through. Pull the third loop through the following second stitch of the previous row, or in the center of the star (i.e., insert the hook under the loop of the chain). Draw the working yarn through and pull it through all 4 loops on the hook at once.

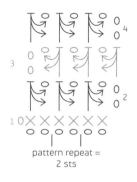

pattern repeat = 2 sts

Work in rows, following the chart; Row 1 is a WS row. Begin with the stitches before the pattern repeat, repeat the marked pattern repeat (2 sts wide) widthwise, and end with the stitches after the pattern repeat. Work Rows 1–4 once, and then repeat Rows 3 and 4 for pattern.

To work the star, at the beginning of the row, pull the first and second loop through the first and third chain, counted from the hook.

155 3-LOOP STARS AND ROWS OF DOUBLE CROCHETS [multiple of 2 + 1 ch + 3 beg-ch]

Chart Key

○ Chain 1

┬ Dc2-in-1: 2 dou-
⫛ ble crochets into the same stitch

† 1 double crochet

⋏ Dc2tog: Double crochet 2 stitches together

⋏ 3-loop-star: For the first loop, insert the hook from the back into the last loop of the previously worked star, and then pull the working yarn through. For the second and third loops, pull 1 loop each through the next 2 stitches of the previous row. Draw the working yarn through all 4 loops on the hook at once.

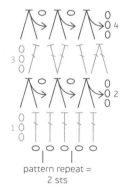

pattern repeat = 2 sts

Work in rows, following the chart; Row 1 is a WS row. Begin with the stitches before the pattern repeat, repeat the marked pattern repeat (2 sts wide) widthwise, and end with the stitches after the pattern repeat. Work Rows 1–4 once, and then repeat Rows 3 and 4 for pattern.

To work the star at the beginning of the row, pull the first loop through the second chain counted from the hook. In Row 3, work the two double crochets into the same insertion point in the center of the star (i.e., in the spot where the loops converge).

156 SMALL STAR PATTERN

[multiple of 2 + 1 beg-ch]

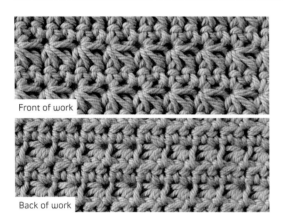

Front of work

Back of work

Work in rows, following the chart; Row 1 is a WS row. Begin with the stitches before the pattern repeat, repeat the marked pattern repeat (2 sts wide) widthwise, and end with the stitches after the pattern repeat. Work Rows 1–3 once, and then repeat Rows 2 and 3 for pattern.

In Row 3, work the first single crochet into the second chain from the hook, which is the spot where the loops of the star converge.

In the back of the work, vertical lines that partition the stitch pattern into small boxes can be seen.

pattern repeat = 2 sts

Chart Key

o   Chain 1   X   1 single crochet

 4-loop-star at the beginning of the row: Pull the first and second loops through the 2 chains of the turning chain, pull the third and fourth loops through the first 2 single crochets of the previous row, draw the working yarn through all 5 loops on the hook at once.

 4-loop-star: Pull the first loop through around the horizontal strand of the chain on the back of the work (this is the strand that holds the loops of the star together). Pull the second loop through the last insertion point of the previously worked star. Pull the third and fourth loops through the next 2 stitches of the previous row. Draw the working yarn through all 5 loops on the hook at once.

157 LARGE STAR PATTERN

[multiple of 2 + 1 beg-ch]

pattern repeat = 2 sts

Work in rows, following the chart; Row 1 is a WS row. Begin with the stitches before the pattern repeat, repeat the marked pattern repeat (2 sts wide) widthwise, and end with the stitches after the pattern repeat. Work Rows 1–3 once, and then repeat Rows 2 and 3 for pattern.

In Row 3, work the first single crochet into the second chain from the hook, which is the spot in which the loops of the star converge.

Chart Key

o   Chain 1   X   1 single crochet

 5-loop-star at the beginning of the row: Pull the first, second, and third loops through one after another through each of the 3 chains of the turning chain; then pull the fourth and fifth loops through the first 2 single crochets of the previous row, draw the working yarn through all 6 loops on the hook at once.

 5-loop-star: Pull the first loop through around the horizontal strand of the chain on the back of the work (this is the strand that holds the loops of the star together). For the second loop, insert the hook from the back into the last loop of the previously worked star, and pull the working yarn through. Pull the third loop through the last insertion point of the previously worked star. Pull the fourth and fifth loops through the next 2 stitches of the previous row. Draw the working yarn through all 6 loops on the hook at once.

158 STAR STITCH IN ROUNDS

[odd st ct]

Work in rounds, following the chart. Join the beginning chain into the round by working 1 slip stitch into the first chain stitch of the beginning chain. Begin with the stitches before the pattern repeat, and then repeat the marked pattern repeat (2 sts wide) widthwise. Join Round 1 with 1 slip stitch into the first single crochet; join all following rounds with a slip stitch into the top chain of the beginning chain. Repeat Round 3 for pattern. With every new round worked, stitches will slant slightly to the right.

To work the star at the beginning of the round, pull the first and second loops through the first and third chains from the hook of the beg-ch; then pull the third and fourth loops through 2 stitches of the previous round, and pull the yarn through all 5 loops on the hook at once.

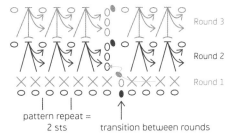

Round 3

Round 2

Round 1

pattern repeat =
2 sts

transition between rounds

Chart Key

o Chain 1

• 1 slip stitch

 ✕ 1 single crochet

 4-loop-star: Pull the first loop through around the horizontal strand of the chain on the back of the work (this is the strand that holds the loops of the star together). For the second loop, insert the hook from the back into the last loop of the previously worked star, and then pull the working yarn through. Pull the third and fourth loops through the next 2 stitches of the previous round. Draw the working yarn through all 5 loops on the hook at once.

 4-loop-star in Round 3: Pull the third loop through only around the back loop of the stitch and the fourth loop around the chain (= center of the star).

Bobble and Nupp Patterns

159 BOBBLE COLUMNS

[multiple of 5 + 4 ch + 2 beg-ch]

Work in rows, following the chart; Row 1 is a WS row. Begin with the stitches before the pattern repeat, repeat the marked pattern repeat (5 sts wide) widthwise, and end with the stitches after the pattern repeat. Work Rows 1–3 once, and then repeat Rows 2 and 3 for pattern.

Chart Key

○ Chain 1

✕ 1 single crochet

T 1 half double crochet

● 1 bobble: Work in RS rows so that the bobble ends up on the RS of the crocheted fabric. Insert the hook into 1 stitch, and pull the yarn through, chain 5. After this, draw the working yarn through again, and pull it through both loops on the hook. Push the resulting chain through to the front of the work.

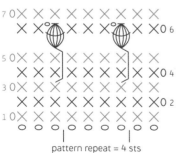

pattern repeat = 5 sts

160 PINEAPPLE SPIKE BOBBLES

[multiple of 4 + 1 ch + 1 beg-ch]

The stitch pattern features bobbles stacked directly atop each other on a single crochet background. Work in rows, following the chart; Row 1 is a WS row. Begin with the stitches before the pattern repeat, repeat the marked pattern repeat (4 sts wide) widthwise, and end with the stitches after the pattern repeat. Work Rows 1–7 once, and then repeat Rows 2–7 for pattern.

Chart Key

○ Chain 1

✕ 1 single crochet

1 bobble: Work in RS rows so that the bobble ends up on the RS of the crocheted fabric. Work 6 double crochets into the same spot, located 2 rows below, and crochet them off together. For the first double cro-chet, yarn over hook once, insert hook into the stitch 2 rows below, draw the working yarn through, and then lengthen the loop to a height just above the top edge of the current row and then yarn over and pull the yarn through the first 2 loops on the hook at once. Work 5 more double crochets the same way into the same insertion point. After you complete these steps, you will have 1 loop for each double crochet plus the working loop on your hook. Draw the working yarn through all 7 loops on the hook at once. The chain worked after this will hold the converging loops together; it will be skipped in the following row.

pattern repeat = 4 sts

161 DRAGON SPIKES

[multiple of 4 + 3 ch + 1 beg-ch]

Work in rows, following the chart; Row 1 is a WS row. Begin with the stitches before the pattern repeat, repeat the marked pattern repeat (4 sts wide) widthwise, and end with the stitches after the pattern repeat. Work Rows 1–5 once, and then repeat Rows 2–5 for pattern.

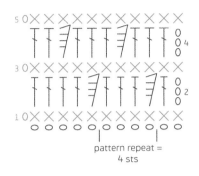

pattern repeat = 4 sts

Chart Key

o Chain 1
X 1 single crochet
⊤ 1 double crochet

1 nupp: Work in RS rows; the nupp is crocheted on the RS of the fabric. Insert the hook into 1 stitch, pull the yarn through, [draw the working yarn through the first loop on the hook] 4 times, making a chain. Pull the working yarn through as follows: Through the back loop of the stitch only, pull 1 loop each through the second, third, and fourth chain of the crocheted chain, slightly lengthen the loops, and then pull 1 additional loop through the stitch from which the crocheted chain emerges. Draw the working yarn through all 6 loops on the hook at once. Push the scale through to the front of the fabric under the joined top. When crocheting over this spot in the following WS row, work 1 single crochet around the joined top, with the scale pointing to the back.

162 SLANTED BOBBLES

[multiple of 18 + 2 + 2 beg-ch]

Chart Key

o Chain 1   ⊤ 1 half double crochet

1 bobble: Work in RS rows so that the bobble is crocheted on the RS of the crocheted fabric. Work 5 double crochets crocheted together around the body of the half double crochet of the previous row. For the first double crochet, yarn over hook once, insert the hook under the top and behind the body of the half double crochet of the previous row located directly below it (so that the half double crochet arcs over the hook), draw the working yarn through, and then yarn over and pull the yarn through the first 2 loops on the hook at once. Work 4 more double crochets the same way, around the half double crochet; they will be located one below the other and completely encapsulate the base stitch. After completion of these steps, you will have 1 loop for each double crochet plus the working loop on your hook. Draw the working yarn through once more and pull it through all 6 loops on the hook at once.

This stitch pattern features bobbles in staggered groups of 3 on a half double crochet background. Work in rows, following the chart. In bobble rows, repeat the marked pattern repeat (18 sts wide) widthwise, and end with the stitches after the pattern repeat. Work Rows 1–5 once, and then repeat Rows 2–5 for pattern. In the final row of the crocheted piece, work half double crochets across (Row 6).

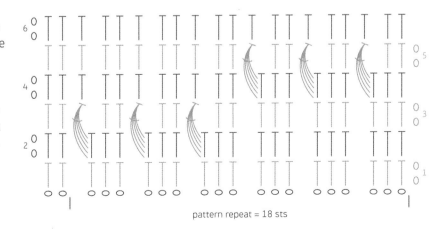

pattern repeat = 18 sts

163 DOUBLE CROCHET BOBBLES

[multiple of 16 + 2 ch + 3 beg-ch]

This stitch pattern features bobbles in staggered groups of 4, arranged on a background of [1 row double crochet, 1 row single crochet]. Work in rows, following the chart. In WS rows, repeat the marked pattern repeat (16 sts wide) widthwise and end with the stitches after the pattern repeat. Work Rows 1–9 once, and then repeat Rows 2–9 for pattern.

BOBBLES IN CONTRASTING COLOR

Bobbles can be worked in one or more contrasting color(s). Work in the main color to the position of the bobble, and then work the final step of the last single crochet in the bobble color, with yarns in front of the work. Work the bobble through the back loop of the next stitch only. After having worked the final step of crocheting the loops of the bobble together, take up the yarn in the main color again and pull it through the working loop; this creates 1 chain. Pull the working yarn taut, and then continue in the background pattern. When crocheting over the bobble spot later, always work 1 double crochet through the second contrasting color loop of the stitch only, while skipping the first one.

Chart Key

o   Chain 1

✕   1 single crochet

⊤   1 double crochet

 1 bobble: Work in WS rows; the bobble will bulge out toward the back on account of the lesser height of the background pattern stitches, so in the finished piece, it will end up on the RS of the crocheted fabric. Work a cluster of 5 double crochets into the same spot and crocheted off together: For each double crochet, yarn over hook once, insert the hook in the same spot again, draw the working yarn through, and then yarn over and pull the yarn through the first two loops on the hook at once. After completion of these steps, you will have 1 loop for each double crochet, plus the working loop on the hook. Draw the working yarn through all 6 loops on the hook at once. Pull the working yarn taut; the bobble will bulge out toward the back.

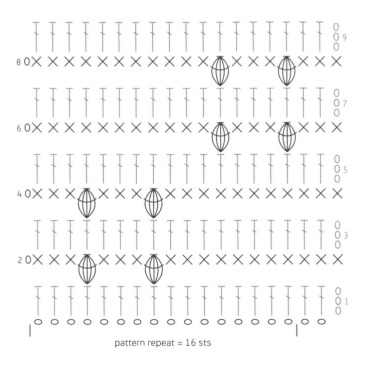

pattern repeat = 16 sts

164 SPIKE STITCH BOBBLES

[13 ch per motif]

This stitch pattern features bobbles worked through the back loop of the stitch only, which are arranged into a diamond motif. Diamonds may be spaced at intervals according to personal preference. The bobble diamond works as an individual motif, lined up either horizontally or vertically into a border, or as an allover pattern.

Work in rows, following the chart. Row 10 marks the heightwise middle of the diamond motif. To complete the upper half of the motif, after Row 11, work Rows 8–3 going backward (i.e., continue to stagger the bobbles, and with every bobble row, decrease the number of bobbles worked = Rows 12–17).

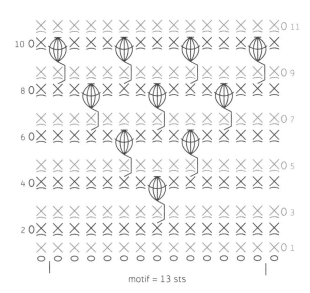

motif = 13 sts

Chart Key

○ Chain 1	✕ 1 single crochet	✕ Blo-sc: 1 single crochet through the back loop only

 1 bobble: Work in WS rows so that in the finished piece, the bobble will end up on the RS of the fabric. Work 5 double crochets 2 rows below and crocheted off together: For the first double crochet, yarn over hook once, insert the hook on the back of the work into the unused loop of the single crochet of the next-to-last row, draw the working yarn through, and then yarn over and pull the yarn through the first 2 loops on the hook at once. Work 4 more double crochets the same way around the same insertion point. After completion of these steps, you will have 1 loop for each double crochet plus the working loop on your hook. Draw the working yarn through all 6 loops on the hook at once.

165 MINI NUPPS IN A RIBBING PATTERN

[multiple of 4 + 1 ch + 1 beg-ch]

This stitch pattern features staggered nupps, which are always worked through the back loop of the stitch only, worked on a single crochet background. Work in rows, following the chart. Begin with the stitches before the pattern repeat, repeat the marked pattern repeat (4 sts wide) widthwise, and end with the stitches after the pattern repeat. Work Rows 1–5 once, and then repeat Rows 2–5 for pattern.

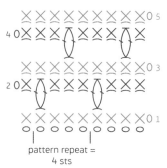

pattern repeat = 4 sts

Chart Key

o   Chain 1   ✕   1 single crochet   ⤬   Blo-sc: 1 single crochet through the back loop only

⟨⟩ 1 nupp: Work in WS rows; the nupp will bulge out toward the back on account of the lesser height of the background pattern stitches and the way the hook is inserted, so in the finished piece, it will end up on the RS of the fabric. Work 2 double crochets through the back loop only into the same stitch, and then crochet them off together.

166 POPCORNS ON AN ARROW PATH

[15 ch per arrow motif]

This stitch pattern features bobbles arranged vertically into arrow motifs on a background of [1 row single crochet, 1 row double crochet]. Arrow motifs may be spaced at intervals according to personal preference.

Work in rows, following the chart; Row 1 is a WS row. Work Rows 1–15 once, and then repeat Rows 4–15 for pattern.

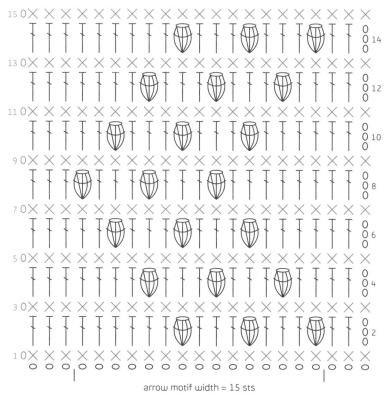

arrow motif width = 15 sts

Chart Key

o   Chain 1

⊤   1 double crochet

✕   1 single crochet

 1 popcorn bobble: Work in RS rows; the bobble will bulge out toward the front of work. Work 5 double crochets into the same stitch, of which the fourth and fifth double crochets are crocheted off together. Remove the hook from the working loop, insert the hook from the front into the first double crochet, place the working loop on the hook again, and pull the yarn through the double crochet. This gathers the loops of the stitches together. Secure the bobble with a tightly worked chain. When crocheting over this spot in the following WS row, work 1 single crochet around the loop of the stitch after the bobble, skipping the single chain.

167 STAGGERED MAXI BOBBLES

[multiple of 6 + 4 ch + 1 beg-ch]

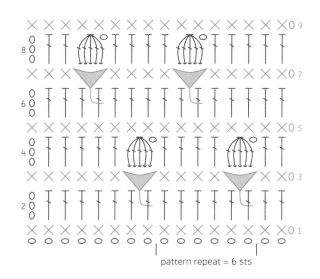

pattern repeat = 6 sts

This stitch pattern features staggered bobbles on a background of [1 row single crochet, 1 row double crochet] alternating. Work in rows, following the chart. Begin with the stitches before the pattern repeat, repeat the marked pattern repeat (6 sts wide) widthwise, and end with the stitches after the pattern repeat. Work Rows 1–9 once, and then repeat Rows 2–9 for pattern.

Chart Key

o   Chain 1

✕   1 single crochet

†   1 double crochet

1 bobble: Worked in RS row and the following WS row, the bobble spans 3 rows of the background pattern.

Step 1: One after another, work [1 single crochet, 1 half double crochet, 2 double crochets, 1 treble crochet] around the body of the double crochet of the previous row. For the first stitch, insert the hook under the top and behind the body of the double crochet of the previous row located directly underneath (the double crochet should bulge out over the hook), pull the working yarn through, and complete the stitch. Work the remaining 4 stitches the same way around the body of the double crochet; they will be located one below the other and completely encapsulate the base stitch.

Step 2: Work 5 double crochets through the front loop only into the bobble stitches of the previous row; crochet them off together. The chain worked after this will hold the converging loops together. When crocheting over this spot in the following row, work 1 single crochet around the chain and 1 single crochet into the joined top of the bobble.

168 POPCORNS UNDER ARCS

[multiple of 8 + 1 ch + 1 beg-ch]

pattern repeat = 8 sts

Work in rows, following the chart; Row 1 is a WS row. Begin with the stitches before the pattern repeat, repeat the marked pattern repeat (8 sts wide) widthwise, and end with the stitches after the pattern repeat. Work Rows 1–5 once, and then repeat Rows 2–5 for pattern.

Chart Key

o Chain 1

✕ 1 single crochet

⫿ 1 double crochet

Dc2tog-in-1: 2 double crochets into the same stitch and crocheted together

1 popcorn bobble: Work in RS rows; the bobble will bulge out toward the front of work. Work 5 double crochets into the same stitch. Remove the hook from the working loop, insert the hook from the front into the first double crochet, place the working loop on the hook again, and pull the yarn through the double crochet. This gathers the loops of the stitches together. Secure the bobble with a tightly worked chain. When crocheting over this spot in the following WS row, work 1 single crochet around the loop of the stitch after the bobble, skipping the single chain.

169 TWIRLY NUPPS

[multiple of 16 + 2 ch + 1 beg-ch]

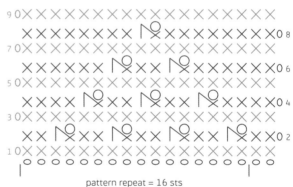

pattern repeat = 16 sts

This stitch pattern features a triangular arrangement of nupps on a background of single crochet. Work in rows, following the chart; Row 1 is a WS row. In RS rows, begin with the stitches before the pattern repeat, and then repeat the marked pattern repeat (16 sts wide) widthwise. Work Rows 1–9 once, and then repeat Rows 2–9 for pattern.

Chart Key

o Chain 1   ✕ 1 single crochet

1 nupp: Worked in RS rows in conjunction with a single crochet, the nupp is crocheted on the RS of the fabric. Insert the hook into 1 stitch, work 1 single crochet, and then crochet a chain of 5. Insert the hook into the left loop of the V-shaped body of the stitch of the previously worked single crochet, and pull a loop through. Insert the hook into the next stitch of the previous row, draw the working yarn through. Draw the working yarn through once more, and then pull the loop through all 3 loops on the hook at once. The crocheted chain loop will first self-adjust outward. When crocheting over this spot in the following WS row, nudge the crocheted chain loop to the back so that it ends up on the RS of the fabric. But before this, work 1 single crochet into the joined top of the 3 loops, as well as 1 single crochet directly into the single crochet after the chain loop.

170 HONEYCOMB PATTERN

[multiple of 3 + 2 ch + 1 beg-ch]

This stitch pattern features staggered bobbles on a single crochet background. Work in rows, following the chart. Begin with the stitches before the pattern repeat, repeat the marked pattern repeat (3 sts wide) widthwise, and end with the stitches after the pattern repeat. Work Rows 1–7 once, and then repeat Rows 2–7 for pattern.

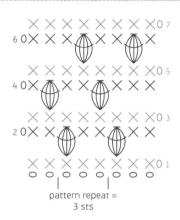

pattern repeat = 3 sts

Chart Key

o   Chain 1   X   1 single crochet

1 bobble: Work in WS rows; the bobble will bulge out toward the back (on account of the lesser height of the background pattern stitches), so in the finished piece, it will end up on the RS of the fabric. Work 5 double crochets into the same stitch and crochet together. For each double crochet, yarn over hook once, insert the hook in the same spot again, draw the working yarn through, and then yarn over and pull the yarn through the first 2 loops on the hook at once. This yields 1 loop for each double crochet on the hook, plus the working loop. Draw the working yarn through once more and pull it through all 6 loops on the hook at once. Pull the working yarn taut; the bobble will bulge out toward the back.

171 FUNNEL NUPPS

[multiple of 4 + 3 ch + 1 beg-ch]

This stitch pattern features nupps stacked directly atop one another on a background of alternating [1 row single crochet, 1 row double crochet]. Work in rows, following the chart. Begin with the stitches before the pattern repeat, repeat the marked pattern repeat (4 sts wide) widthwise, and end with the stitches after the pattern repeat. Work Rows 1–5 once, and then repeat Rows 2–5 for pattern.

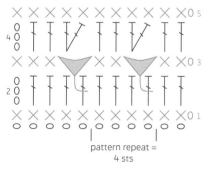

Chart Key

o   Chain 1

X   1 single crochet

T   1 double crochet

V   Dc2-in-1: 2 double crochets into the same stitch

1 nupp: Work in RS rows so that the nupp ends up on the RS of the crocheted fabric. One after another, work [1 single crochet, 1 half double crochet, 2 double crochets, 1 treble crochet] around the body of the double crochet of the previous row. For the first stitch, insert the hook under the joined top and behind the body of the double crochet of the previous row located directly underneath so that the double crochet bulges out over the hook, pull the working yarn through, and complete the stitch. Work the remaining 4 stitches the same way around the body of the double crochet; they will be located one below the other and completely encapsulate the base stitch. In the following WS row, leave the nupp stitches unworked, instead working 2 double crochets into each skipped individual double crochet of the next-to-last row.

pattern repeat = 4 sts

172 BOBBLES ON A DIAGONAL

[multiple of 5 + 2 ch + 1 beg-ch]

The stitch pattern features bobbles arranged in diagonal lines on a single crochet background. Work in rows, following the chart; Row 1 is a WS row. Begin with the stitches before the pattern repeat, repeat the marked pattern repeat (5 sts wide) widthwise, and end with the stitches after the pattern repeat. Work Rows 1–12 once, and then repeat Rows 3–12 for pattern.

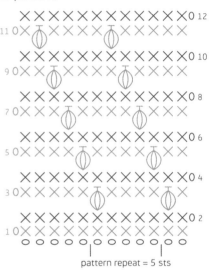

Chart Key

o   Chain 1   X   1 single crochet

 1 bobble: Work in WS rows; the bobble will bulge out toward the back (on account of the smaller height of the background stitches), so in the finished piece it will end up on the RS of the crocheted fabric. Work [yarn over hook once, insert hook, pull the working yarn through] 4 times, slightly lengthen the loops, draw the working yarn through all loops on the hook at once (except for the working loop). Draw the working yarn through the remaining 2 loops on the hook.

pattern repeat = 5 sts

173 FLOWER PATTERN BANDS

[multiple of 6 + 1 ch + 1 beg-ch]

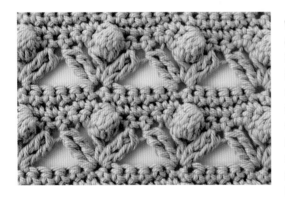

Work in rows, following the chart; Row 1 is a WS row. Begin with the stitches before the pattern repeat, repeat the marked pattern repeat (6 sts wide) width-wise, and end with the stitches after the pattern repeat. Work Rows 1–9 once, and then repeat Rows 2–9 for pattern.

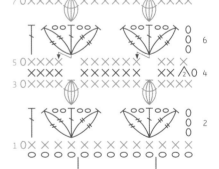

pattern repeat = 6 sts

Chart Key

o   Chain 1   ⊤   1 double crochet

X   1 single crochet

⚂   Sc2tog: Single crochet 2 stitches together

 1 bobble: Work in WS rows; the bobble will bulge out toward the back (on account of the lesser height of the background pattern stitches), so in the finished piece, it will end up on the RS of the fabric. Work 5 double crochets into the same stitch and crochet together. For each double crochet, yarn over hook once, insert the hook in the same spot again, draw the working yarn through, and then yarn over and pull the yarn through the first 2 loops on the hook at once. After completion of these steps, you will have 1 loop for each double crochet plus the working loop on your hook. Draw the working yarn through all 6 loops on the hook at once. Pull the working yarn taut; the bobble will bulge out toward the back. When crocheting over this spot in the following row, skip the joined top of the bobble.

1 group of stitches all worked into the same stitch: 2 treble crochets crocheted off together, chain 2, 1 double crochet, chain 2, 2 treble crochets crocheted off together.

174 BOBBLES BREAKING THROUGH

[multiple of 5 + 3 ch + 1 beg-ch]

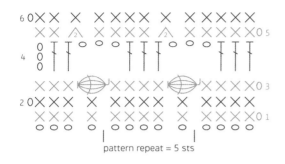

pattern repeat = 5 sts

Chart Key

○   Chain 1

✕   1 single crochet

⋀   Sc2tog: 2 single crochets crocheted together

𝖙   1 double crochet

 1 bobble: Work in RS rows; the bobble is crocheted on the RS of the crocheted fabric. Chain 2; then work 5 double crochets around the body of the single crochet worked last, and crochet them off together. For each double crochet, yarn over hook once, insert the hook between the last 2 single crochets, draw the working yarn through, and then yarn over and pull the yarn through the first 2 loops on the hook at once. After completion of these steps, you will have 1 loop for each double crochet plus the working loop on your hook. Draw the working yarn through once more, pulling it through all 6 loops on the hook at once.

Work in rows, following the chart. Begin with the stitches before the pattern repeat, repeat the marked pattern repeat (5 sts wide) width-wise, and end with the stitches after the pattern repeat. Work Rows 1–6 once, and then repeat Rows 3–6 for pattern.

In Row 5, when crocheting over the chain, always grasp both the back loop of the stitch and the horizontal bar on the back of the chain.

175 FLORAL HEM BORDER

[multiple of 8 + 1 ch + 1 beg-ch]

The funnel-shaped nupp is open at the top and extends over 3 heightwise rows of the background pattern. It is worked mainly in 2 consecutive WS rows. This version is not a typical bobble, because the stitches are not gathered at the top and therefore don't create a closed shape. However, because the overall appearance of this stitch is three-dimensional, it can still be considered a variation of the traditional bobble.

Work in rows, following the chart. Begin with the stitches before the pattern repeat, repeat the marked pattern repeat (8 sts wide) widthwise, and end with the stitches after the pattern repeat. The border is finished after Row 8 is complete, after which you can either continue the background pattern of single crochets or work any other stitch pattern.

In Row 4, skip the individual chain that holds the loops of the double treble crochets together. In Row 5, work into the single crochet of the previous row and bridge the distance behind the nupp stitches with a single chain. In Row 7, work into the single crochet of the previous row and bridge the distance behind the nupp stitches with a chain of 3.

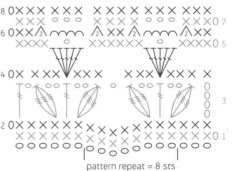

pattern repeat = 8 sts

Chart Key

○   Chain 1

✕   1 single crochet

⋀   Sc2tog: 2 single crochets crocheted together

𝖙   1 treble crochet

Dtr3-tog-in-1: 3 double treble crochets into the same stitch and crocheted together

Dc5-in-1: 5 double crochets into the same stitch

Work an arced edging into the 5 double crochets of the next-to-last row: 1 single crochet, chain 3, [1 slip stitch, chain 3] 3 times, 1 single crochet

SPIKE STITCH PATTERNS

176 STAGGERED V-STITCH
[multiple of 2 + 1 beg-ch]

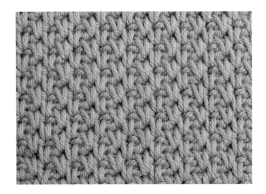

Work in rows, following the chart; Row 1 is a WS row. Begin with the stitches before the pattern repeat, repeat the marked pattern repeat (2 sts wide) widthwise, and end with the stitches after the pattern repeat. Work Rows 1–4 once, and then repeat Rows 3 and 4 for pattern.

Chart Key

○ Chain 1   ✕ 1 single crochet

✕⌇ 1 spike stitch in single crochet: In Row 2 insert the hook into the corresponding chain of the beginning chain; from Row 3 onward, insert the hook into the stitch 2 rows below (i.e., under the top loop of the single crochet of the next-to-last row). Draw the working yarn through and lengthen the loop to a height of just above the top edge of the current row. Pull the working yarn through both loops at once.

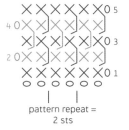

pattern repeat =
2 sts

177 BRIOCHE PATTERN
[multiple of 2 + 1 beg-ch]

Work in rows, following the chart. Begin with the stitches before the pattern repeat, repeat the marked pattern repeat (2 sts wide) widthwise, and end with the stitches after the pattern repeat. Work Rows 1–5 once, and then repeat Rows 4 and 5 for pattern. Work the pattern loosely so that it will be easier to insert the hook into the stitch.

Chart Key

○ Chain 1   ✕ 1 single crochet

✕⌇ 1 spike stitch in single crochet: In Rows 3 and 4 (= WS row), insert the hook into the stitch 2 rows below (i.e., under the top loop of the single crochet of the next-to-last row); draw the working yarn through, lengthen the loop to a height of just above the top edge of the current row, and crochet these 2 loops off together—the hook is inserted into the same spot as it was for the single crochet of the previous row. In Row 5 (= RS row), insert the hook into the body of the single crochet worked 2 rows below—this spot is located between the 2 strands of the stitch that diverge like the two legs of the letter V.

pattern repeat =
2 sts

SERGED STRIPS

[any st ct + 1 beg-ch]

Work in rows, following the chart. Work Rows 1–8 once, and then repeat Rows 5–8 for pattern.

Two-color pattern, option A: Work in rows, following the chart for the one-color pattern. Change color for the first time after Row 1 and then after every 2 rows. Spike stitches are always worked in the same color. Carry up unused yarns at the edge of the work.

Two-color pattern, option B: Work in rows, following the chart for the one-color pattern. Change color for the first time after Row 3 and then after every 4 rows. Spike stitches are worked alternatingly in two colors. Carry up unused colors at the edge of the work.

Chart Key

○ Chain 1　　　　● 1 slip stitch

✕ 1 single crochet

✕ 1 spike stitch in single crochet: Insert the hook into the stitch 3 rows below, draw the working yarn through, and lengthen the loop to a height of just above the top edge of the current row; the loop should be loose enough to not draw the enclosed rows together and make them pucker. Pull the working yarn through both loops at once.

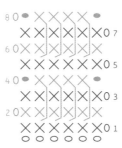

FANGS

[multiple of 4 + 2 ch + 1 beg-ch]

Work in rows, following the chart. Begin with the stitches before the pattern repeat, repeat the marked pattern repeat (4 sts wide) width-wise, and end with the stitches after the pattern repeat. Work Rows 1–10 once, and then repeat Rows 3–10 for pattern.

Two-color pattern: Work in rows, following the chart for the one-color pattern. Change color every 2 rows; carry up unused colors at the edge.

Chart Key

○ Chain 1　　　　✕ 1 single crochet

✕ 1 spike stitch in single crochet: In Rows 3 and 7, insert the hook into the stitch 2 rows below (i.e., under the top loop of the single crochet of the the next-to-last row); draw the working yarn through and lengthen the loop to a height of just above the top edge of the current row; crochet these 2 loops off together—the hook has been inserted in the same spot as for the single crochet of the previous row. In Rows 5 and 9, insert the hook into the body of the single crochet worked 2 rows below—this spot is located between the 2 strands of the stitch that diverge like the two legs of the letter V. If the spike stitch tightly encloses the previous row, rows will be constricted, which will result in a slightly wavy look; more loosely worked spike stitches will create straight rows.

pattern repeat =
4 sts

180 EMBRACED RIDGE PATTERN, ONE COLOR [multiple of 6 + 5 ch + 1 beg-ch]

Work in rows, following the chart. Begin with the stitches before the pattern repeat, repeat the marked pattern repeat (6 sts wide) width-wise, and end with the stitches after the pattern repeat. Work Rows 1–6 once, and then repeat Rows 3–6 for pattern.

Chart Key

○ Chain 1   ✕ 1 single crochet

╳ Blo-sc: 1 single crochet through the back loop only

1 spike stitch in single crochet: Insert the hook into the stitch 2 rows below (i.e., under the top loop of the single crochet of the the next-to-last row); draw the working yarn through and lengthen the loop to a height of just above the top edge of the current row—this loop encloses the outer ridgeline. Pull the working yarn through both loops at once.

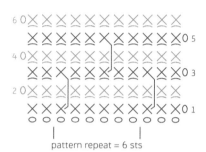

pattern repeat = 6 sts

181 EMBRACED RIDGE PATTERN, TWO COLORS [multiple of 2 + 1 ch + 1 beg-ch]

Work in rows, following the chart. Begin with the stitches before the pattern repeat, repeat the marked pattern repeat (2 sts wide) width-wise, and end with the stitches after the pattern repeat. Work Rows 1–6 once, and then repeat Rows 3–6 for pattern. Change color every 2 rows; carry up unused colors at the edge.

Chart Key

○ Chain 1   ✕ 1 single crochet

╳ Blo-sc: 1 single crochet through the back loop only

1 spike stitch in single crochet: Insert the hook into the stitch 2 rows below (i.e., under the top loop of the single crochet of the the next-to-last row); draw the working yarn through and lengthen the loop to a height of just above the top edge of the current row—this loop encloses the outer ridgeline. Crochet these 2 loops off together.

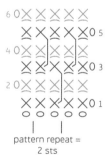

pattern repeat = 2 sts

TWO-COLORED BASKETWEAVE

[multiple of 6 + 3 ch + 1 beg-ch]

Chart Key

- ○   Chain 1
- ✕   1 single crochet
- ⤬   Flo-sc: 1 single crochet through the front loop only
- ⤬   Blo-sc: 1 single crochet through the back loop only
- ⊤   1 half double crochet

   1 treble crochet, worked below, placed in front: Insert the hook 3 rows below into the unused front loop of the single crochet in Row 1 so that it is placed loosely on top of the background stitches

   1 double treble crochet, worked below, placed in front: Insert the hook 4 rows below into the same spot as the single crochet atop the differently colored half double crochet, with the double treble crochet to the left of the single crochet and at the same time placed loosely on top of the background stitches

   Carry the yarn at the edge

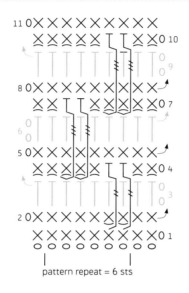

Work in rows, following the chart. Begin with the stitches before the pattern repeat, repeat the marked pattern repeat (6 sts wide) widthwise, and end with the stitches after the pattern repeat. Work Rows 1–11 once, and then repeat Rows 6–11 for pattern. The half double crochet rows alternate between the RS and the WS. Carry up unused colors at the edge of the work.

TWO-COLOR VERTICAL STRIPES

[multiple of 6 + 5 ch + 1 beg-ch]

Work in rows, following the chart. Begin with the stitches before the pattern repeat, repeat the marked pattern repeat (6 sts wide) widthwise, and end with the stitches after the pattern repeat. Work Rows 1–7 once, and then repeat Rows 4–7 for pattern, alternating [2 RS rows, 2 WS rows], while at the same time changing colors after every row. Carry up unused colors at the edge of the work. Row 8 in the chart is the final row at the upper edge of the crocheted piece.

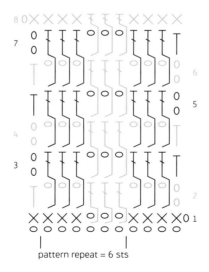

pattern repeat = 6 sts

Chart Key

- ○   Chain 1
- ✕   1 single crochet
- ⊤   1 half double crochet

   1 double crochet worked below: Yarn over hook once; in Row 2 insert the hook into a chain of the beginning chain, from Row 3 on insert hook into the skipped stitch of the previous row; pull the working yarn through, and then crochet 2 loops on the hook off together while grasping the chain of the previous row and pulling it closer toward the edge of the work located below. Crochet the 2 loops on the hook off together to finish the last step of the double crochet.

184 PINSTRIPES

[multiple of 4 + 2 ch + 1 beg-ch]

Work in rows, following the chart. Begin with the stitches before the pattern repeat, repeat the marked pattern repeat (4 sts wide) width-wise, and end with the stitches after the pattern repeat. Work Rows 1–7 once, and then repeat Rows 6 and 7 for pattern.

Two-color pattern: Work in rows, following the chart for the one-color pattern. Change color for the first time after Row 3 and then after every 2 rows, and carry up unused colors at the edge. A stepped-up effect is clearly visible in the pattern. The first and last rows of the crocheted piece will turn out slightly slanted.

Chart Key

○   Chain 1   ✕   1 single crochet

✕   1 slanted spike stitch in single crochet: Insert the hook into the stitch 3
rows below, but 1 stitch farther to
the right (i.e., under the top loop of
the single crochet), draw the working yarn through, and lengthen the
loop to a height of just above the top
edge of the current row—the loop
should be loose enough to not draw
the enclosed rows together and
make them pucker. Pull the working
yarn through both loops at once.

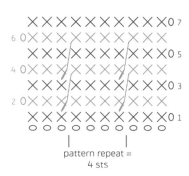

pattern repeat =
4 sts

185 STAGGERED PAWS

[multiple of 5 + 2 ch + 1 beg-ch]

Work in rows, following the chart; Row 1 is a WS row. Begin with the stitches before the pattern repeat, repeat the marked pattern repeat (5 sts wide) widthwise, and end with the stitches after the pattern repeat. Work Rows 1–9 once, and then repeat Rows 2–9 for pattern.

Two-color pattern: Work in rows, following the chart for the one-color pattern. Always work Rows 4 and 8 on the RS, changing color in these rows. Work the 3 rows in between in the main color, alternating between beginning with a RS or with a WS row, to avoid having to break the working yarn.

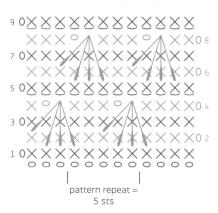

pattern repeat =
5 sts

Chart Key

○   Chain 1

✕   1 single crochet

⋉   Flo-sc: 1 single crochet
through the front loop only

 4 spike stitches in single crochet crocheted together: One after another, insert the hook into 3 consecutive stitches 3 rows below, and then in 1 stitch 2 rows below, drawing the working yarn through every time and lengthening the loop to a height of just above the top edge of the current row every time. The loops should be placed loosely in front of the background stitches to avoid constricting the enclosed rows. Finally, pull the working yarn through all 5 loops on the hook at once.

BRIDGED RIDGES

[multiple of 6 + 5 ch + 1 beg-ch]

Chart Key

o   Chain 1   ✕   1 single crochet

⤬   Blo-sc: 1 single crochet through the back loop only

⟩   1 spike stitch in single crochet: Insert the hook into the stitch 2 rows below (i.e., under the top loop of the single crochet of the the next-to-last row); draw the working yarn through and lengthen the loop to a height of just above the top edge of the current row—this loop encloses the outer ridgeline. Pull the working yarn through both loops at once. On the right side of the fabric, the loops of the deeper stitches lie on the front between the outer ridge lines.

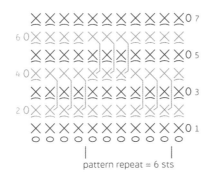

pattern repeat = 6 sts

Work in rows, following the chart. Begin with the stitches before the pattern repeat, repeat the marked pattern repeat (6 sts wide) widthwise, and end with the stitches after the pattern repeat. Work Rows 1–7 once, and then repeat Rows 4–7 for pattern.

SMOCKED RIBBING

[multiple of 8 + 3 ch + 1 beg-ch]

Work in rows, following the chart; Row 1 is a WS row. Repeat the marked pattern repeat (8 sts wide) widthwise, and end with the stitches after the pattern repeat. Work Rows 1–9 once, and then repeat Rows 2–9 for pattern.

Chart Key

o   Chain 1   ✕   1 single crochet

⤬   Blo-sc: 1 single crochet through the back loop only

⟩   1 single crochet worked below: First, insert the hook 3 rows below in the unused front loop of the single crochet. Immediately after, insert the hook through the back loop of the stitch of the previous row. Now, pull the working yarn through and finish working the single crochet.

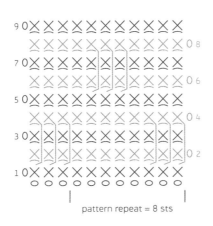

pattern repeat = 8 sts

188 TWO-COLOR TEARDROPS

[multiple of 4 + 2 ch + 3 beg-ch]

Work in rows, following the chart. Begin with the stitches before the pattern repeat, repeat the marked pattern repeat (4 sts wide) width-wise, and end with the stitches after the pattern repeat. Work Rows 1–6 once, and then repeat Rows 3–6 for pattern, alternating [2 RS rows, 2 WS rows] and at the same time changing color after every row. Carry up unused colors at the edge of the work.

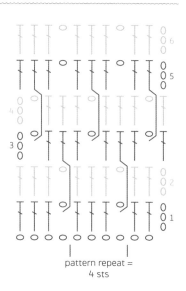

pattern repeat = 4 sts

Chart Key

○ Chain 1

⊤ 1 double crochet

1 spike stitch in double crochet: Yarn over hook once; insert hook 2 rows below (i.e., below the chain of the next-to-last row); draw the working yarn through and loosely lengthen the loop to a height of just above the top edge of the current row—this loop encloses the chains from the 2 previous rows. Now [pull the working yarn through 2 loops on the hook at once] twice to finish the double crochet.

189 EMBRACED STRIPES IN THREE COLORS

[multiple of 6 + 4 ch + 3 beg-ch]

Work in rows, following the chart; Row 1 is a WS row. Begin with the stitches before the pattern repeat, repeat the marked pattern repeat (6 sts wide) widthwise, and end with the stitches after the pattern repeat. Work Rows 1–8 once, and then repeat Rows 5–8 for pattern, continuing the color sequence. Use the 3 colors one after another, changing colors after every 2 rows; carry up unused colors at the edge.

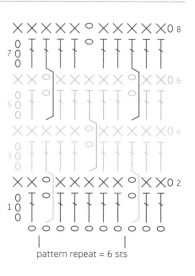

pattern repeat = 6 sts

Chart Key

○ Chain 1

✕ 1 single crochet

⊤ 1 double crochet

1 spike stitch in double crochet: Yarn over hook once; in Row 3 insert the hook into a chain of the beginning chain; in Rows 5 and 7, in the skipped stitch located 3 rows below, insert the hook, draw the working yarn through, and loosely lengthen the loop to a height of just above the top edge of the current row—this loop encloses the chains from the 2 previous rows. Now [pull the working yarn through 2 loops on the hook at once] twice to finish the double crochet.

TWO-COLOR EYELASHES

[multiple of 4 + 1 ch + 1 beg-ch]

Work in rows, following the chart. Begin with the stitches before the pattern repeat, repeat the marked pattern repeat (4 sts wide) widthwise, and end with the stitches after the pattern repeat. Work Rows 1–9 once, and then repeat Rows 2–9 for pattern. Change color every 4 rows and carry up unused colors at the edge.

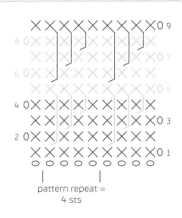

pattern repeat = 4 sts

Chart Key

o Chain 1

X 1 single crochet

X (spike bracket) 1 spike stitch in single crochet: Insert the hook into the stitch 2, 3, or 4 rows below (i. e., under the top loops of the appropriate single crochet); draw the working yarn through and lengthen the loop to a height of just above the top edge of the current row—the loop should be loose enough to not draw the enclosed rows together and make them pucker. Pull the working yarn through both loops at once.

TWO-COLOR RIB GRID

[multiple of 4 + 2 ch + 1 beg-ch]

Work in rows, following the chart. Begin with the stitches before the pattern repeat, repeat the marked pattern repeat (4 sts wide) width-wise, and end with the stitches after the pattern repeat. Work Rows 1–7 once, and then repeat Rows 4–7 for pattern. Change color every 2 rows and carry up unused colors at the edge.

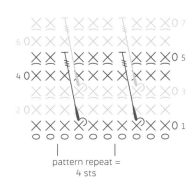

pattern repeat = 4 sts

Chart Key

o Chain 1

X 1 single crochet

X (Blo) Blo-sc: 1 single crochet through the back loop only

T (dtr symbol) 1 double treble crochet, worked below, placed in front: Insert the hook 4 rows below, but 1 stitch farther to the right, loosely on top of the background of single crochets. To do this, work as follows: [Yarn over hook] 3 times, insert the hook directly underneath the top loop of the stitch to the right of the stitch, exit the hook to the left of the stitch, pull the working yarn through, and then [pull the yarn through 2 loops on the hook at once] 4 times to finish the double treble crochet.

192 TWO-COLOR GEARWHEEL PATTERN

[multiple of 4 + 2 ch + 1 beg-ch]

Work in rows, following the chart. Begin with the stitches before the pattern repeat, repeat the marked pattern repeat (4 sts wide) width-wise, and end with the stitches after the pattern repeat. Work Rows 1–6 once, and then repeat Rows 3–6 for pattern. Change color every 2 rows and carry up unused colors at the edge. The final row of the crocheted piece will be 1 row of single crochet and treble crochet worked below (shown as Row 7 in the Chart Key).

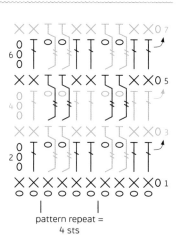

pattern repeat = 4 sts

Chart Key

○ Chain 1

✕ 1 single crochet

| 1 double crochet

↑ Carry the yarn at the edge

1 treble crochet worked below, worked into the skipped stitch of the previous row. The height of the treble crochet bridges the distance between the gap and the top edge of the current row. The single chain stays loosely in back of work.

193 DIAMOND PATTERN

[multiple of 4 + 3 ch + 1 beg-ch]

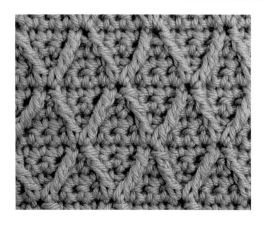

Work in rows, following the chart. Begin with the stitches before the pattern repeat, repeat the marked pattern repeat (4 sts wide) widthwise, and end with the stitches after the pattern repeat. Work Rows 1–13 once, and then repeat Rows 6–13 for pattern. Add 1 row of single crochets as the final row of the cro-cheted piece.

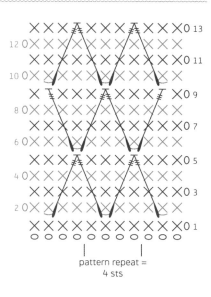

pattern repeat = 4 sts

Chart Key

○ Chain 1   ✕ 1 single crochet

✕ Flo-sc: 1 single crochet through the front loop only

1 double treble crochet, worked below, placed in front: Work 4 rows below in the spot where the double treble crochets converge, inserting the hook between the double treble crochets below the last loop of the right double treble crochet, and then move the tip of the hook above the un-used front loop of the stitch to the front of the work again. Draw the working yarn through and finish the last step of the double treble crochet.

2 double treble crochets worked below, placed in front, and crocheted together: Always insert the hook 4 rows below and shifted 2 stitches to the right or left into the unused front loop of the single crochet as shown on the chart, and then pull the work-ing yarn through all but the last 2 loops on the hook at once. After this, pull the yarn through 3 loops together at once. The com-pleted double treble crochets should lie flat on top of the back-ground stitches. At crossing points in Rows 9 and 13, insert the hook as described for individually worked double treble crochet.

BOXY HOLE PATTERN WITH INTERMITTENT ROWS [multiple of 3 + 2 ch + 1 beg-ch]

Work in rows, following the chart; Row 1 is a WS row. Begin with the stitches before the pattern repeat, repeat the marked pattern repeat (3 sts wide) widthwise, and end with the stitches after the pattern repeat. Work Rows 1–6 once, and then repeat Rows 4–6 for pattern, always working Row 4 of the pattern repeat on the RS, changing color in this row. Carry the unused main color at the edge.

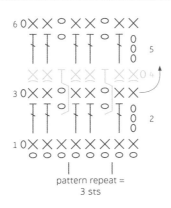

pattern repeat = 3 sts

Chart Key

○ Chain 1

✕ 1 single crochet

⊤ 1 double crochet

⋉ Blo-sc: 1 single crochet through the back loop only

↱ Carry the yarn at the edge

⊺ 1 spike stitch in half double crochet: Yarn over hook once, insert hook 2 rows below (below the chain of the next-to-last row), draw the working yarn through, and loosely lengthen the loop to a height of just above the top edge of the current row; this loop wraps around the chains from the 2 previous rows. Pull the working yarn through all 3 loops on the hook at once.

SERGED LADDERS

[any st ct + 1 beg-ch]

Work in rows, following the chart. Work Rows 1–9 once, and then repeat Rows 4–9 for pattern, working Rows 4 and 7 with spike stitches in single crochet in color 2 and alternating on the RS and the WS. Carry up unused yarns at the edge of the work.

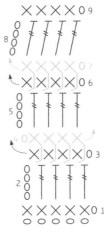

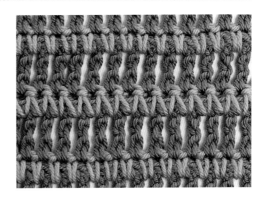

Chart Key

○ Chain 1

✕ 1 single crochet

✕ 1 spike stitch in single crochet: Insert the hook into the same spot as for the single crochet of the previous row (i.e., between the treble crochets of the next-to-last row); draw the working yarn through and lengthen the loop to a height of just above the top edge of the current row—this loop wraps around the single crochet of the previous row. Pull the working yarn through both loops at once.

⊤ 1 treble crochet

↱ Carry the yarn at the edge

196 WOVEN BLOCK PATTERN

Work in rows, following the chart. Begin with the stitches before the pattern repeat, repeat the marked pattern repeat (24 sts wide) width-wise, and end with the stitches after the pattern repeat. Work Rows 1–13 once, and then repeat Rows 2–13 for pattern, always changing the back/front positioning of the triple treble crochets (i.e., alternately working the triple treble crochets in front of and behind the chains). Change color every 6 rows.

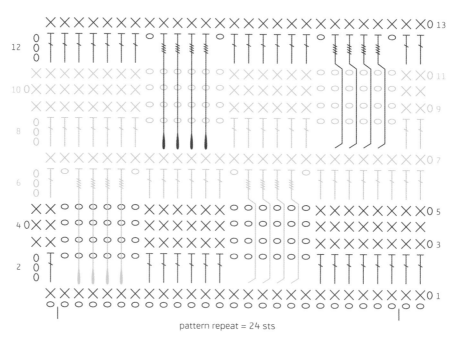

pattern repeat = 24 sts

Chart Key

○ Chain 1   ✕ 1 single crochet   ┬ 1 double crochet

┬ 1 triple treble crochet worked below, behind the chains: Insert the hook into the skipped stitch located 4 rows below and work in back of the chains, with the height of the triple treble crochet bridging the distance between the gap and the top edge of the current row. On the front of the crocheted piece, the triple treble crochets are on top of the background stitches, with the chains loosely behind them.

┬ 1 triple treble crochet worked below, in front of the chains: Insert the hook into the skipped stitch located 4 rows below and work in front of the chains, with the height of the triple treble crochet bridging the distance between the gap and the top edge of the current row. On the front of the crocheted piece, the triple treble crochets are behind the background stitches, with the chains loosely in front.

SPIKE STITCH DOUBLE CROCHET VS

[multiple of 2 + 1 ch + 1 beg-ch]

Work in rows, following the chart; Row 1 is a WS row. Begin with the stitches before the pattern repeat, repeat the marked pattern repeat (2 sts wide) widthwise, and end with the stitches after the pattern repeat. Work Rows 1–5 once, and then repeat Rows 4 and 5 for pattern.

Two-color pattern: Work in rows, following the chart for the one-color pattern. Work alternating [2 WS rows, 2 RS rows] for pattern, changing color after every row. Carry up unused colors at the edge of the work.

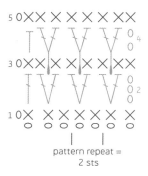

pattern repeat = 2 sts

Chart Key

o   Chain 1

X   1 single crochet

Y   Dc2-in-1: 2 double crochets into the same stitch

T   1 half double crochet

T   1 double crochet

Y   Spike stitch from 2 double crochets into the same stitch: For the first double crochet, yarn over hook once, insert the hook between double crochets of the next-to-last row, draw the working yarn through, and loosely lengthen the loop to a height of just above the top edge of the current row; this loop wraps around the single crochet of the previous row. Now [pull the working yarn through 2 loops on the hook at once] twice to finish the double crochet. Work the second double crochet into the same spot.

STAGGERED SPIKE STITCH DOUBLE CROCHET VS

[multiple of 4 + 3 beg-ch]

Work in rows, following the chart. Begin with the stitches before the pattern repeat, repeat the marked pattern repeat (4 sts wide) widthwise, and end with the stitches after the pattern repeat. Work Rows 1–4 once, and then repeat Rows 3 and 4 for pattern. In the final row of the crocheted piece, work single crochet instead of double crochet.

Two-color pattern: Work in rows, following the chart for the one-color pattern. Work alternating [2 RS rows, 2 WS rows] for pattern, changing color after every row. Carry up unused colors at the edge of the work. This pattern creates a vertical stripe effect.

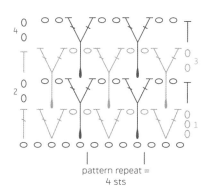

pattern repeat = 4 sts

Chart Key

o   Chain 1

T   1 double crochet

T   1 half double crochet

Y   Dc2-in-1: 2 double crochets into the same stitch

Y   Spike stitch from 2 double crochets into the same stitch: For the first double crochet, yarn over hook once; in Row 2, insert the hook into a chain of the beginning chain, in Rows 3 and 4, insert the hook between double crochets of the next-to-last row; draw the working yarn through and loosely lengthen the loop to a height of just above the top edge of the current row—this loop encloses the single chain of the previous row. Now [pull the working yarn through 2 loops on the hook at once] twice to finish the double crochet. Work the second double crochet into the same spot.

199 OPEN DIAMOND PATTERN

[multiple of 7 + 1 ch + 3 beg-ch]

Work in rows, following the chart. Begin with the stitches before the pattern repeat, repeat the marked pattern repeat (either 7 or 9 sts wide) widthwise from Row 1 on, and end with the stitches after the pattern repeat. Work Rows 1–7 once, and then repeat Rows 2–7 for pattern. Always work the groups of stitches in the chain space of the previous row, around the chain.

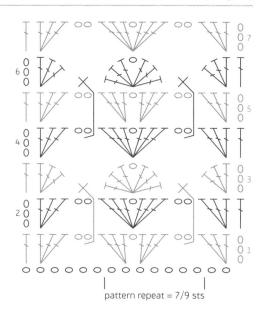

pattern repeat = 7/9 sts

Chart Key

 Chain 1

 1 double crochet

Dc3-in-1: 3 double crochets into the same stitch

 [3 double crochets, chain 1, 3 double crochets] into the same stitch

✕ 1 single crochet worked below: Insert the hook 2 rows below—under the chains of the next-to-last row—draw the working yarn through both loops on the hook at once so that the newly worked single crochet holds the chains from the 2 previous rows tightly together.

200 STAGGERED LITTLE WOVEN BOXES

[multiple of 10 + 2 ch + 1 beg-ch]

Work in rows, following the chart. Begin with the stitches before the pattern repeat, repeat the marked pattern repeat (10 sts wide) widthwise, and end with the stitches after the pattern repeat. Work Rows 1–9 once, and then repeat Rows 2–9 for pattern. Change color every 2 rows and carry up unused colors at the edge.

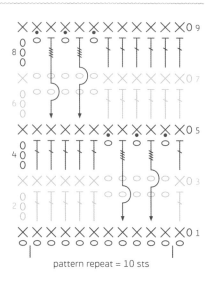

pattern repeat = 10 sts

Chart Key

o Chain 1

✕ 1 single crochet

✕ 1 single crochet around both horizontal bumps (front and back) of the chain

| 1 double crochet

 2 spike stitches in triple treble crochet with chain 1 between them, in front of and behind the chains: Work the first triple treble crochet 2 rows below, into the skipped stitch, by moving the hook from the back to the front between the chains where it will be inserted. The height of the triple treble crochet bridges the distance between the gap and the top edge of the current row. Chain 1. Work the second triple treble crochet in the stitch located 2 rows below, after the next one, now moving the hook from the front to the back between the chains where it will be inserted. This stitch pattern creates a woven effect.

BIG PAW PATTERNS [multiple of 5 + 3 beg-ch]

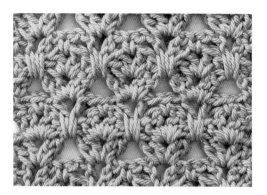 

Work in rows, following the chart. Begin with the stitches before the pattern repeat, repeat the marked pattern repeat (5 sts wide) widthwise, and end with the stitches after the pattern repeat. Work Rows 1–7 once, and then repeat Rows 2–7 for pattern. Always work the groups of stitches in the chain spaces of the previous row, around the chain.

Two-color pattern: Work in rows, following the chart for the one-color pattern. Work Rows 1 and 2 in color 1, and then alternate working [3 rows in color 2, 3 rows in color 1]. When changing color, always take up the color hanging at the edge and carry the unused color at the edge.

Chart Key

○   Chain 1

✕   1 single crochet

T   1 double crochet

V   Dc2-in-1: 2 double crochets into the same stitch

ToT / V   [2 double crochets, chain 1, 2 double crochets] into the same stitch

Spike stitch from 2 double crochets into the same stitch with chain 1 between them: For the first double crochet, yarn over hook once, insert the hook between the double crochet groups of the next-to-last row, draw the working yarn through, and then yarn over and pull it through 2 loops on the hook at once so that the newly created stitch pulls the gap from the 2 previous rows together. Finish the last step of the double crochet, chain 1, and work the second double crochet into the same spot.

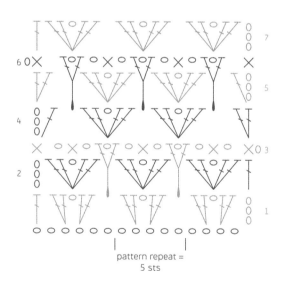

pattern repeat = 5 sts

202 ZIGZAG STRIPS ON A SWIRL BACKGROUND [multiple of 6 + 1 ch + 1 beg-ch]

Work in rows, following the chart; Row 1 is a WS row. Begin with the stitches before the pattern repeat, repeat the marked pattern repeat (6 sts wide) widthwise, and end with the stitches after the pattern repeat. Work Rows 1–10 once, and then repeat Rows 5–10 for pattern. Work colors 1, 2, and 3 in this order, changing color after every row. Carry up unused colors at the edge.

Chart Key

○   Chain 1   ✕   1 single crochet

1 double crochet worked below: In a WS row, work into the unused front loop of the single crochet from the next-to-last row. In a RS row, work into the unused back loop of the single crochet from the next-to-last row.

1 treble crochet worked below, worked around the body of a stitch: Work 3 rows below, but 1 stitch farther to the right, loosely on the background of single crochets. To do this, work as follows: [Yarn over hook] twice, insert the hook directly underneath the top loop of the stitch to the right of the stitch, exit the hook to the left of the stitch, pull the working yarn through, and then [pull the yarn through 2 loops on the hook at once] 3 times to finish the treble crochet.

1 treble crochet worked below, worked in an unused loop of the stitch: 3 rows below, but 1 stitch farther to the right into the unused loop at the top of the treble crochet located at the top edge of the work, inserting the hook in WS rows from the back and in RS rows from the front.

Carry the yarn at the edge

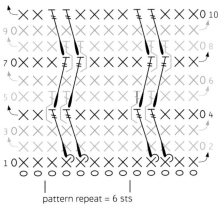

pattern repeat = 6 sts

203 ARROWHEAD PATTERN [multiple of 5 + 2 ch + 1 beg-ch]

Work in rows, following the chart; Row 1 is a WS row. Begin with the stitches before the pattern repeat, repeat the marked pattern repeat (5 sts wide) widthwise, and end with the stitches after the pattern repeat. Work Rows 1–10 once, and then repeat Rows 7–10 for pattern. Add 1 row of single crochets as the final row.

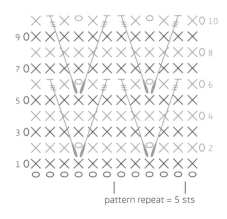

pattern repeat = 5 sts

Chart Key

○   Chain 1
✕   1 single crochet

1 double treble crochet worked below, worked into the gap between stitches: [Yarn over hook] 3 times, on the RS of the fabric insert the hook into the unused stitch located 4 rows below, lead the tip of the crochet hook to the front of the fabric through the gap between stitches, and pull the working yarn through. Now, finish the double treble crochet, taking care to watch out for its length so that after the last step, the finished double treble crochet lies flat on the crocheted background and the top of the stitch reaches the top of the current row.

FRAMED FANS

[multiple of 6 + 1 ch + 1 beg-ch]

Work in rows, following the chart; Row 1 is a WS row. Begin with the stitches before the pattern repeat, repeat the marked pattern repeat (6 sts wide) widthwise, and end with the stitches after the pattern repeat. Work Rows 1–6 once, and then repeat Rows 3–6 for pattern.

Two-color pattern: Work in rows, following the chart for the one-color pattern. Change color after every 2 rows and carry up unused colors at the edge.

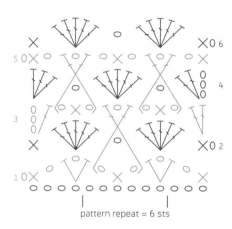

pattern repeat = 6 sts

Chart Key

○   Chain 1

  [1 half double crochet, chain 1, 1 half double crochet] into the same stitch

1 double crochet

  Dc2-in-1: 2 double crochets into the same stitch

  Dc3-in-1: 3 double crochets into the same stitch

✕   1 single crochet

  Dc5-in-1: 5 double crochets into the same stitch

2 crossed spike stitches in double crochet with chain 1 between them: For the first double crochet, yarn over hook once, insert hook 2 rows below under the chain of the next-to-last row into the gap after the single crochet, draw the working yarn through 2 loops on the hook at once so that the newly created stitch pulls the gap from the 2 previous rows together. Finish the last step of the double crochet, and then chain 1. Work the second double crochet 2 rows below and cross over back into the gap before the single crochet, while enclosing the preceding double crochet.

RAISED STITCH PATTERNS

205 TALL RAISED HORIZONTAL RIDGES

[any st ct + 3 beg-ch]

Work in rows, following the chart. Work Rows 1–3 once, and then repeat Rows 2 and 3 for pattern.

Chart Key

○ Chain 1

⊤ 1 half double crochet

⊤ 1 double crochet

Fpdc: 1 front post double crochet

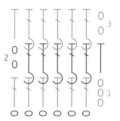

206 NARROW RAISED HORIZONTAL RIDGES

[any st ct + 3 beg-ch]

Work in rows, following the chart. Work Rows 1–3 once, and then repeat Rows 2 and 3 for pattern.

Chart Key

○ Chain 1

⊤ 1 half double crochet

⊤ 1 double crochet

Fpdc: 1 front post double crochet

Bpdc: 1 back post double crochet

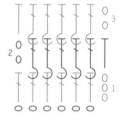

207 RAISED VERTICAL RIDGES

[any st ct + 3 beg-ch]

Work in rows, following the chart. Work Rows 1–3 once, and then repeat Rows 2 and 3 for pattern.

Chart Key

○ Chain 1

⊤ 1 half double crochet

Fpdc: 1 front post double crochet

Bpdc: 1 back post double crochet

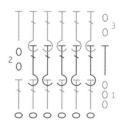

208 WICKER BASKET PATTERN

[multiple of 6 + 4 ch + 3 beg-ch]

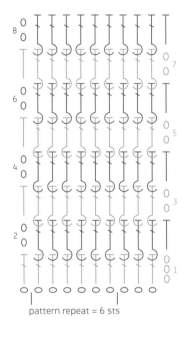

pattern repeat = 6 sts

Chart Key

○ Chain 1

| 1 half double crochet

┬ 1 double crochet

Fpdc: 1 front post double crochet

Bpdc: 1 back post double crochet

Work in rows, following the chart. Begin every row with the stitches before the pattern repeat, repeat the marked pattern repeat (6 sts wide) widthwise, and end with the stitches after the pattern repeat. Work Rows 1–8 once, and then repeat Rows 3–8 for pattern.

209 RAISED DIAGONAL PATTERN

[multiple of 4 + 1 ch + 3 beg-ch]

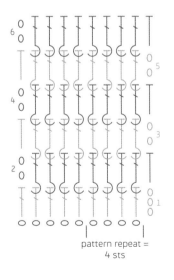

pattern repeat = 4 sts

Chart Key

○ Chain 1

| 1 half double crochet

┬ 1 double crochet

Fpdc: 1 front post double crochet

Bpdc: 1 back post double crochet

Work in rows, following the chart. Begin every row with the stitches before the pattern repeat, repeat the marked pattern repeat (4 sts wide) widthwise, and end with the stitches after the pattern repeat. Work Rows 1–6 once, and then repeat Rows 3–6 for pattern.

210 SLAT PATTERN

[multiple of 7 + 4 ch + 3 beg-ch]

Work in rows, following the chart; Row 1 is a WS row. Begin every row with the stitches before the pattern repeat, repeat the marked pattern repeat (7 sts wide) widthwise, and end with the stitches after the pattern repeat. Work Rows 1–3 once, and then repeat Rows 2 and 3 for pattern.

Chart Key

○ Chain 1

⊤ 1 double crochet

✗ 2 front post double crochets crossed to the left: Skip 1 double crochet of the previous row, work the first front post double crochet around the body of the following double crochet, and then insert the hook for the second front post double crochet before the first raised double crochet, going back around the skipped double crochet of the previous row.

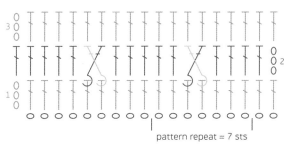

pattern repeat = 7 sts

211 CROW'S FEET

[multiple of 10 + 9 ch + 3 beg-ch]

Work in rows, following the chart. Begin every row with the stitches before the pattern repeat, repeat the marked pattern repeat (10 sts wide) widthwise, and end with the stitches after the pattern repeat. Work Rows 1–10 once, and then repeat Rows 3–10 for pattern.

Chart Key

○ Chain 1

✗ 1 single crochet

⊤ 1 double crochet

Λ Fpdc-bel-2tog (2 spike stitches in front post double crochet crocheted together): Always work 2 rows below around the body of the double crochet.

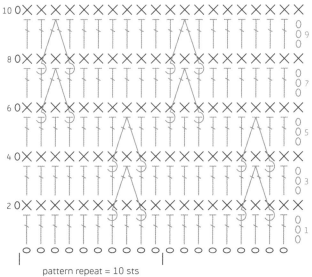

pattern repeat = 10 sts

212 STAGGERED RAISED PATTERN

[even st ct + 3 beg-ch]

Work in rows, following the chart. Work Rows 1–5 once, and then repeat Rows 2–5 for pattern.

Chart Key

○ Chain 1

✕ 1 single crochet

⊤ 1 double crochet

⌡ Fptr-bel (front post treble crochet worked below): Insert the hook 2 rows below around the double crochet.

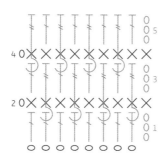

213 RAISED STRIPS WITH DIAMONDS

[multiple of 8 + 2 ch + 3 beg-ch]

Work in rows, following the chart. Begin every row with the stitches before the pattern repeat, repeat the marked pattern repeat (8 sts wide) widthwise, and end with the stitches after the pattern repeat. Work Rows 1–13 once, and then repeat Rows 4–13 for pattern.

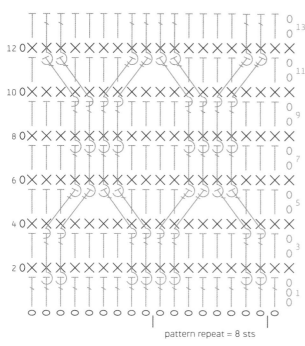

pattern repeat = 8 sts

Chart Key

○ Chain 1

✕ 1 single crochet

⊤ 1 half double crochet

⊤ 1 double crochet

Fpdc-bel: 1 front post double crochet worked below: In Row 3, work around the double crochet 2 rows below; from Row 5 on, work 2 rows below around the raised double crochet. In Rows 5 and 11, when working the front post double crochets worked below, always work going forward or back as shown.

214 FURROW PATTERN

[any st ct + 3 beg-ch]

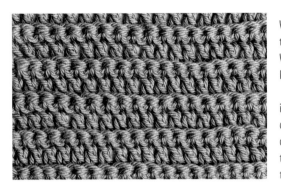

Work in rows, following the chart, never turning work, always working on the RS. Work Rows 1–5 once, and then repeat Rows 4 and 5 for pattern.

Work Rows 2 and 4 from left to right, inserting the hook through the front loop of the double crochet of the previous row only. Work Rows 3 and 5 again from right to left, inserting the hook 2 rows below through the back loop of the double crochet only.

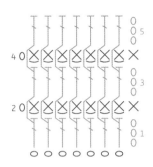

Chart Key

○ Chain 1

✕ 1 single crochet

⤢ Flo-sc: 1 single crochet through the front loop only

⊤ 1 double crochet

} Blo-dc-bel: 1 double crochet through the back loop only, worked below: Insert the hook 2 rows below through the back loop of the double crochet only

215 BROAD RAISED RIDGES

[multiple of 2 + 3 beg-ch]

Chart Key

○ Chain 1

✕ 1 single crochet

⊤ 1 double crochet

} Fpdc-bel: 1 front post double crochet worked below: In Row 3, insert the hook 2 rows below around the double crochet; from Row 5 on, insert the hook 2 rows below around the raised double crochet

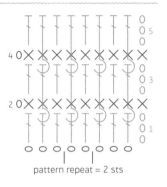

pattern repeat = 2 sts

Work in rows, following the chart. Begin every row with the stitches before the pattern repeat, repeat the marked pattern repeat (2 sts wide) widthwise, and end with the stitches after the pattern repeat. Work Rows 1–5 once, and then repeat Rows 4 and 5 for pattern.

216 RAISED STITCHES IN PAIRS

[multiple of 8 + 4 ch + 2 bg-ch]

Chart Key

○ Chain 1

⊤ 1 half double crochet

} Fpdc-bel (1 front post double crochet worked below): Insert the hook 2 rows below from the front around the half double crochet

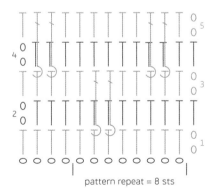

pattern repeat = 8 sts

Work in rows, following the chart. Begin every row with the stitches before the pattern repeat, repeat the marked pattern repeat (8 sts wide) widthwise, and end with the stitches after the pattern repeat. Work Rows 1–5 once, and then repeat Rows 2–5 for pattern.

217 RAISED STITCH DIAGONALS

[multiple of 3 + 2 ch + 1 beg-ch]

Work in rows, following the chart; Row 1 is a WS row. Begin every row with the stitches before the pattern repeat, repeat the marked pattern repeat (3 sts wide) widthwise, and end with the stitches after the pattern repeat. Work Rows 1–6 once, and then repeat Rows 5 and 6 for pattern.

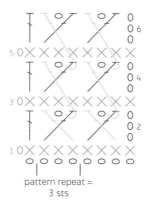

pattern repeat = 3 sts

Chart Key

○   Chain 1

✕   1 single crochet

T   1 double crochet

 2 double crochets crossed to the left with chain 1 between them: Skip 2 single crochets of the previous row, work the first double crochet in the following single crochet, chain 1, and then insert hook for the second double crochet before the first double crochet, going back in the first one of the 2 skipped stitches so that 1 stitch between the double crochets stays unused.

 1 double crochet and 1 front post double crochet worked below crossed to the left with chain 1 between them: Skip 2 single crochets of the previous row, work 1 double crochet in the following single crochet, chain 1, and then go back in front of the double crochet and work the raised double crochet worked below from the front around the double crochet under the first one of the 2 skipped single crochets.

218 RAISED STITCHES WITH EYELETS

[multiple of 4 + 1 ch + 1 beg-ch]

Work in rows, following the chart; Row 1 is a WS row. Begin every row with the stitches before the pattern repeat, repeat the marked pattern repeat (4 sts wide) widthwise, and end with the stitches after the pattern repeat. Work Rows 1–4 once, and then repeat Rows 3 and 4 for pattern.

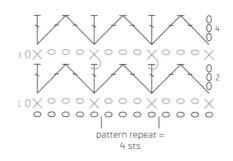

pattern repeat = 4 sts

Chart Key

○ Chain 1

✕ 1 single crochet

T 1 double crochet

✕ Fpsc: 1 front post single crochet

 2 double crochets crocheted together, working the first double crochet into the first single crochet of the previous row; skip 3 chains of the previous row; work the second double crochet into the next single crochet; * work 2 double crochets into the same single crochet as the second one of the double crochets that were crocheted together, but do not finish the last step of the last double crochet, skip 3 chains of the previous row, work 1 double crochet into the next single crochet of the previous row, and crochet both double crochets together; repeat from * to end of row; 1 double crochet into the last single crochet of the previous row.

219 WAFFLE PATTERN
[multiple of 4 + 2 ch + 3 beg-ch]

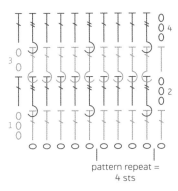

pattern repeat = 4 sts

Chart Key
○ Chain 1

T 1 half double crochet

T 1 double crochet

Bpdc: 1 back post double crochet

Fpdc: 1 front post double crochet

Fptr: 1 front post treble crochet

Work in rows, following the chart; Row 1 is a WS row. Begin every row with the stitches before the pattern repeat, repeat the marked pattern repeat (4 sts wide) widthwise, and end with the stitches after the pattern repeat. Work Rows 1–4 once, and then repeat Rows 3 and 4 for pattern.

220 RIDGES BOTH WAYS
[any st ct + 3 beg-ch]

Work in rows, following the chart; Row 1 is a WS row. Work Rows 1–4 once, and then repeat Rows 3 and 4 for pattern.

Chart Key
○ Chain 1

T 1 double crochet

Fpdc: 1 front post double crochet

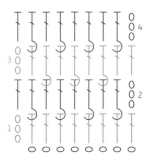

221 STAGGERED RAISED STITCHES
[odd st ct + 2 beg-ch]

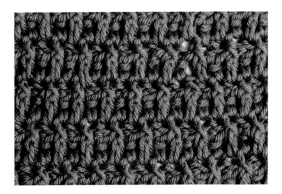

Work in rows, following the chart; Row 1 is a WS row. Work Rows 1–5 once, and then repeat Rows 2–5 for pattern.

Chart Key
○ Chain 1

× Fpsc: 1 front post single crochet

× Bpsc: 1 back post single crochet

T 1 half double crochet

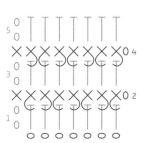

222 STACKED SHELLS

[multiple of 10 + 3 beg-ch]

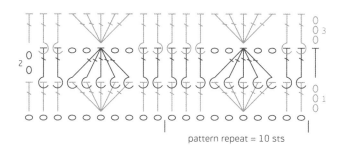

pattern repeat = 10 sts

Chart Key

○ Chain 1

| 1 double crochet

| Fpdc: 1 front post double crochet

| Bpdc: 1 back post double crochet

 Dc5-in-1: 5 double crochets into the same stitch

 Bpdc-5tog: Back post double crochet 5 stitches together

Work in rows, following the chart. Begin every row with the stitches before the pattern repeat, repeat the marked pattern repeat (10 sts wide) widthwise, and end with the stitches after the pattern repeat. Work Rows 1–3 once, and then repeat Rows 2 and 3 for pattern.

223 RAISED PAIRS AND CROSSINGS

[multiple of 5 + 2 ch + 1 beg-ch]

Chart Key

○ Chain 1

✕ 1 single crochet

| Fptr: 1 front post treble crochet

Cross 2 treble crochets to the left with chain 1 between them: Skip 2 single crochets of the previous row, work the first treble crochet into the following single crochet, chain 1, and then work the second treble crochet before the first treble crochet, going back into the first of the 2 skipped stitches so that 1 stitch between the treble crochets stays unused.

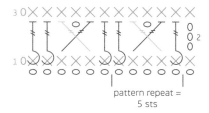

pattern repeat = 5 sts

Work in rows, following the chart; Row 1 is a WS row. Begin every row with the stitches before the pattern repeat, repeat the marked pattern repeat (5 sts wide) widthwise, and end with the stitches after the pattern repeat. Work Rows 1–3 once, and then repeat Rows 2 and 3 for pattern.

224 RAISED DIAMONDS

[multiple of 6 + 2 ch + 1 beg-ch]

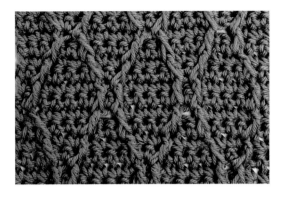

Chart Key

○ Chain 1   ✕ 1 single crochet

Fpdc-bel: 1 front post double crochet worked
below: In Row 4, work around the body of the
single crochet 2 rows below; from Row 6 on,
work 2 rows below around the raised double
crochet worked below.

Work in rows, fol-
lowing the chart;
Row 1 is a WS row.
Begin every row
with the stitches
before the pattern
repeat, repeat the
marked pattern
repeat (6 sts wide)
widthwise, and end
with the stitches
after the pattern
repeat. Work Rows
1–16 once, and then
repeat Rows 7–16
for pattern.

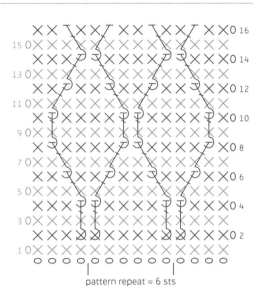

pattern repeat = 6 sts

225 EYELET CABLES

[multiple of 6 + 3 beg-ch]

Work in rows, following
the chart. Begin every row
with the stitches before
the pattern repeat, repeat
the marked pattern repeat
(6 sts wide) widthwise,
and end with the stitches
after the pattern repeat.
Work Rows 1–5 once, and
then repeat Rows 4 and 5
for pattern.

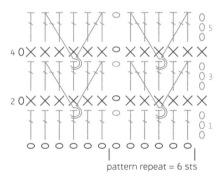

pattern repeat = 6 sts

Chart Key

○ Chain 1

✕ 1 single crochet

╎ 1 double crochet

 1 double crochet and 1 front post double
crochet worked below, crocheted together:
Always work the raised double crochet 2
rows below, going 2 stitches forward,
around the double crochet.

1 front post double crochet worked below
and 1 double crochet crocheted together.
Always work the raised double crochet 2
rows below, going 2 stitches back, around
the double crochet.

125

226 BROAD STRIPES OF RAISED CABLES

[12 ch per pattern strip]

Work in rows, following the chart; Row 1 is a WS row. As background pattern, work double crochets in Row 1; from Row 2 on, work raised double crochet (front or back post) as shown. Space the pattern strips on the background as desired; they should be at least 2 background stitches apart from each other. Work Rows 1–10 once, and then repeat Rows 3–10 for pattern.

Chart Key

○ Chain 1

 1 double crochet

Bpdc: 1 back post double crochet

Fpdc: 1 front post double crochet

6 front post treble crochets crossed to the right: Skipping 3 raised double crochets of the previous row, work 1 front post double crochet each around the following 3 raised double crochets; going back behind the already worked raised double crochets, work 1 front post treble crochet each around the 3 skipped raised double crochets of the previous row.

6 front post treble crochets crossed to the left: Skipping 3 raised double crochets of the previous row, work 1 front post double crochet each around the following 3 raised double crochets; going back in front of the already worked raised double crochets, work 1 front post treble crochet each around the 3 skipped raised double crochets of the previous row.

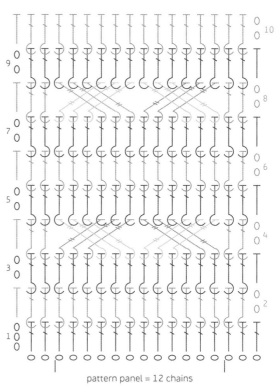

pattern panel = 12 chains

227 RAISED TEXTURED PATTERN

[multiple of 2 + 1 ch + 1 beg-ch]

Work in rows, following the chart. Begin every row with the stitches before the pattern repeat, repeat the marked pattern repeat (2 sts wide) widthwise, and end with the stitches after the pattern repeat. Work Rows 1–6 once, and then repeat Rows 3–6 for pattern.

Chart Key

○ Chain 1

✕ 1 single crochet

Fpdc-bel: 1 front post double crochet worked below: Insert the hook 2 rows below around the single crochet

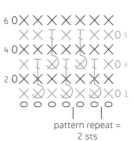

pattern repeat = 2 sts

228 RAISED CABLES WITH CORDS

[multiple of 12 + 8 ch + 3 beg-ch]

Work in rows, following the chart; Row 1 is a WS row. Begin every row with the stitches before the pattern repeat, repeat the marked pattern repeat (12 sts wide) widthwise, and end with the stitches after the pattern repeat. Work Rows 1–6 once, and then repeat Rows 3–6 for pattern.

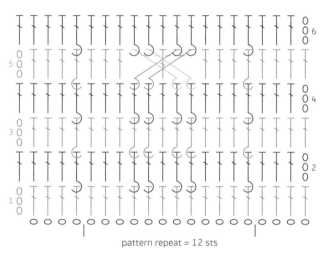

pattern repeat = 12 sts

Chart Key

○ Chain 1

| 1 double crochet

Fpdc: 1 front post double crochet

Bpdc: 1 back post double crochet

2 back post double crochets and 2 crossed front post double crochets with 1 double crochet in between: Skip 2 raised double crochets and 1 double crochet of the previous row, and then work 1 back post double crochet around each of the next 2 raised double crochets, 1 double crochet into the skipped double crochet, and 2 front post double crochets, going back around the 2 skipped raised double crochets of the previous row. Raised double crochets shown in color in the chart lie in front of the crocheted background on the RS of the crocheted fabric.

229 RAISED WAFFLE PATTERN

[multiple of 3 + 1 ch + 1 beg-ch]

Work in rows, following the chart. Begin every row with the stitches before the pattern repeat, repeat the marked pattern repeat (3 sts wide) widthwise, and end with the stitches after the repeat. Work Rows 1–7 once, and then repeat Rows 4–7 for pattern.

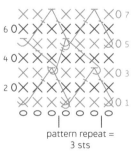

pattern repeat = 3 sts

Chart Key

○ Chain 1

✕ 1 single crochet

Fpdc-bel (1 front post double crochet worked below): Insert the hook 2 rows below around the joined top of the raised double crochets, which were crocheted together.

Fpdc-bel-2tog (2 spike stitches in front post double crochet crocheted together): In Row 3, work as shown 2 rows below around the single crochets; from Row 5 on, work as shown 2 rows below around the joined tops of the raised double crochets, which were crocheted together.

230 TWO-COLOR RAISED STITCH PATTERN

[multiple of 6 + 2 ch + 1 beg-ch]

Work in rows, following the chart. Begin every row with the stitches before the pattern repeat, repeat the marked pattern repeat (6 sts wide), and end with the stitches after the repeat. Work Rows 1–7 once, and then repeat Rows 2–7 for pattern.

Change color every 2 rows as shown. Carry unused colors at the edge.

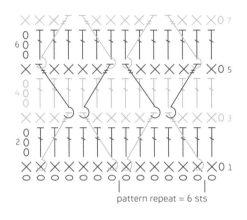

pattern repeat = 6 sts

Chart Key

○   Chain 1

✕   1 single crochet

⊤   1 double crochet

Fptr-bel (front post treble crochet worked below): In Row 3, work 2 rows below around the single crochet; from Row 5 on, work 2 rows below around the raised treble crochet that had been worked below, always going forward or back as shown

231 TWO-COLOR SPIKE STITCH PATTERN

[multiple of 6 + 2 ch + 1 beg-ch]

Work in rows, following the chart. Begin every row with the stitches before the pattern repeat, repeat the marked pattern repeat (6 sts wide) widthwise, and end with the stitches after the pattern repeat. Work Rows 1–6 once, and then repeat Rows 3–6 for pattern. Change color every 2 rows as shown. Carry unused colors at the edge.

Chart Key

○   Chain 1

✕   1 single crochet

⊤   1 double crochet

Fpdc-bel (1 front post double crochet worked below): Insert the hook 2 rows below around the single crochet

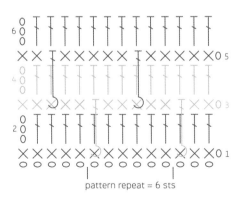

pattern repeat = 6 sts

232 RAISED TRIANGLES

[multiple of 6 + 2 ch + 3 beg-ch]

Chart Key

○ Chain 1

⊤ 1 double crochet

Fpdc: 1 front post double crochet

Bpdc: 1 back post double crochet

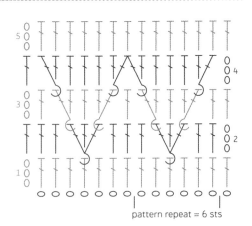

pattern repeat = 6 sts

Work in rows, following the chart; Row 1 is a WS row. Begin every row with the stitches before the pattern repeat, repeat the marked pattern repeat (6 sts wide) widthwise, and end with the stitches after the pattern repeat. Work Rows 1–5 once, and then repeat Rows 2–5 for pattern.

233 INTERWOVEN PATTERN

[multiple of 4 + 1 ch + 3 beg-ch]

Work in rows, following the chart; Row 1 is a WS row. Begin every row with the stitches before the pattern repeat, repeat the marked pattern repeat (4 sts wide) widthwise, and end with the stitches after the pattern repeat. Work Rows 1–6 once, and then repeat Rows 3–6 for pattern.

Chart Key

○ Chain 1

✕ 1 single crochet

⊤ 1 half double crochet

⊤ 1 double crochet

pattern repeat = 4 sts

4 front post treble crochets crossed to the right: In Row 2, skip 2 double crochets of the previous row and work 1 front post treble crochet around each of the following 2 double crochets; go back behind the 2 already worked raised treble crochets and work 1 front post treble crochet around each of the 2 skipped double crochets of the previous row.

4 front post treble crochets worked below crossed to the left: Skip 2 stitches of the previous row and work 1 front post treble crochet 2 rows below around each of the 2 raised treble crochets (at the end of the row only, around the two half double crochets); then go back in front of the 2 already worked raised treble crochets and work 1 front post treble crochet 2 rows below around each of the 2 raised treble crochets, going under the skipped single crochets.

4 front post treble crochets worked below crossed to the right: Skip 2 stitches of the previous row and work 1 front post treble crochet 2 rows below around each of the 2 raised treble crochets; then go back behind the 2 already worked raised treble crochets and work 1 front post treble crochet 2 rows below around each of the 2 raised treble crochets (at the beginning of the row only, around the 2 half double crochets), going under the skipped single crochets.

234 CROSSWISE PATTERN

[multiple of 8 + 1 beg-ch]

Chart Key

○ Chain 1

✕ 1 single crochet

⊤ 1 half double crochet

Fpdc: 1 front post double crochet

Bpdc: 1 back post double crochet

4 front post double crochets crossed to the left: Skip 2 raised double crochets of the previous row and work 1 front post double crochet around each of the following 2 raised double crochets; then go back in front of the 2 raised double crochets and work 1 front post double crochet around each of the 2 skipped raised double crochets of the previous row.

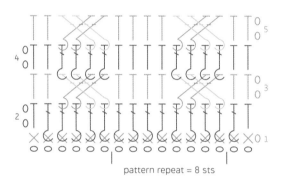

pattern repeat = 8 sts

Work in rows, following the chart. Begin every row with the stitches before the pattern repeat, repeat the marked pattern repeat (8 sts wide) widthwise, and end with the stitches after the pattern repeat. Work Rows 1–5 once, and then repeat Rows 4 and 5 for pattern.

235 RAISED LINES

[11 ch per pattern strip]

The strips are worked on a background of single crochets. Space the pattern strips on the background as desired, with a minimum distance of 2 single crochets between 2 pattern strips. Work in rows, following the chart. Work Rows 1–15 once, and then repeat Rows 4–15 for pattern.

For ease of work, raised double crochets worked below in Rows 7–13 are shown in color in the chart.

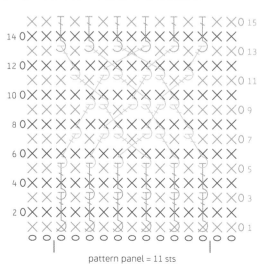

pattern panel = 11 sts

Chart Key

○ Chain 1   ✕ 1 single crochet

Fpdc-bel (1 front post double crochet worked below): In Row 3, work 2 rows below around the single crochet; from Row 5 on, work 2 rows below around the raised double crochet. In Rows 7–13, when working the front post double crochets worked below, always work going forward or backward as shown to cross them.

236 HORIZONTAL STRIPES WITH RIDGES

[multiple of 3 + 1 ch + 1 beg-ch]

Work in rows, following the chart; Row 1 is a WS row. Begin every row with the stitches before the pattern repeat, repeat the marked pattern repeat (3 sts wide) widthwise, and end with the stitches after the pattern repeat. Work Rows 1–3 once, and then repeat Rows 2 and 3 for pattern.

Chart Key

o Chain 1

X 1 single crochet

⊤ 1 double crochet

⊥ Fpdc: 1 front post double crochet

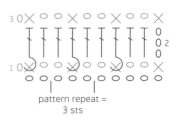

pattern repeat =
3 sts

237 TWO-COLOR FANS AND RIDGES

[multiple of 8 + 1 ch + 1 beg-ch]

Work in rows, following the chart. Begin every row with the stitches before the pattern repeat, repeat the marked pattern repeat (8 sts wide) widthwise, and end with the stitches after the pattern repeat. Work Rows 1–7 once, and then repeat Rows 4–7 for pattern. Change color every 2 rows as shown. Carry unused colors at the edge.

Chart Key

o Chain 1

X 1 single crochet

⊤ 1 double crochet

[1 double crochet, chain 1, 1 double crochet, chain 1, 1 double crochet, chain 1, 1 double crochet] into the same stitch

Fpdc-bel (1 front post double crochet worked below): In Row 4, work around the double crochet 2 rows below; from Row 6 on, work 2 rows below around the raised double crochet.

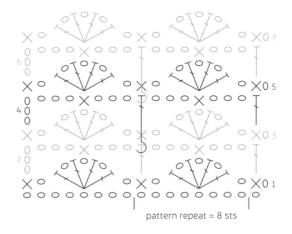

pattern repeat = 8 sts

238 BRICKWORK

[multiple of 4 + 2 ch + 3 beg-ch]

Chart Key

○   Chain 1

┬   1 half double crochet

┬   1 double crochet

Bpdc: 1 back post double crochet

Fpdc: 1 front post double crochet

Fptr: 1 front post treble crochet

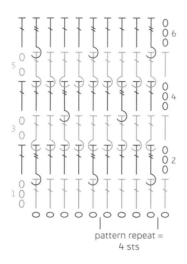

pattern repeat = 4 sts

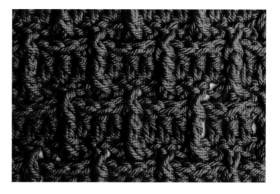

Work in rows, following the chart; Row 1 is a WS row. Begin every row with the stitches before the pattern repeat, repeat the marked pattern repeat (4 sts wide) widthwise, and end with the stitches after the pattern repeat. Work Rows 1–6 once, and then repeat Rows 3–6 for pattern.

239 OWL

[8 ch per motif]

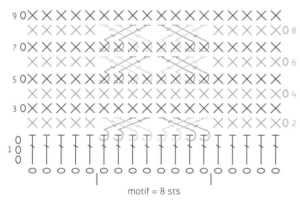

motif = 8 sts

Work in rows, following the chart; Row 1 is a WS row. The background pattern is double crochet for Row 1; from Row 2 on, single crochet as shown. Motifs may be spaced as desired; they should be at least 2 background stitches apart from each other. Work Rows 1–9 once.

Embellish each owl motif with two eyes attached at the level of Row 6 between the cable crossings as shown in the photo, using either beads or small buttons.

Chart Key

○   Chain 1

✕   1 single crochet

┬   1 double crochet

   4 front post double crochets crossed to the right: Skip 2 stitches of the previous row and work 1 front post double crochet around each of the following 2 stitches, and then go back behind the 2 raised double crochets and work 1 front post double crochet around each of the 2 skipped stitches of the previous row.

4 front post double crochets crossed to the left: Skip 2 stitches of the previous row and work 1 front post double crochet around each of the following 2 stitches, and then go back in front of the 2 raised double crochets, work 1 front post double crochet each around the two skipped stitches of the previous row.

MESH AND TRELLIS PATTERNS

240 LARGE DOUBLE CROCHET GRID

[multiple of 3 + 3 beg-ch]

Work in rows, following the chart. Begin every row with the stitches before the pattern repeat, repeat the marked pattern repeat (3 sts wide) widthwise, and end with the stitches after the pattern repeat. Work Rows 1–3 once, and then repeat Rows 2 and 3 for pattern.

Chart Key

o Chain 1

T 1 double crochet

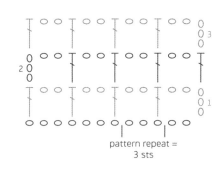

pattern repeat =
3 sts

241 LACE WITH PICOTS

[multiple of 6 + 1 ch + 1 beg-ch]

Work in rows, following the chart. Begin every row with the stitches before the pattern repeat, repeat the marked pattern repeat (6 sts wide) widthwise, and end with the stitches after the pattern repeat. Work Rows 1–9 once, and then repeat Rows 2–9 for pattern.

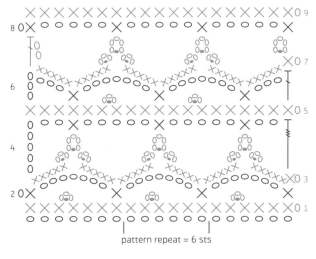

pattern repeat = 6 sts

Chart Key

o Chain 1

X 1 single crochet

T 1 double crochet

 1 double treble crochet

1 picot of 3: Chain 3, and then join with 1 slip stitch back into the first chain

1 picot of 5: Chain 5, and then join with 1 slip stitch back into the first chain

242 NET OF FLOWERS

[multiple of 6 + 2 ch + 1 beg-ch]

Work in rows, following the chart. Begin every row with the stitches before the pattern repeat, repeat the marked pattern repeat (6 sts wide) widthwise, and end with the stitches after the pattern repeat. Work Rows 1–6 once, and then repeat Rows 3–6 for pattern. In Rows 2, 4, and 6, always work the single crochet into the middle (fifth) chain of the chain-9 arc.

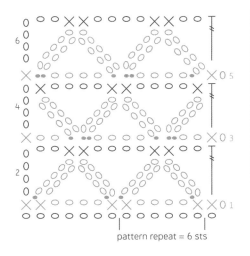

pattern repeat = 6 sts

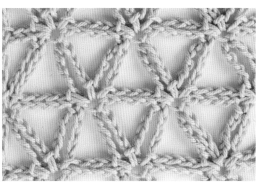

Chart Key

○ Chain 1

● 1 slip stitch

✕ 1 single crochet

⊥ 1 treble crochet

243 MESH WITH HEXAGONS

[multiple of 18 + 6 ch + 3 beg-ch]

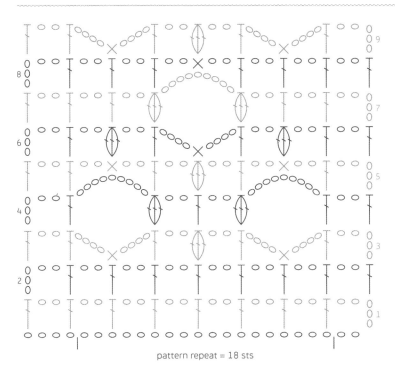

pattern repeat = 18 sts

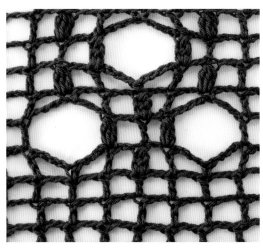

Chart Key

○ Chain 1

⊤ 1 double crochet

✕ 1 single crochet

⬥ Dc3tog-in-1: 3 double crochets into the same stitch and crocheted together

Work in rows, following the chart. Begin every row with the stitches before the pattern repeat, repeat the marked pattern repeat (18 sts wide) widthwise, and end with the stitches after the pattern repeat. Work Rows 1–9 once, and then repeat Rows 4–9 for pattern.

244 DOUBLE CROCHET CHAINS

[multiple of 6 + 4 ch + 3 beg-ch]

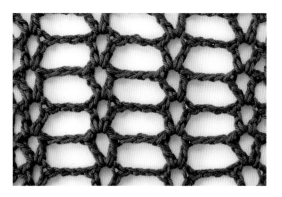

Work in rows, following the chart. Begin every row with the stitches before the pattern repeat, repeat the marked pattern repeat (6 sts wide) widthwise, and end with the stitches after the pattern repeat. Work Rows 1–3 once, and then repeat Rows 2 and 3 for pattern.

From Row 2 on, always work the double crochets from the group of [1 double crochet, 2 chains, 1 double crochet] in the chain space of the previous row, around the chain.

Chart Key

o Chain 1

⌶ 1 double crochet

 [1 double crochet, chain 2, 1 double crochet] into the same stitch

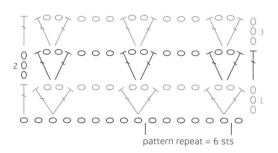

pattern repeat = 6 sts

245 MESH WREATHS

[multiple of 9 + 6 ch + 3 beg-ch]

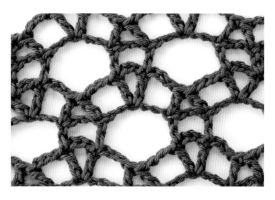

Work in rows, following the chart. Begin every row with the stitches before the pattern repeat, repeat the marked pattern repeat (9 sts wide) widthwise, and end with the stitches after the pattern repeat. Work Rows 1–5 once, and then repeat Rows 2–5 for pattern.

Chart Key

o Chain 1

⌶ 1 double crochet

⋀ Dc2tog: Double crochet 2 stitches together

[1 double crochet, chain 3, 1 double crochet] into the same stitch

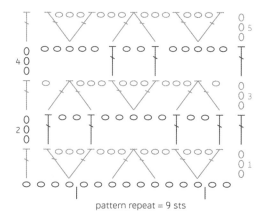

pattern repeat = 9 sts

246 SIMPLE TRELLIS PATTERN

[multiple of 4 + 1 ch + 1 beg-ch]

Work in rows, following the chart. Begin every row with the stitches before the pattern repeat, repeat the marked pattern repeat (4 sts wide) widthwise, and end with the stitches after the pattern repeat. Work Rows 1–3 once, and then repeat Rows 2 and 3 for pattern.

Chart Key

o Chain 1

✕ 1 single crochet

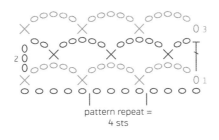

pattern repeat = 4 sts

247 SPINDLE MESH

[multiple of 10 + 3 beg-ch]

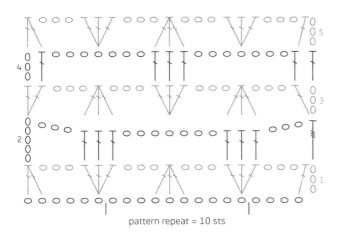

pattern repeat = 10 sts

Chart Key

o Chain 1

⊤ 1 double crochet

⊤ 1 double treble crochet

Dc3tog: Double crochet 3 stitches together

Dc3-in-1: 3 double crochets into the same stitch

Dc2tog: Double crochet 2 stitches together

Dc2-in-1: 2 double crochets into the same stitch

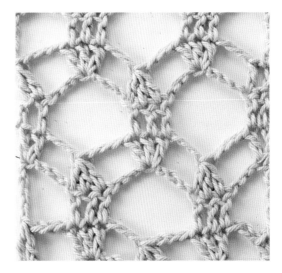

Work in rows, following the chart. Begin every row with the stitches before the pattern repeat, repeat the marked pattern repeat (10 sts wide) widthwise, and end with the stitches after the pattern repeat. Work Rows 1–5 once, and then repeat Rows 2–5 for pattern.

248 NETWORK [multiple of 5 + 1 ch + 4 beg-ch]

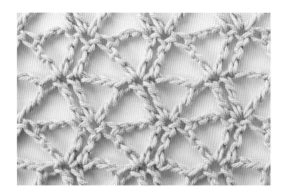

Work in rows, following the chart. Begin every row with the stitches before the pattern repeat, repeat the marked pattern repeat (5 sts wide) widthwise, and end with the stitches after the pattern repeat. Work Rows 1–3 once, and then repeat Rows 2 and 3 for pattern.

Chart Key

Chain 1

1 treble crochet

[1 treble crochet, chain 3, 1 treble crochet] into the same stitch

2 treble crochets crocheted off together; for the first treble crochet, skip 1 chain of the beginning chain; from Row 3 on, skip 1 chain of the previous row

2 treble crochets crocheted off together; for the second treble crochet, skip 3 chains of the beginning chain; from Row 2 on, skip 3 chains of the previous row, chain 3, and work 1 treble crochet into the same spot as the previous treble crochet

2 treble crochets crocheted off together; for the second treble crochet skip 3 chains of the previous row, chain 2, and work 1 treble crochet into the same spot as the previous treble crochet

pattern repeat = 5 sts

249 CLOISTER [multiple of 7 + 3 beg-ch]

Chart Key

○ Chain 1

✕ 1 single crochet

┃ 1 double crochet

Dc2tog-in-1: 2 double crochets into the same stitch and crocheted together

Dc2tog: Double crochet 2 stitches together

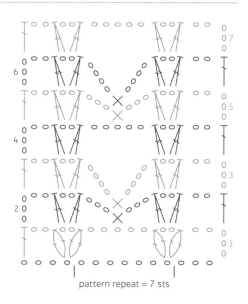

pattern repeat = 7 sts

Work in rows, following the chart. Begin every row with the stitches before the pattern repeat, repeat the marked pattern repeat (7 sts wide) widthwise, and end with the stitches after the pattern repeat. Work Rows 1–7 once, and then repeat Rows 2–7 for pattern.

From Row 2 on, work the double crochets from the groups of [2 double crochets, 2 chains, 2 double crochets], which are crocheted off together, always in the chain space of the previous row, around the chain.

250 COLUMN GRID

[multiple of 4 + 2 ch + 1 beg-ch]

Work in rows, following the chart; Row 1 is a WS row. Begin every row with the stitches before the pattern repeat, repeat the marked pattern repeat (4 sts wide) widthwise, and end with the stitches after the pattern repeat. Work Rows 1–3 once, and then repeat Rows 2 and 3 for pattern.

Chart Key

o   Chain 1
X   1 single crochet
T   1 double crochet

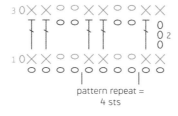

pattern repeat =
4 sts

251 ROSEBUD TRELLIS

[multiple of 5 + 1 ch + 1 beg-ch]

Work in rows, following the chart. Begin every row with the stitches before the pattern repeat, repeat the marked pattern repeat (5 sts wide) widthwise, and end with the stitches after the pattern repeat. Work Rows 1–3 once, and then repeat Rows 2 and 3 for pattern.

Chart Key

o   Chain 1
X   1 single crochet
T   1 treble crochet

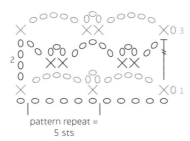

pattern repeat =
5 sts

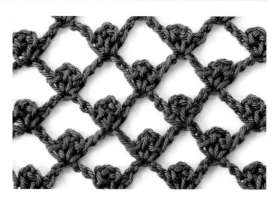

252 KNOTTED GRID [multiple of 6 + 4 ch + 3 beg-ch]

Work in rows, following the chart. Begin every row with the stitches before the pattern repeat, repeat the marked pattern repeat (6 sts wide) widthwise, and end with the stitches after the pattern repeat. Work Rows 1–3 once, and then repeat Rows 2 and 3 for pattern.

From Row 2 on, always work the double crochets from the group of [1 double crochet, 1 chain, 1 double crochet] in the chain space of the previous row, around the chain.

Chart Key

○ Chain 1

┬ 1 half double crochet

┬ 1 double crochet

V̄ [1 double crochet, chain 1, 1 double crochet] into the same stitch

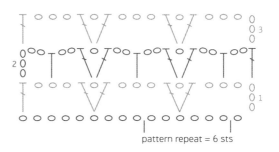

pattern repeat = 6 sts

253 BRAIDED DIAMONDS [multiple of 4 + 1 ch + 1 beg-ch]

Work in rows, following the chart; Row 1 is a WS row. Begin every row with the stitches before the pattern repeat, repeat the marked pattern repeat (4 sts wide) widthwise, and end with the stitches after the pattern repeat. Work Rows 1–4 once, and then repeat Rows 3 and 4 for pattern.

Chart Key

○ Chain 1

✕ 1 single crochet

┼ 1 double crochet

╪ 1 treble crochet

[1 double crochet, 1 treble crochet, and 1 double crochet with 3 different bases] crocheted together: Always work the first double crochet into the same chain of the previous row as the previous double crochet, skip 2 chains of the previous row (Row 2), work the treble crochet into the next single crochet of the previous row and in later rows into the top of the [1 double crochet, 1 treble crochet, 1 double crochet] of the previous row, skip 2 chains of the previous row, work the next double crochet into the next chain of the previous row.

[1 double crochet and 1 treble crochet] crocheted together: Work the double crochet into the same chain of the previous row as the previous double crochet, skip 2 chains of the previous row, work the treble crochet into the last stitch of the previous row.

pattern repeat = 4 sts

254 FLORAL LATTICE

[multiple of 8 + 1 ch + 1 beg-ch]

Work in rows, following the chart; Row 1 is a WS row. Begin every row with the stitches before the pattern repeat, repeat the marked pattern repeat (8 sts wide) widthwise, and end with the stitches after the pattern repeat. Work Rows 1–6 once, and then repeat Rows 3–6 for pattern.

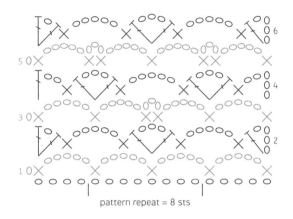

pattern repeat = 8 sts

Chart Key

○ Chain 1

✕ 1 single crochet

⊤ 1 double crochet

 [1 double crochet, chain 3, 1 double crochet] into the same stitch

[1 double crochet, chain 1, 1 double crochet] into the same stitch

255 ROCOCO LATTICE

[multiple of 11 + 7 ch + 3 beg-ch]

Work in rows, following the chart. Begin every row with the stitches before the pattern repeat, repeat the marked pattern repeat (11 sts wide) widthwise, and end with the stitches after the pattern repeat. Work Rows 1–3 once, and then repeat Rows 2 and 3 for pattern.

From Row 2 on, always work the single crochet and double crochet in the chain space of the previous row, around the chain, except for the double crochet at the end of the row, which is worked into the top chain of the beginning chain.

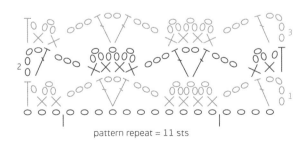

pattern repeat = 11 sts

Chart Key

○ Chain 1

✕ 1 single crochet

⊤ 1 double crochet

⊤ 1 half double crochet

 [1 double crochet, chain 2, 1 double crochet] into the same stitch

256 DOUBLE DIAMOND MESH
[multiple of 6 + 2 beg-ch]

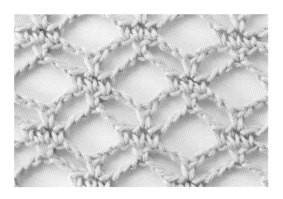

Work in rows, following the chart. Begin every row with the stitches before the pattern repeat, repeat the marked pattern repeat (6 sts wide) widthwise, and end with the stitches after the pattern repeat. Work Rows 1–5 once, and then repeat Rows 2–5 for pattern.

Chart Key

○ Chain 1

✕ 1 single crochet

⊤ 1 half double crochet

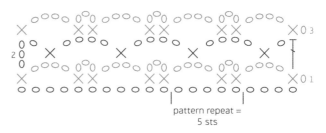

pattern repeat = 6 sts

257 DOT NET
[multiple of 5 + 1 beg-ch]

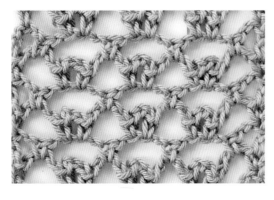

Work in rows, following the chart. Begin every row with the stitches before the pattern repeat, repeat the marked pattern repeat (5 sts wide) widthwise, and end with the stitches after the pattern repeat. Work Rows 1–3 once, and then repeat Rows 2 and 3 for pattern.

From Row 2 on, always work the single crochet in the chain space of the previous row, around the chain.

Chart Key

○ Chain 1

✕ 1 single crochet

⊤ 1 double crochet

pattern repeat = 5 sts

258 TILES AND PICOTS

[multiple of 6 + 3 beg-ch]

Work in rows, following the chart; Row 1 is a WS row. Begin every row with the stitches before the pattern repeat, repeat the marked pattern repeat (6 sts wide) widthwise, and end with the stitches after the pattern repeat. Work Rows 1–3 once, and then repeat Rows 2 and 3 for pattern.

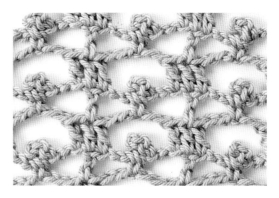

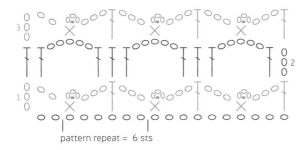

pattern repeat = 6 sts

Chart Key

○ Chain 1

╳ 1 single crochet

┬ 1 double crochet

₀Ꮬₒ 1 picot of 3: Chain 3, and then join with 1 slip stitch back into the first chain

259 SHELL DIAMONDS

[multiple of 10 + 6 ch + 3 beg-ch]

Work in rows, following the chart. Begin every row with the stitches before the pattern repeat, repeat the marked pattern repeat (10 sts wide) widthwise, and end with the stitches after the pattern repeat. Work Rows 1–7 once, and then repeat Rows 2–7 for pattern.

From Row 2 on, work the double crochets from the groups of [4 double crochets, 2 chains, 4 double crochets] always in the chain space of the previous row, around the chain. Single crochets worked below are always worked around the chain from 2 rows below.

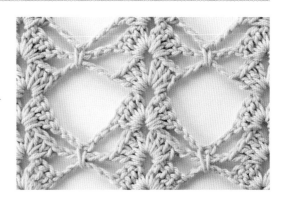

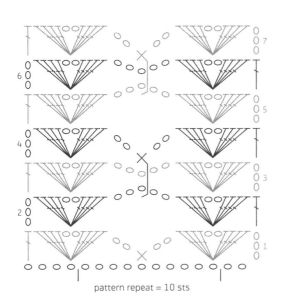

pattern repeat = 10 sts

Chart Key

○ Chain 1

╳ 1 single crochet

┬ 1 double crochet

⟋⟍ [4 double crochets, chain 2, 4 crochets] into the same stitch

╳ 1 single crochet worked below around the chain arc

260 OYSTER GRID

[multiple of 10 + 3 beg-ch]

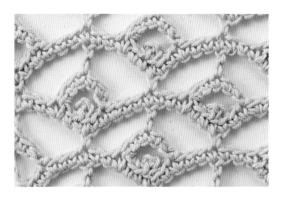

Chart Key

o   Chain 1

✕   1 single crochet

⌐   1 double crochet

o⟡o   1 picot of 3: Chain 3, and then join with 1 slip stitch back into the first chain

Work in rows, following the chart; Row 1 is a WS row. Begin every row with the stitches before the pattern repeat, repeat the marked pattern repeat (10 sts wide) widthwise, and end with the stitches after the repeat. In Rows 2 and 4, always follow the arrows. Work Rows 1–5 once, and then repeat Rows 2–5 for pattern.

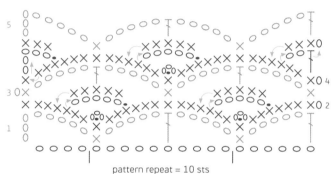

pattern repeat = 10 sts

261 DIAMOND NET

[multiple of 17 + 4 ch + 3 beg-ch]

Chart Key

o   Chain 1

✕   1 single crochet

⌐   1 double crochet

↑   1 treble crochet

Ⓥ   Dc3-in-1: 3 double crochets into the same stitch

Work in rows, following the chart. Begin every row with the stitches before the pattern repeat, repeat the marked pattern repeat (17 sts wide) widthwise, and end with the stitches after the pattern repeat. Work Rows 1–8 once, and then repeat Rows 3–8 for pattern.

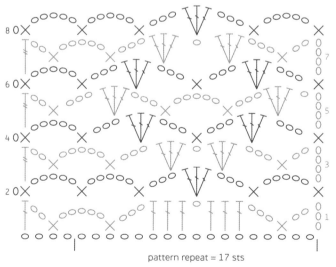

pattern repeat = 17 sts

262 ARROW MESH

[multiple of 6 + 4 beg-ch]

Work in rows, following the chart. Begin every row with the stitches before the pattern repeat, repeat the marked pattern repeat (6 sts wide) widthwise, and end with the stitches after the pattern repeat. Work Rows 1–3 once, and then repeat Rows 2 and 3 for pattern.

Chart Key

○　Chain 1

✕　1 single crochet

†　1 treble crochet

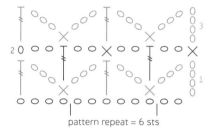

pattern repeat = 6 sts

263 HYDRANGEA PATTERN

[multiple of 16 + 9 ch + 3 beg-ch]

Work in rows, following the chart; Row 1 is a WS row. Begin every row with the stitches before the pattern repeat, repeat the marked pattern repeat (16 sts wide) widthwise, and end with the stitches after the pattern repeat. Work Rows 1–7 once, and then repeat Rows 2–7 for pattern.

pattern repeat = 16 sts

Chart Key

○　Chain 1

✕　1 single crochet

†　1 double crochet

4 double crochets into the same stitch, but not yet finishing the last step of the last double crochet, in Row 1, skip 7 chains of the beginning chain, and work 1 double crochet into the next chain of the beginning chain; or from Row 2 on, 1 double crochet into the double crochet of the previous row (as shown on the chart), crochet both double crochets together, and then work 3 additional double crochets into the same spot as the last one of the double crochets that were crocheted together.

264 BOX GRID

[multiple of 4 + 2 ch + 3 beg-ch]

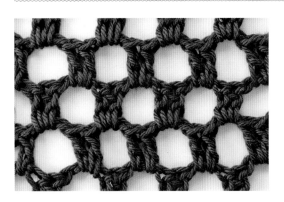

Work in rows, following the chart. Begin every row with the stitches before the pattern repeat, repeat the marked pattern repeat (4 sts wide) widthwise, and end with the stitches after the pattern repeat. Work Rows 1–3 once, and then repeat Rows 2 and 3 for pattern.

From Row 2 on, always work the double crochets in the chain space of the previous row, around the chain, except for the double crochet at the end of the row, which is worked into the top chain of the beginning chain.

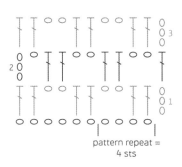

pattern repeat = 4 sts

Chart Key

○ Chain 1

⊤ 1 double crochet

265 ARCED NET WITH SMALL KNOTS

[multiple of 7 + 1 ch + 1 beg-ch]

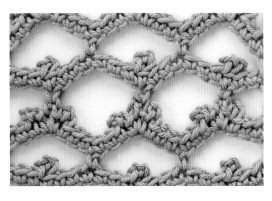

Work in rows, following the chart. Begin every row with the stitches before the pattern repeat, repeat the marked pattern repeat (7 sts wide) widthwise, and end with the stitches after the pattern repeat. Work Rows 1–5 once, and then repeat Rows 2–5 for pattern.

In Row 4, always work the single crochet around the chain of the middle picot of the previous row.

Chart Key

○ Chain 1

✕ 1 single crochet

⊤ 1 double crochet

⸰⸰⸰ 1 picot of 3: Chain 3, and then join with 1 slip stitch back into the first chain

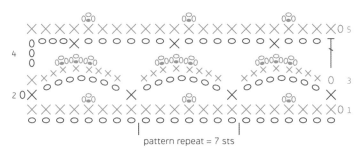

pattern repeat = 7 sts

266 TRELLIS MESH

[multiple of 5 + 6 beg-ch]

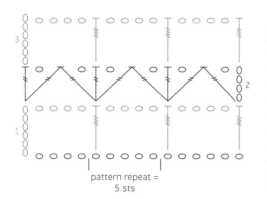

Work in rows, following the chart; Row 1 is a WS row. Begin every row with the stitches before the pattern repeat, repeat the marked pattern repeat (5 sts wide) width-wise, and end with the stitches after the pattern repeat. Work Rows 1–3 once, and then repeat Rows 2 and 3 for pattern.

pattern repeat = 5 sts

Chart Key

○ Chain 1

⊤ 1 treble crochet

⫢ 1 triple treble crochet

2 treble crochets crocheted off together: Place the first treble crochet into the first triple treble crochet of the previous row (but do not complete the last step of the treble crochet), and then skip 4 chains of the previous row before working the second treble crochet and finishing them off together, * chain 1, 1 treble crochet into the triple treble crochet of the previous row, chain 1, 1 treble crochet into the same triple treble crochet—but do not complete the last step of the last treble crochet—skip 4 chains of the previous row, and then work 1 treble crochet into the next triple treble crochet of the previous row, and crochet both together; repeat from * to end of row. Here the last insertion spot is the top chain of the turning chain of the previous row.

267 FORKED DOUBLE CROCHETS AND PICOTS

[multiple of 4 + 4 beg-ch]

Work in rows, following the chart; Row 1 is a WS row. Begin every row with the stitches before the pattern repeat, repeat the marked pattern repeat (4 sts wide) widthwise, and end with the stitches after the pattern repeat. Work Rows 1–3 once, and then repeat Rows 2 and 3 for pattern.

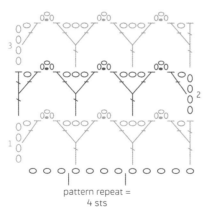

pattern repeat = 4 sts

Chart Key

○ Chain 1

⊤ 1 double crochet

 1 picot of 3: Chain 3, and then join with 1 slip stitch back into the first chain

 1 forked double crochet with 3 chains in between: [Yarn over hook] twice, insert hook, and finish as for a treble crochet. Chain 3, [yarn over hook] once, insert the hook in the middle of the treble crochet directly above the diagonal loop at the bottom, and pull the working yarn through. Continue working the 3 loops on the hook as done for a regular double crochet in two steps.

1 forked double crochet with chain 1 between them: [Yarn over hook] twice, insert hook, and finish as for a treble crochet. Chain 1, [yarn over hook] once, insert the hook in the middle of the treble crochet directly above the diagonal loop at the bottom, and pull the working yarn through. Continue working the 3 loops on the hook as done for a regular double crochet in two steps.

268 FILIGREE NET

[multiple of 7 + 3 beg-ch]

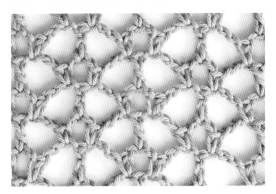

Work in rows, following the chart. Begin every row with the stitches before the pattern repeat, repeat the marked pattern repeat (7 sts wide) widthwise, and end with the stitches after the pattern repeat. Work Rows 1–3 once, and then repeat Rows 2 and 3 for pattern.

Chart Key

○ Chain 1

✕ 1 single crochet

T 1 half double crochet

T 1 double crochet

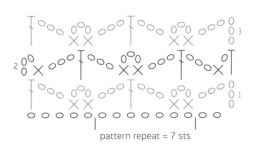

pattern repeat = 7 sts

269 SIMPLE ZIGZAG GRID

[multiple of 3 + 1 ch + 1 beg-ch]

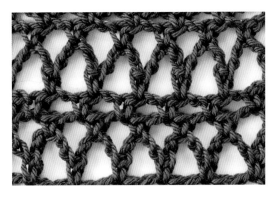

Work in rows, following the chart. Begin every row with the stitches before the pattern repeat, repeat the marked pattern repeat (3 sts wide) widthwise, and end with the stitches after the pattern repeat. Work Rows 1–7 once, and then repeat Rows 2–7 for pattern.

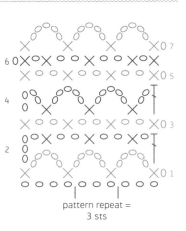

pattern repeat = 3 sts

Chart Key

○ Chain 1   ✕ 1 single crochet   T 1 double crochet

270 DENSE V-MESH

[multiple of 3 + 2 ch + 1 beg-ch]

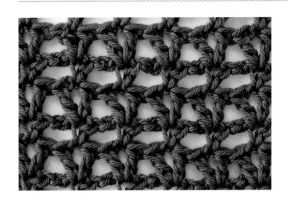

Work in rows, following the chart; Row 1 is a WS row. Begin every row with the stitches before the pattern repeat, repeat the marked pattern repeat (3 sts wide) widthwise, and end with the stitches after the pattern repeat. Work Rows 1–4 once, and then repeat Rows 3 and 4 for pattern.

Chart Key

○ Chain 1

✕ 1 single crochet

T 1 double crochet

V [1 double crochet, chain 1, 1 double crochet] into the same stitch

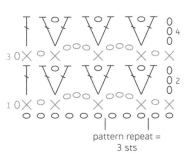

pattern repeat = 3 sts

271 WIDE-MESH NET

[multiple of 10 + 1 ch + 1 beg-ch]

Work in rows, following the chart. Begin every row with the stitches before the pattern repeat, repeat the marked pattern repeat (10 sts wide) widthwise, and end with the stitches after the pattern repeat. Work Rows 1–3 once, and then repeat Rows 2 and 3 for pattern.

In Row 3, place the single crochets in the pattern repeat always between two double crochets of the previous row.

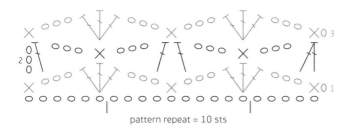

pattern repeat = 10 sts

Chart Key

o   Chain 1

✕   1 single crochet

⊤   1 double crochet

Dc3-in-1: 3 double crochets into the same stitch

Dc2tog: Double crochet 2 stitches together

272 STAR GRID

[multiple of 10 + 1 ch + 4 beg-ch]

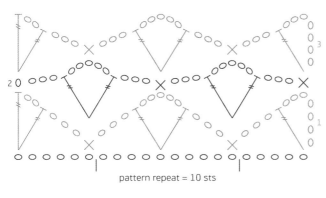

pattern repeat = 10 sts

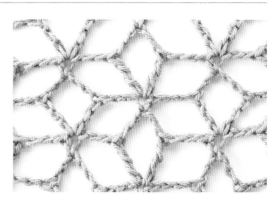

Work in rows, following the chart. Begin every row with the stitches before the pattern repeat, repeat the marked pattern repeat (10 sts wide) widthwise, and end with the stitches after the pattern repeat. Work Rows 1–3 once, and then repeat Rows 2 and 3 for pattern.

Chart Key

o   Chain 1

✕   1 single crochet

⊤   1 treble crochet

 [1 treble crochet, chain 5, 1 treble crochet] into the same stitch

 [1 treble crochet, chain 2, 1 treble crochet] into the same stitch

273 KALEIDOSCOPE

[multiple of 8 + 5 ch + 1 beg-ch]

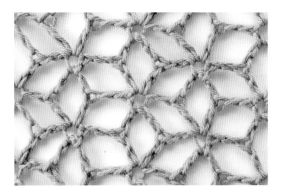

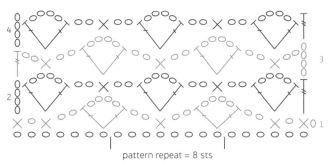

pattern repeat = 8 sts

Work in rows, following the chart. Begin every row with the stitches before the pattern repeat, repeat the marked pattern repeat (8 sts wide) widthwise, and end with the stitches after the pattern repeat. Work Rows 1–4 once, and then repeat Rows 3 and 4 for pattern.

Chart Key

○ Chain 1

✕ 1 single crochet

⊤ treble crochet

⌄ [1 double crochet, chain 4, 1 double crochet] into the same stitch

274 DIAMONDS IN A NET

[multiple of 10 + 3 beg-ch]

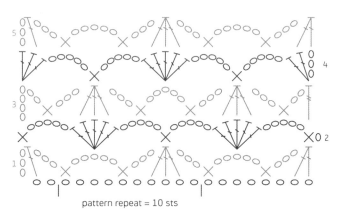

pattern repeat = 10 sts

Work in rows, following the chart; Row 1 is a WS row. Begin every row with the stitches before the pattern repeat, repeat the marked pattern repeat (10 sts wide) widthwise, and end with the stitches after the pattern repeat. Work Rows 1–5 once, and then repeat Rows 2–5 for pattern.

Chart Key

○ Chain 1

✕ 1 single crochet

⊤ 1 double crochet

⋀ Dc2tog: Double crochet 2 stitches together

 Dc3tog: Double crochet 3 stitches together

Dc5-in-1: 5 double crochets into the same stitch

Dc2-in-1: 2 double crochets into the same stitch

275 STAGGERED DOUBLE CROCHET GRID

[multiple of 2 + 3 beg-ch]

Work in rows, following the chart. Begin every row with the stitches before the pattern repeat, repeat the marked pattern repeat (2 sts wide) widthwise, and end with the stitches after the pattern repeat. Work Rows 1–3 once, and then repeat Rows 2 and 3 for pattern.

From Row 2 on, work the double crochets in the chain space of the previous row, around the chain.

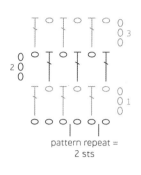

pattern repeat = 2 sts

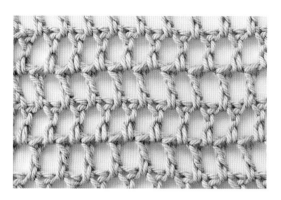

Chart Key

○ Chain 1   ⊤ 1 double crochet

276 SMALL DOUBLE CROCHET GRID

[multiple of 2 + 3 beg-ch]

Work in rows, following the chart. Begin every row with the stitches before the pattern repeat, repeat the marked pattern repeat (2 sts wide) widthwise, and end with the stitches after the pattern repeat. Work Rows 1–3 once, and then repeat Rows 2 and 3 for pattern.

Chart Key

○ Chain 1   ⊤ 1 double crochet

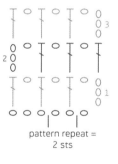

pattern repeat = 2 sts

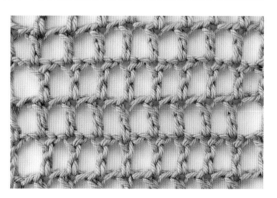

277 HONEYCOMB PATTERN

[multiple of 4 + 2 ch + 3 beg-ch]

Work in rows, following the chart. Begin every row with the stitches before the pattern repeat, repeat the marked pattern repeat (4 sts wide) widthwise, and end with the stitches after the pattern repeat. Work Rows 1–3 once, and then repeat Rows 2 and 3 for pattern.

From Row 2 on, always work the double crochets into the chain space of the previous row, around the chain, except for the double crochet at the end of the row, which is worked into the top chain of the beginning chain.

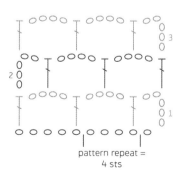

pattern repeat = 4 sts

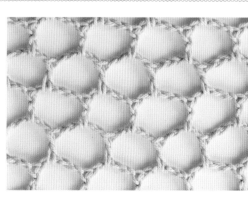

Chart Key

○ Chain 1   ⊤ 1 double crochet

278 SOLOMON'S KNOT NET

[number of knots a multiple of 2 + 1 knot]

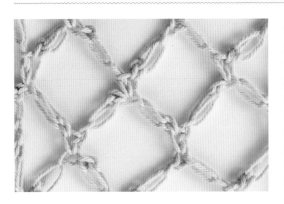

Work in rows, following the chart. Begin every row with the stitches and knot before the pattern repeat, repeat the marked pattern repeat (2 knots wide) widthwise, and end with the stitches and knot after the pattern repeat. Follow the working direction shown by the arrows. Work Rows 1–3 once, and then repeat Rows 2 and 3 for pattern.

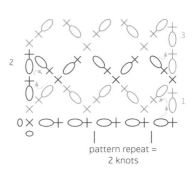

pattern repeat = 2 knots

Chart Key

o   Chain 1

×   1 single crochet

O+ 1 Solomon's knot: Make a beginning slipknot on the crochet hook, chain 1, and pull it out to a length of about 10 mm [0.4 inch]. Draw the working yarn through and pull it in regular length through the elongated loop, holding the two strands of the elongated loop so that they are separate from the drawn-through working yarn. Now, lead the crochet hook between the single working yarn and the strands of the elongated loop (like working in the back of a chain) and pull the working yarn through. There are 2 loops on the hook. Draw the working yarn through once more, and then pull the yarn through both loops on the hook as for a single crochet.

To make the knot out of the beginning chain and at the edges, always pull the elongated loop to a length of about 10 mm [0.4 inch]. For the knot within the net, always pull the elongated loop to a length of about 15 mm [0.6 inch].

To crochet a net with this stitch, work single crochets between knots into the knots of the previous row as shown in the chart.

279 FRETWORK

[multiple of 12 + 1 ch + 3 beg-ch]

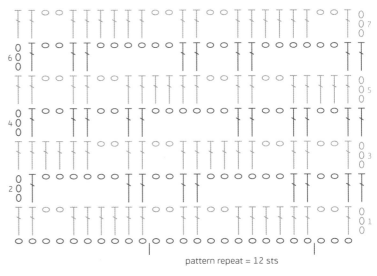

pattern repeat = 12 sts

Work in rows, following the chart. Begin every row with the stitches before the pattern repeat, repeat the marked pattern repeat (12 sts wide) widthwise, and end with the stitches after the pattern repeat. Work Rows 1–7 once, and then repeat Rows 2–7 for pattern.

Chart Key

o   Chain 1

T   1 double crochet

280 LADDER PATTERN

[multiple of 4 + 1 ch + 1 beg-ch]

Work in rows, following the chart. Begin every row with the stitches before the pattern repeat, repeat the marked pattern repeat (4 sts wide) widthwise, and end with the stitches after the pattern repeat. Work Rows 1–3 once, and then repeat Rows 2 and 3 for pattern.

Chart Key

o   Chain 1

✕   1 single crochet

⟋⟍   Blo-sc: 1 single crochet through the back loop only

pattern repeat = 4 sts

281 TRUSSES

[multiple of 4 + 3 beg-ch]

Work in rows, following the chart. Begin every row with the stitches before the pattern repeat, repeat the marked pattern repeat (4 sts wide) widthwise, and end with the stitches after the pattern repeat. Work Rows 1–3 once, and then repeat Rows 2 and 3 for pattern.

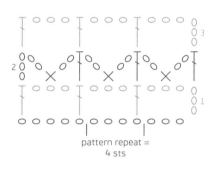

pattern repeat = 4 sts

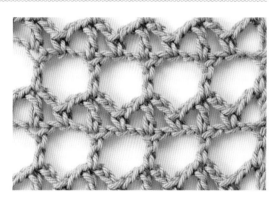

Chart Key

o   Chain 1   ✕   1 single crochet   ⊤   1 double crochet

282 STURDY HONEYCOMB NET

[multiple of 5 + 1 ch + 1 beg-ch]

Work in rows, following the chart. Begin every row with the stitches before the pattern repeat, repeat the marked pattern repeat (5 sts wide) widthwise, and end with the stitches after the repeat. Work Rows 1–6 once, and then repeat Rows 3–6 for pattern.

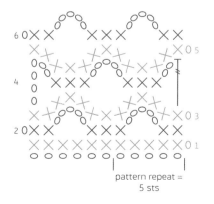

pattern repeat = 5 sts

Chart Key

o   Chain 1

✕   1 single crochet

⟊   1 treble crochet

283 NORDIC LATTICE

[multiple of 12 + 9 ch + 3 beg-ch]

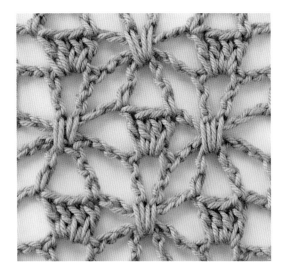

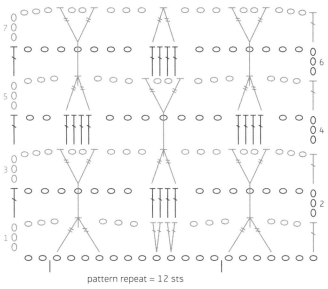

pattern repeat = 12 sts

Work in rows, following the chart; Row 1 is a WS row. Begin every row with the stitches before the pattern repeat, repeat the marked pattern repeat (12 sts wide) widthwise, and end with the stitches after the repeat. Work Rows 1–7 once, and then repeat Rows 4–7 for pattern.

In Rows 4 and 6, always work the groups of 4 double crochets into the chain space of the previous row, around the chain.

Chart Key

○   Chain 1

│   1 double crochet

V   Dc2-in-1: 2 double crochets into the same stitch

⋏   Tr2tog: Treble crochet 2 stitches together

[1 treble crochet worked below, chain 2, 1 treble crochet worked below] into the same stitch

284 CHAIN GRID

[multiple of 6 + 1 ch + 1 beg-ch]

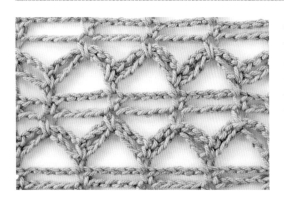

Chart Key

○   Chain 1

✕   1 single crochet

│   1 double crochet

✕   Sc-bel: 1 single crochet worked below

Work in rows, following the chart; Row 1 is a WS row. Begin every row with the stitches before the pattern repeat, repeat the marked pattern repeat (6 sts wide) widthwise, and end with the stitches after the pattern repeat. Work Rows 1–10 once, and then repeat Rows 3–10 for pattern.

Always work stitches below into the chain space 2 rows below, around the chain.

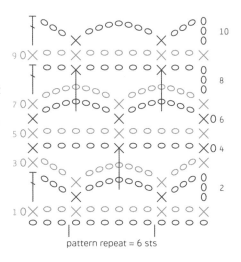

pattern repeat = 6 sts

285 CROSSBILL GRID

[multiple of 3 + 3 beg-ch]

Work in rows, following the chart. Begin every row with the stitches before the pattern repeat, repeat the marked pattern repeat (3 sts wide) widthwise, and end with the stitches after the pattern repeat. Work Rows 1–3 once, and then repeat Rows 2 and 3 for pattern.

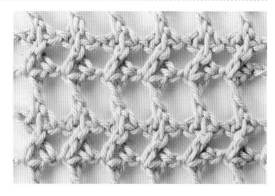

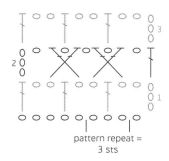

pattern repeat =
3 sts

Chart Key

○   Chain 1

†   1 double crochet

2 crossed double crochets with chain 1 in between: Work the first double crochet into the chain after the next double crochet of the previous row, chain 1, work the second double crochet going back in front of the double crochet into the chain of the previous row

286 ORNAMENTAL BANDS

[multiple of 14 + 3 beg-ch]

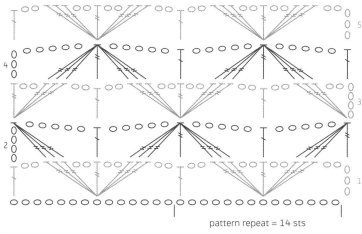

pattern repeat = 14 sts

Chart Key

○ Chain 1

 3 treble crochets worked in 3 treble crochets of the previous row and crocheted together

† 1 double crochet

 [3 treble crochets, chain 2, 1 treble crochet] into the same stitch

† 1 treble crochet

 Tr4tog: 4 treble crochets crocheted off together: Work the first 3 treble crochets into 3 treble crochets of the previous row, skip 2 chains of the previous row, work 1 treble crochet into the third chain of the beginning chain of the previous row

Tr7tog: 7 treble crochets worked into 3 different spots and crocheted together: Work the first 3 treble crochets into 3 treble crochets of the previous row, skip 2 chains of the previous row, work 1 treble crochet into the next double crochet of the previous row, skip 2 chains of the previous row, work 3 treble crochets into 3 treble crochets of the previous row

 [3 treble crochets, chain 2, 1 treble crochet, chain 2, 3 treble crochets] into the same stitch

Work in rows, following the chart. Begin every row with the stitches before the pattern repeat, repeat the marked pattern repeat (14 sts wide) widthwise, and end with the stitches after the pattern repeat. Work Rows 1–5 once, and then repeat Rows 2–5 for pattern.

287 ZIGZAG BANDS

[multiple of 7 + 3 ch + 4 beg-ch]

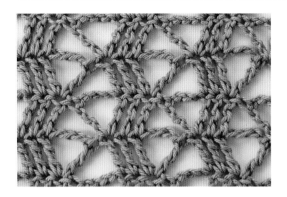

Work in rows, following the chart. Begin every row with the stitches before the pattern repeat, repeat the marked pattern repeat (7 sts wide) widthwise, and end with the stitches after the pattern repeat. Work Rows 1–3 once, and then repeat Rows 2 and 3 for pattern.

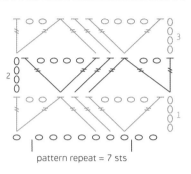

pattern repeat = 7 sts

Chart Key

○ Chain 1

| 1 treble crochet

[1 treble crochet, chain 4, 1 treble crochet] into the same stitch

2 treble crochets crocheted together, chain 2, 1 treble crochet: for the second treble crochet in Row 1, skip 4 chains of the beginning chain, or from Row 2 on, skip 4 chains and 1 treble crochet of the previous row, and then [chain 2, 1 treble crochet] into the same spot as the last one of the treble crochets that were crocheted together

288 TREE MESH

[multiple of 12 + 3 beg-ch]

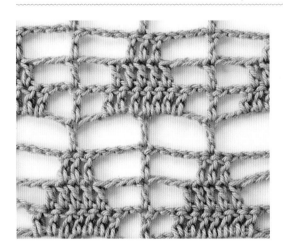

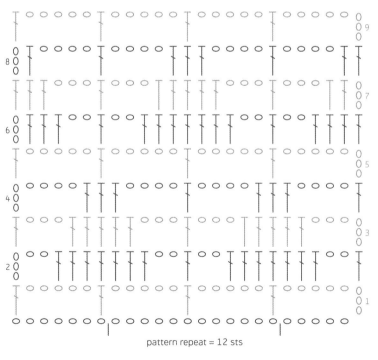

pattern repeat = 12 sts

Work in rows, following the chart. Begin every row with the stitches before the pattern repeat, repeat the marked pattern repeat (12 sts wide) widthwise, and end with the stitches after the pattern repeat. Work Rows 1–9 once, and then repeat Rows 2–9 for pattern.

Chart Key

○ Chain 1 | 1 double crochet

289 PINEAPPLE MESH

[multiple of 20 + 9 ch + 3 beg-ch]

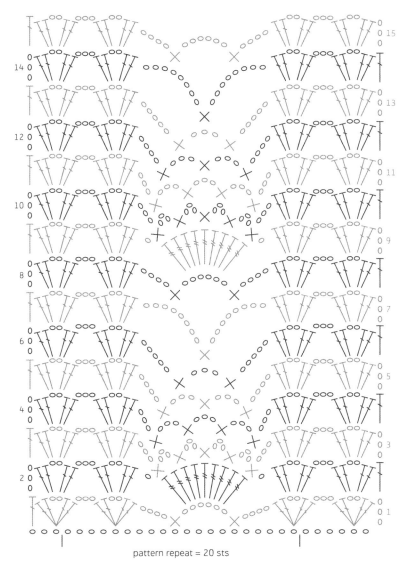

pattern repeat = 20 sts

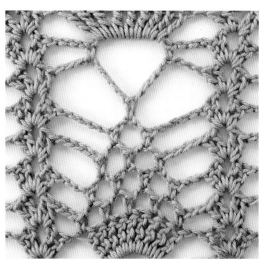

Work in rows, following the chart. Begin every row with the stitches before the pattern repeat, repeat the marked pattern repeat (20 sts wide) widthwise, and end with the stitches after the pattern repeat. Work Rows 1–15 once, and then repeat Rows 2–15 for pattern.

From Row 2 on, always work the double crochets from the groups of [2 double crochets, 2 chains, 2 double crochets] as well as the sequence of 9 treble crochets into the chain space of the previous row, around the chain.

Chart Key

o Chain 1

✕ 1 single crochet

⊤ 1 treble crochet

⊤ 1 double crochet

 [2 double crochets, chain 2, 2 double crochets] into the same stitch

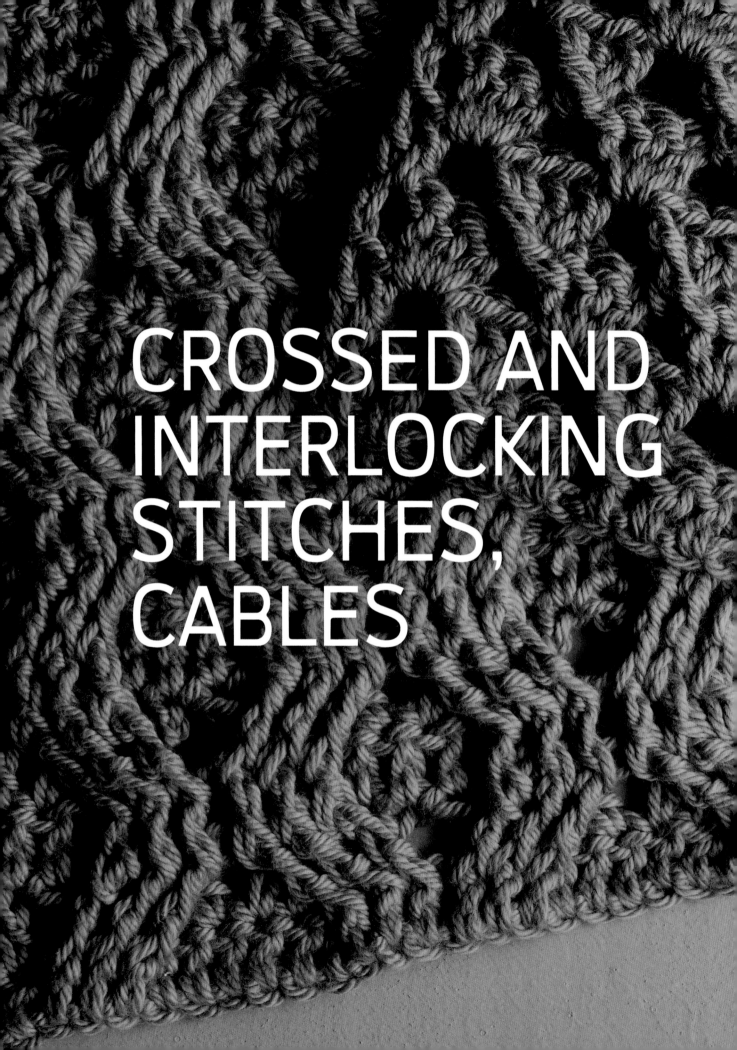

CROSSED AND INTERLOCKING STITCHES, CABLES

Stitch Patterns with **Crossed Stitches**

290 CROSSED SINGLE CROCHETS

[multiple of 2 + 1 beg-ch]

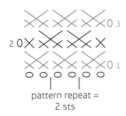

pattern repeat =
2 sts

Work in rows, following the chart. Begin with the stitches before the pattern repeat, repeat the marked pattern repeat (2 sts wide) widthwise, and end with the stitches after the pattern repeat. Work Rows 1–3 once, and then repeat Rows 2 and 3 for pattern.

Chart Key

○ Chain 1   ✕ 1 single crochet

✕✕ 2 crossed single crochets: In Row 1, work the first single crochet into the third chain from the hook; for the second single crochet, insert hook into the chain before the first single crochet, pull the working yarn through, and finish the last step of the single crochet. The second single crochet encloses the body of the first single crochet. For every following pair of crossed stitches, in the first row for the first single crochet always skip 1 chain of the beginning chain. From Row 2 on, when crossing 2 single crochets, for the first single crochet, always skip 1 stitch of the previous row and work the second single crochet into the skipped stitch and around the previously worked single crochet.

291 RAISED TRIANGLES

[base row: multiple of 4 + 2 ch + 3 beg-ch]

Work in rows, following the chart; Row 1 is a WS row. Begin with the stitches before the pattern repeat, repeat the marked pattern repeat (4 sts wide; or in Rows 2 and 4, 5 sts wide) widthwise, and end with the stitches after the pattern repeat. Work Rows 1–4 once, and then repeat Rows 3 and 4 for pattern.

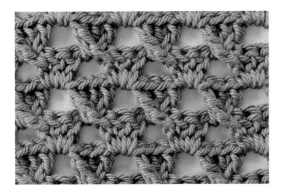

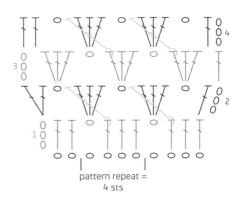

pattern repeat =
4 sts

Chart Key

○ Chain 1   ⊤ 1 double crochet   Dc2-in-1: 2 double crochets into the same stitch

Fptr-cr-l (1 front post treble crochet, crossed to the left): Work around the third double crochet of a group of 3 double crochets of the previous row. Work [yarn over hook] twice, insert the hook before the double crochet, lead the hook behind the shaft of the double crochet to the front again, pull the working yarn through, and finish the treble crochet. The finished raised treble crochet will end up in front of the background stitches and leans to the left.

CROSSED DOUBLE CROCHETS [multiple of 2 + 1 ch + 3 beg-ch]

Work in rows, following the chart. Begin with the stitches before the pattern repeat, repeat the marked pattern repeat (2 sts wide) widthwise, and end with the stitches after the pattern repeat. Work Rows 1–3 once, and then repeat Rows 2 and 3 for pattern.

Chart Key

pattern repeat = 2 sts

o   Chain 1   1 double crochet

2 crossed double crochets: In Row 1, work the first double crochet into the fifth chain from the hook; for the second double crochet, yarn over hook once, insert the hook into the chain before the first double crochet, and pull the working yarn through; then finish the double crochet. The second double crochet crosses over the body of the first double crochet. For every following pair of crossed stitches, in Row 1, for the first double crochet, always skip 1 chain of the beginning chain. From Row 2 on, when crossing 2 double crochets, for the first double crochet, always skip 1 stitch of the previous row and work the second double crochet into the skipped stitch and around the previously worked double crochet.

CROSSED DOUBLE CROCHETS WITH INTERMITTENT ROWS [multiple of 2 + 1 ch + 3 beg-ch]

Work in rows, following the chart. Begin with the stitches before the pattern repeat, repeat the marked pattern repeat (2 sts wide) widthwise, and end with the stitches after the pattern repeat. Work Rows 1–5 once, and then repeat Rows 2–5 for pattern.

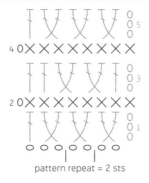 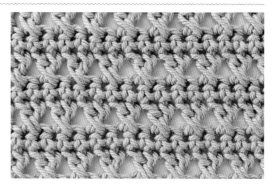

pattern repeat = 2 sts

Chart Key

o   Chain 1

✕   1 single crochet   1 double crochet

2 crossed double crochets: In Row 1, work the first double crochet into the fifth chain from the hook; for the second double crochet, yarn over hook once, insert the hook into the chain before the first double crochet, and pull the working yarn through; then finish the double crochet. The second double crochet crosses over the body of the first double crochet. For every following pair of crossed stitches, in Row 1, for the first double crochet, always skip 1 chain of the beginning chain. From Row 2 on, when crossing 2 double crochets, for the first double crochet, always skip 1 stitch of the previous row and work the second double crochet into the skipped stitch and around the previously worked double crochet.

CROSSED DOUBLE CROCHET GROUPS [multiple of 4 + 1 ch + 3 beg-ch]

Work in rows, following the chart; Row 1 is a WS row. Begin with the stitches before the pattern repeat, repeat the marked pattern repeat (4 sts wide) widthwise, and end with the stitches after the pattern repeat. Work Rows 1–4 once, and then repeat Rows 3 and 4 for pattern.

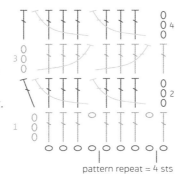 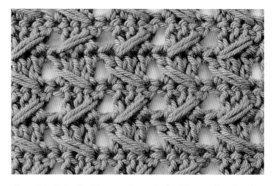

pattern repeat = 4 sts

Chart Key

o   Chain 1

1 double crochet

Group of 3 double crochets crossed with a double crochet: Work [3 double crochets, 1 double crochet back into the stitch in front of the 3 double crochets]. For this, yarn over hook once, insert the hook into the stitch before the first double crochet, pull the working yarn through, and pull the loop until long enough to loosely span the 3 double crochets without pulling them together; then finish the double crochet.

SWINGY RIBBON GRID

[base row: multiple of 8 + 3 ch + 1 beg-ch]

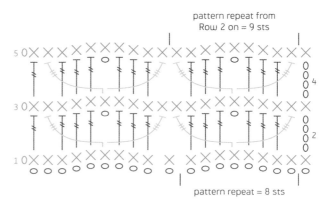

pattern repeat from
Row 2 on = 9 sts

pattern repeat = 8 sts

Chart Key

○ Chain 1

✕ 1 single crochet

 1 treble crochet

1 double treble crochet crossed to the right in front of a group of 3 treble crochets: Work 1 double treble crochet into the fourth insertion spot of the group (i.e., skip the 3 spots for the treble crochets), and then, behind this double treble crochet, work 3 treble crochets into the skipped stitches so that the double treble crochet ends up on top and leans to the right.

1 double treble crochet crossed to the left in front of a group of 3 treble crochets: First work 1 treble crochet each into the second, third, and fourth insertion spots of the group, and then work 1 double treble crochet before the first treble crochet into the same spot as the previous double treble crochet, inserting the hook from back to front. The finished double treble crochet will end up in front of the background stitches and lean to the left.

Work in rows, following the chart; Row 1 is a WS row. Begin with the stitches before the pattern repeat, repeat the marked pattern repeat (8 sts; from Row 2 on, 9 sts wide) widthwise, and end with the stitches after the pattern repeat. Work Rows 1–5 once, and then repeat Rows 4 and 5 for pattern.

ENTRELAC PATTERN

[multiple of 6 + 1 ch + 3 beg-ch]

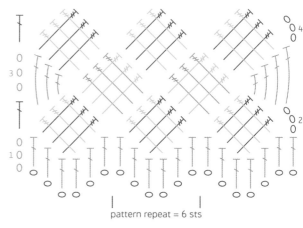

pattern repeat = 6 sts

Chart Key

○ Chain 1

 1 double crochet

2 groups of 3 treble crochets cabled to the left: Skip 3 stitches of the previous row, work 1 treble crochet into each of the next 3 stitches of the previous row, and then, going back in front of the already worked treble crochets, work 3 treble crochets into the skipped stitches so that they end up in front of the background stitches and lean to the left.

2 groups of 3 treble crochets cabled to the right: Skip 3 stitches of the previous row, work 1 treble crochet into each of the next 3 stitches of the previous row, and then, going back behind the already worked treble crochets, work 3 treble crochets into the skipped stitches. The treble crochets in front lean to the right.

Work in rows, following the chart; Row 1 is a WS row. Begin with the stitches before the pattern repeat, repeat the marked pattern repeat (6 sts wide) widthwise, and end with the stitches after the pattern repeat. Work Rows 1–4 once, and then repeat Rows 3 and 4 for pattern. The treble crochets that are located in front on the RS of the crocheted fabric are shown in color on the chart.

WRAPPED DOUBLE CROCHET GROUPS

[multiple of 5 + 1 ch + 3 beg-ch]

Work in rows, following the chart. Begin with the stitches before the pattern repeat, repeat the marked pattern repeat (5 sts wide) widthwise, and end with the stitches after the pattern repeat. Work Rows 1–3 once, and then repeat Rows 2 and 3 for pattern.

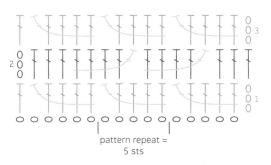

pattern repeat =
5 sts

Chart Key

o   Chain 1

†   1 double crochet

 Group of 4 double crochets wrapped with a horizontal double crochet: Yarn over hook once, insert the crochet hook into the gap between stitches before the first double crochet, draw the working yarn through, and pull the loop to a length loosely spanning the 4 double crochets without pulling them together; [pull the yarn through 2 loops on the hook at once] twice to finish the double crochet

ZIGZAG LADDERS

[multiple of 4 + 1 beg-ch]

Work in rows, following the chart; Row 1 is a WS row. Begin with the stitches before the pattern repeat, repeat the marked pattern repeat (4 sts wide) widthwise, and end with the stitches after the pattern repeat. Work Rows 1–4 once, and then repeat Rows 3 and 4 for pattern.

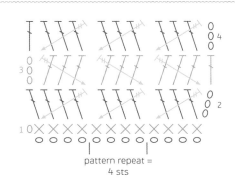

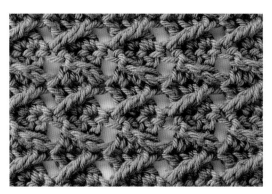

pattern repeat =
4 sts

Chart Key

o   Chain 1

✕   1 single crochet

†   1 double crochet

1 treble crochet crossed to the left in front of a group of 3 double crochets: Work 1 treble crochet into the following fourth stitch (i.e., skip 3 stitches of the previous row), and then, behind this treble crochet, work 3 double crochets into the skipped stitches so that on the right side of the crocheted fabric the treble crochet ends up in front and leans to the right.

1 treble crochet crossed to the right in front of a group of 3 double crochets: Work 1 treble crochet into the following fourth stitch (i.e., skip 3 stitches of the previous row), and then, behind this treble crochet, work 3 double crochets into the skipped stitches so that on the right side of the crocheted fabric the treble crochet ends up in the front and leans to the left.

299 STAGGERED X-SHAPED TREBLE CROCHETS [multiple of 6 + 4 ch + 4 beg-ch]

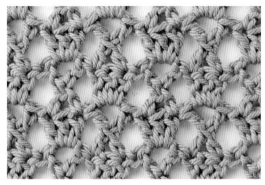

Work in rows, following the chart. Begin with the stitches before the pattern repeat, repeat the marked pattern repeat (6 sts wide) widthwise, and end with the stitches after the pattern repeat. Work Rows 1–3 once, and then repeat Rows 2 and 3 for pattern.

Work the 3 double crochets atop the X-shaped stitches into the chain space, around the chain.

Chart Key

o — Chain 1

⊥ — 1 double crochet

‡ — 1 treble crochet

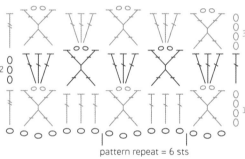

1 X-shaped treble crochet with chain 2 in between: [Yarn over hook] twice, insert the hook into the first insertion spot and draw the working yarn through, yarn over and pull the yarn through 2 loops on the hook at once; 3 loops remain on the hook. Yarn over hook once, draw the working yarn through the second insertion spot, and then [yarn over and pull the yarn through 2 loops on the hook at once] 4 times. Now chain 2, yarn over hook once, and insert the hook into the middle of the X-shaped treble crochet (the 2 loops from "drawing the working yarn through" the second time). Draw the working yarn through these 2 loops at once, and then [yarn over and pull the yarn through 2 loops on the hook at once] twice to finish the X-shaped treble crochet.

pattern repeat = 6 sts

300 FILIGREE HOLE GRID [multiple of 6 + 5 ch + 1 beg-ch]

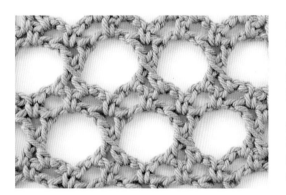

Work in rows, following the chart; Row 1 is a WS row. Begin with the stitches before the pattern repeat, repeat the marked pattern repeat (6 sts wide) widthwise, and end with the stitches after the pattern repeat. Work Rows 1–5 once, and then repeat Rows 2–5 for pattern.

In Rows 3 and 5, work the single crochets atop the chain 3 into the chain space (around the chain), and work the single crochets between the X-shaped treble crochets into the middle chain. In the final row of the crocheted piece, instead of 3 chains between the single crochets, only chain 2.

Chart Key

o — Chain 1   ✕ — 1 single crochet

⊥ — 1 treble crochet

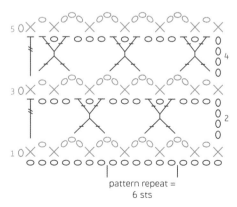

pattern repeat = 6 sts

1 X-shaped treble crochet with chain 1 in between: [Yarn over hook] twice, insert the hook into the first insertion point (into the chain space), pull the working yarn through, and yarn over and pull the yarn through 2 loops on the hook at once; 3 loops remain on the hook. Yarn over hook once, insert the hook into the second insertion spot (around the chain), yarn over and pull the working yarn through, and [pull the yarn through 2 loops on the hook at once] 4 times. Now chain 1, yarn over hook once, and insert the hook into the middle of the X-shaped treble crochet (i.e., the 2 loops from "drawing the working yarn through" the second time). Draw the working yarn through these 2 loops at once, and [pull the yarn through 2 loops on the hook at once] twice to finish the last step of the X-shaped treble crochet.

CROSSED COLUMNS

[multiple of 2 + 1 ch + 3 beg-ch]

Work in rows, following the chart. Begin with the stitches before the pattern repeat, repeat the marked pattern repeat (2 sts wide) width-wise, and end with the stitches after the pattern repeat. Work Rows 1–3 once, and then repeat Rows 2 and 3 for pattern.

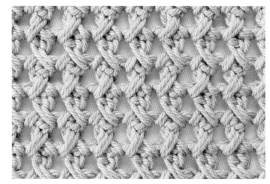

Chart Key

o   Chain 1   1 double crochet

2 crossed double crochets: In Row 1, work the first double crochet into the fifth chain from the hook; for the second double crochet, yarn over hook once, insert the hook in the chain before the first double crochet, pull the working yarn through, and finish the double crochet. The second double crochet crosses the body of the first double crochet. For every following pair of crossed stitches, in Row 1, for the first double crochet, al-ways skip 1 chain of the beginning chain. From Row 2 on, when crossing 2 double cro-chets, always insert the hook into the gap between stitches—the first double crochet after a pair of double crochets and the second double crochet going back in front of the pair of double crochets of the previous row so that it crosses the previously worked double crochet.

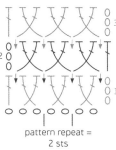

pattern repeat =
2 sts

ALLOVER MINI CABLES

[base row: multiple of 3 + 3 beg-ch]

Work in rows, following the chart; Row 1 is a WS row. Begin with the stitches before the pattern repeat, repeat the marked pattern repeat (3 sts; or from Row 2 on, 4 sts wide) widthwise, and end with the stitches after the pattern repeat. Work Rows 1–4 once, and then repeat Rows 3 and 4 for pattern.

Those treble crochets that are located in front on the RS of the crocheted fabric are shown in color on the chart.

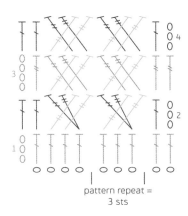

pattern repeat =
3 sts

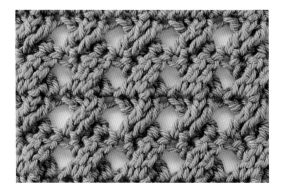

Chart Key

o   Chain 1

       1 double crochet

       1 treble crochet

 2 times 2 treble crochets crossed to the right: Work 1 treble crochet into each of the follow-ing second and third stitches (i.e., skip 1 stitch of the previous row), and then go be-hind these 2 treble crochets and work 2 tre-ble crochets into the 1 skipped stitch so that the first 2 treble crochets end up on top and lean to the right.

2 times 2 treble crochets crossed to the right: Work 1 treble crochet each in the following third and fourth stitches (i.e., skip 2 stitches of the previous row), and then go behind these 2 treble crochets and work 2 treble crochets into the 2 skipped stitches so that the first 2 treble crochets end up on top and lean to the right.

CROSSBILL

[multiple of 3 + 3 beg-ch]

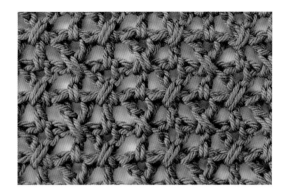

Chart Key

○ Chain 1

┬ 1 double crochet

┐ 1 double crochet around
the chain between the
crossed double crochets

V Dc2-in-1: 2 double crochets
into the same stitch

pattern repeat =
3 sts

2 crossed double crochets with chain 1 between them: Work the first double crochet into the fifth chain from the hook, chain 1; for the second double crochet, yarn over hook once, insert the hook in the chain before the first double crochet, pull the working yarn through, and finish the double crochet. The second double crochet crosses the body of the first double crochet. From Row 2 on, when crossing the 2 double crochets, always insert the hook into the gap between stitches—for the first double crochet, after the individual double crochet; for the second double crochet, go back in front of the individual double crochet of the previous row so that it crosses the previously worked double crochet.

Work in rows, following the chart. Begin with the stitches before the pattern repeat, repeat the marked pattern repeat (3 sts wide) widthwise, and end with the stitches after the pattern repeat. Work Rows 1–3 once, and then repeat Rows 2 and 3 for pattern.

CROSS STITCH RIBBONS

[multiple of 2 + 1 ch + 1 beg-ch]

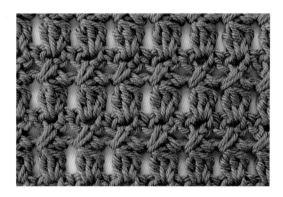

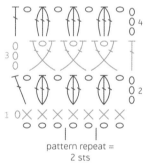

pattern repeat =
2 sts

Chart Key

○ Chain 1

✕ 1 single crochet

┬ 1 double crochet

 Dc3tog-in-1: 3 double crochets into the same stitch and crocheted together

2 crossed double crochets with chain 1 between them: Work the first double crochet after a group of double crochets of the previous row into the chain space (around the chain), chain 1, and then work the second double crochet, going back in front of the group of double crochets and into the chain space (around the chain), so that it crosses the previously worked double crochet

3 double crochets worked into the chain space between the crossed double crochets and crocheted together

Work in rows, following the chart; Row 1 is a WS row. Begin with the stitches before the pattern repeat, repeat the marked pattern repeat (2 sts wide) widthwise, and end with the stitches after the pattern repeat. Work Rows 1–4 once, and then repeat Rows 3 and 4 for pattern.

TILE PATTERN

[multiple of 6 + 5 ch + 1 beg-ch]

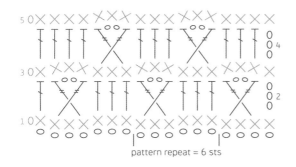

pattern repeat = 6 sts

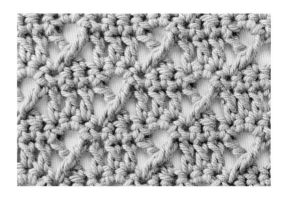

Chart Key

○   Chain 1   ✕   1 single crochet   ⊤   1 double crochet

 2 crossed treble crochets with chain 2 in between: Work the first treble crochet in the second insertion spot (i.e., skip 2 stitches of the previous row), chain 2, and then work the second treble crochet going back behind the first treble crochet into the second stitch, located in front of it, so that 1 stitch between the treble crochets stays unused

Work in rows, following the chart; Row 1 is a WS row. Begin with the stitches before the pattern repeat, repeat the marked pattern repeat (6 sts wide) width-wise, and end with the stitches after the pattern repeat. Work Rows 1–5 once, and then repeat Rows 2–5 for pattern.

Work the 3 single crochets atop the crossed treble crochets into the chain space, around the chain.

CANE WEBBING PATTERN

[multiple of 5 + 1 beg-ch]

Work in rows, following the chart. Begin with the stitches before the pattern repeat, repeat the marked pattern repeat (5 sts wide) width-wise, and end with the stitches after the pattern repeat. Work Rows 1–14 once, and then repeat Rows 7–14 for pattern. Change color every 2 rows as shown and carry up unused colors at the edge.

In Rows 3, 7, and 11, work the half double crochets into the back loop of the slip stitch only so that the top loops of the single crochets and double treble crochets end up in front.

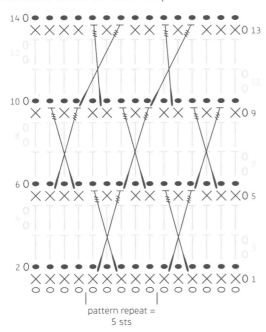

pattern repeat =
5 sts

Chart Key

○   Chain 1   ✕   1 single crochet

●   1 slip stitch   ⊤   1 half double crochet

 2 double treble crochets, crossed and worked below, with 1 single crochet in between: Work 1 double treble crochet into the second insertion spot—4 rows below, either in the top loop of the single crochet located on top or in the top loop of the double treble crochet located below—then work 1 single crochet in the top edge of the current row. Work the second double treble crochet 4 rows below, crossing back into the second stitch, which is located in front of the first double treble crochet, working into the top loop of the single crochet located in front. Between these 2 double treble crochets, 1 stitch stays unused.

Patterns with **Interlocking Stitches**

307 STAGGERED SHELLS

[multiple of 4 + 1 ch + 1 beg-ch]

Work in rows, following the chart; Row 1 is a WS row. Begin with the stitches before the pattern repeat, repeat the marked pattern repeat (4 sts wide) widthwise, and end with the stitches after the pattern repeat. Work Rows 1–4 once, and then repeat Rows 3 and 4 for pattern.

In Rows 2 and 4, place the single crochet between the double crochet and chain.

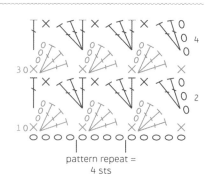

pattern repeat = 4 sts

Chart Key

o   Chain 1

✕   1 single crochet

| 1 double crochet

 Dc2-in-1: 2 double crochets into the same spot

 Dc3-in-1: 3 double crochets into the same spot

1 group of stitches: [1 single crochet, chain 3, 3 double crochets] into the same stitch

308 LEAFY VINES

[multiple of 6 + 2 ch + 3 beg-ch]

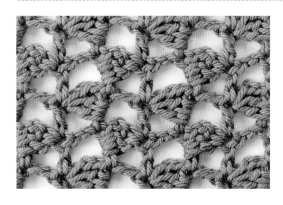

Work in rows, following the chart. Begin with the stitches before the pattern repeat, repeat the marked pattern repeat (6 sts wide) widthwise, and end with the stitches after the pattern repeat. Work Rows 1–3 once, and then repeat Rows 2 and 3 for pattern.

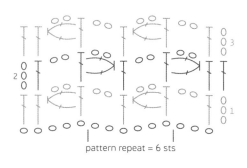

pattern repeat = 6 sts

Chart Key

o   Chain 1

| 1 double crochet

 1 horizontal group of stitches: [Chain 2, and then work 2 double crochets crocheted together around the double crochet worked last] so that the pair of double crochets ends up horizontally in the row

VERTICAL BANDS OF SHELLS

[multiple of 5 + 3 ch + 3 beg-ch]

Work in rows, following the chart. Begin with the stitches before the pattern repeat, repeat the marked pattern repeat (5 sts wide) widthwise, and end with the stitches after the pattern repeat. Work Rows 1–3 once, and then repeat Rows 2 and 3 for pattern.

From Row 2 on, work the single crochet into the chain space close to the double crochet.

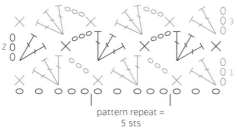

pattern repeat = 5 sts

Chart Key

○ Chain 1

✕ 1 single crochet

Dc2-in-1: 2 double crochets into the same stitch

Dc3-in-1: 3 double crochets into the same stitch

LITTLE DIAMOND PATTERN

[multiple of 4 + 1 ch + 1 beg-ch]

Work in rows, following the chart. Begin with the stitches before the pattern repeat, repeat the marked pattern repeat (4 sts wide) widthwise, and end with the stitches after the pattern repeat. Work Rows 1–3 once, and then repeat Rows 2 and 3 for pattern.

From Row 2 on, always work the stitches into the chain space of the previous row, around the chain.

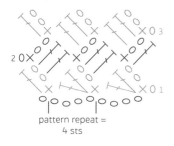

pattern repeat = 4 sts

Chart Key

○ Chain 1

✕ 1 single crochet

┬ 1 double crochet

1 group of stitches: [1 single crochet, chain 2, 2 double crochets] into the same stitch

TWO-PART SHELLS

[multiple of 6 + 1 ch + 1 beg-ch]

Work in rows, following the chart. Begin with the stitches before the pattern repeat, repeat the marked pattern repeat (6 sts wide) widthwise, and end with the stitches after the pattern repeat. Work Rows 1–3 once, and then repeat Rows 2 and 3 for pattern.

From Row 2 on, work the single crochet between the groups of stitches into the single crochet of the previous row.

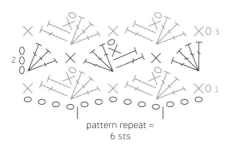

pattern repeat = 6 sts

Chart Key

○ Chain 1

✕ 1 single crochet

Dc3-in-1: 3 double crochets into the same stitch

Dc4-in-1: 4 double crochets into the same stitch

1 group of stitches around the double crochet worked last: [3 double crochets into the same stitch, chain 1, 1 single crochet, 1 half double crochet, 1 double crochet]

312 PEAKED MOUNTAINS

[multiple of 4 + 1 ch + 1 beg-ch]

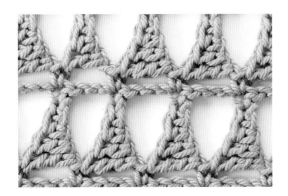

Chart Key

○ Chain 1

● 1 slip stitch

✕ 1 single crochet

⊤ 1 half double crochet

╪ 1 double crochet

╪ 1 treble crochet

╪ 1 double treble crochet

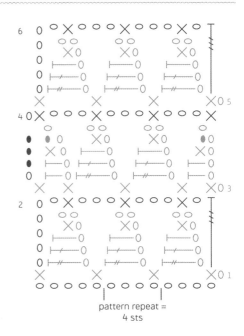

pattern repeat = 4 sts

Work in rows, following the chart. Begin with the stitches before the pattern repeat, repeat the marked pattern repeat (4 sts wide) width-wise, and end with the stitches after the pattern repeat. Work Rows 1–6 once, and then repeat Rows 3–6 for pattern.

313 OPEN DIAMOND PATTERN

[multiple of 4 + 1 ch + 3 beg-ch]

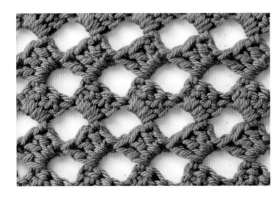

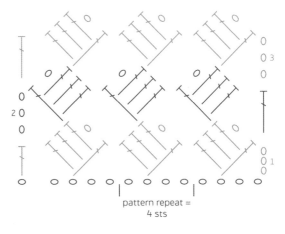

pattern repeat = 4 sts

Work in rows, following the chart. Begin with the stitches before the pattern repeat, repeat the marked pattern repeat (4 sts wide) width-wise, and end with the stitches after the pattern repeat. Work Rows 1–3 once, and then repeat Rows 2 and 3 for pattern.

Chart Key

○ Chain 1

╪ 1 double crochet

 1 group of stitches: [1 double crochet worked diagonally, chain 1, and then 3 double crochets around the diagonal double crochet worked last]

ALTERNATING PATTERN BLOCKS

[multiple of 6 + 2 ch + 1 beg-ch]

Work in rows, following the chart. Begin with the stitches before the pattern repeat, repeat the marked pattern repeat (6 sts wide) widthwise, and end with the stitches after the pattern repeat. Work Rows 1–4 once, and then repeat Rows 3 and 4 for pattern.

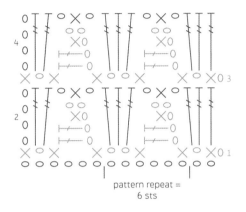

pattern repeat =
6 sts

Chart Key

○ Chain 1

✕ 1 single crochet

⊤ 1 double crochet

⊤ 1 treble crochet

RAGGED STRIPES

[multiple of 3 + 1 ch + 1 beg-ch]

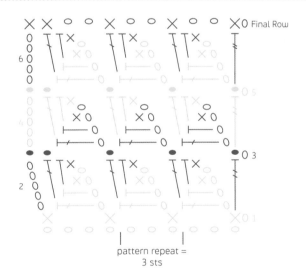

pattern repeat =
3 sts

Chart Key

○ Chain 1

● 1 slip stitch

✕ 1 single crochet

⊤ 1 half double crochet

⊤ 1 double crochet

⊤ 1 treble crochet

Work in rows, following the chart. Begin with the stitches before the pattern repeat, repeat the marked pattern repeat (3 sts wide) widthwise, and end with the stitches after the pattern repeat. Work Rows 1–6 once, and then repeat Rows 3–6 for pattern. Change color for the first time after Row 1, and then after every 2 rows as shown. Carry unused colors at the edge; if needed, weave them into the turning chain to avoid long floats. To do this, before every chain move the strand in the unused color alternatingly to the back or to the front over the working yarn. Finish the crocheted piece by working the final row shown in the chart.

316 SPIKE ROWS

[base row: multiple of 3 + 2 ch + 1 beg-ch]

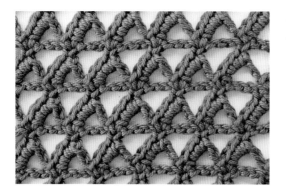

Work in rows, following the chart; Row 1 is a WS row. Begin with the stitches before the pattern repeat, repeat the marked pattern repeat (3 sts wide; or from Row 3 on, 4 sts wide) widthwise, and end with the stitches after the pattern repeat. Work Rows 1–7 once, and then repeat Rows 4–7 for pattern.

In Row 3, 5, and 7, work the single crochet into the single crochet at the point of the spike of the previous row.

Chart Key

○ Chain 1

● 1 slip stitch

✕ 1 single crochet

⊤ 1 double crochet

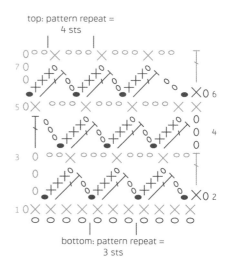

top: pattern repeat = 4 sts

bottom: pattern repeat = 3 sts

317 LOCKED DIAMOND PATTERN

[multiple of 6 + 1 ch + 1 beg-ch]

Work in rows, following the chart. Begin with the stitches before the pattern repeat, repeat the marked pattern repeat (6 sts wide) widthwise, and end with the stitches after the pattern repeat. Work Rows 1–4 once, and then repeat Rows 3 and 4 for pattern. To work the pattern as shown here, change color after every 2 rows, carrying unused colors at the edge.

From Row 2 on, work the single crochet into the chain space of the previous row, around the chain; only at the beginning of the row, work the single crochet into the joined top of the double crochets.

Chart Key

○ Chain 1

✕ 1 single crochet

⊤ 1 double crochet

⋁ Dc2-in-1: 2 double crochets into the same spot

⋀ Dc3tog: Double crochet 3 stitches together

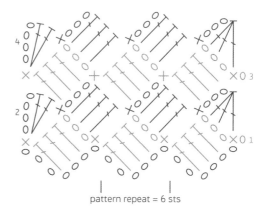

pattern repeat = 6 sts

FRAMED TRIANGLES

[multiple of 4 + 1 ch + 1 beg-ch]

Work in rows, following the chart. Begin with the stitches before the pattern repeat, repeat the marked pattern repeat (4 sts wide) widthwise, and end with the stitches after the pattern repeat. Work Rows 1–7 once, and then repeat Rows 2–7 for pattern. Change color as shown: Work 2 rows in color 1, and 1 row in color 2. Carry unused colors at the edge. Work individual rows of double crochet in color 2 (see Rows 3 and 6) alternatingly on the RS and WS to avoid having to break the working yarn frequently.

At the end of Rows 3 and 5, pull the working loop longer, pass the skein of yarn through, and then pull the working yarn snug to secure the loop.

At the beginning of Rows 4 and Row 6, join the working yarn in the new color: Insert the hook either into the top chain of the turning chain or into the single crochet and pull the working yarn through.

Finish the crocheted piece by working the final row as shown in the chart.

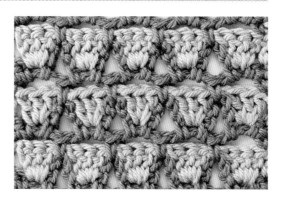

Chart Key

o Chain 1	✕ 1 single crochet	↱ Carry the yarn at the edge
/5\ Chain arc of 5 chains	⟩ Sc-bel: 1 single crochet worked below	⊤ 1 double crochet

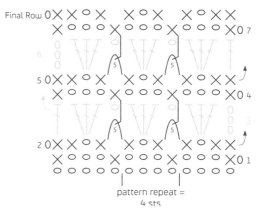

pattern repeat = 4 sts

BOXES IN LATTICE FRAMEWORK

[multiple of 6 + 3 beg-ch]

Work in rows, following the chart. Begin with the stitches before the pattern repeat, repeat the marked pattern repeat (6 sts wide) widthwise, and end with the stitches after the pattern repeat. Work Rows 1–4 once, and then repeat Rows 3 and 4 for pattern.

In Rows 2 and 4, place the single crochet between the double crochet and the chain.

Chart Key

o Chain 1	✕ 1 single crochet	⊤ 1 double crochet

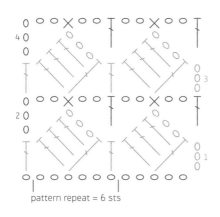

pattern repeat = 6 sts

Cable Patterns

NARROW CABLES

[multiple of 17 + 1 ch + 3 beg-ch]

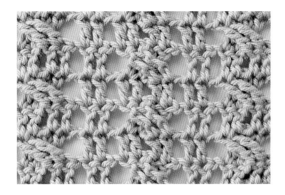

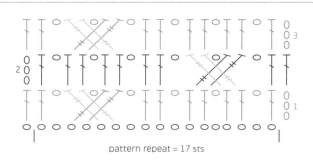

pattern repeat = 17 sts

Work in rows, following the chart. Begin with the stitches before the pattern repeat, repeat the marked pattern repeat (17 sts wide) width-wise, and end with the stitch after the pattern repeat. In Row 1, 1 stitch is increased in every repeat on account of the crossed stitch group. Work Rows 1–3 once, and then repeat Rows 2 and 3 for pattern.

Chart Key

○ Chain 1   ⊤ 1 double crochet

2 pairs of 2 treble crochets crossed to the left with chain 1 between them: Work 1 treble crochet in both the third and the fourth insertion spots (i.e., in the first row, skip 2 chains of the beginning chain, and from Row 2 on, skip 3 stitches of the previous row); chain 1, and then in front of the 2 treble crochets, work 1 treble crochet into each skipped chain of the beginning chain, and from Row 2 on, into each skipped 2 double crochets so that they end up in front and lean to the left.

BROAD CABLE IN A DOUBLE CROCHET PATTERN [multiple of 13 + 6 ch + 3 beg-ch]

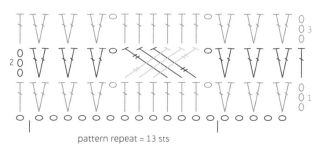

pattern repeat = 13 sts

Work in rows, following the chart. Begin with the stitches before the pattern repeat, repeat the marked pattern repeat (13 sts wide) width-wise, and end with the stitches after the pattern repeat. In Row 1, 1 stitch is increased in every repeat in the double crochet pattern. Work Rows 1–3 once, and then repeat Rows 2 and 3 for pattern.

From Row 2 on, always work the [2 double crochets into the same spot] between the pairs of double crochets of the previous row.

Chart Key

○ Chain 1   ⊤ 1 double crochet   V Dc2-in-1: 2 double crochets into the same stitch

2 groups of 3 treble crochets cabled to the right: Skip 3 stitches of the previous row, and work 1 treble crochet into each of the next 3 stitches of the previous row; then, going back behind the already worked treble crochets, work 1 treble crochet into each of the 3 skipped stitches. The treble crochets in front lean to the right.

EASY LOOP CABLE

[multiple of 4 + 1 beg-ch]

Work in rows, following the chart; Row 1 is a WS row. Begin with the stitches before the pattern repeat, repeat the marked pattern repeat (4 sts wide) widthwise, and end with the stitches after the pattern repeat. Work Rows 1–5 once, and then repeat Rows 2–5 for pattern, working the first 3 rows in color 1 and then alternating [2 rows in color 2, 2 rows in color 1]. Finish the crocheted piece by adding Final Rows a and b at the end.

Braiding the cable: Start at the bottom of the piece. Pull the crochet chain loops into one another row by row, using a crochet hook to aid if needed. First, twist the first loop to the left so that the beginning and end of the loop overlap, and then pull the second loop through the first loop from back to front and toward the top. Twist the passed-through loop to the left; then take up the next loop and pull it through, twist it, and so on. The chain loops will be secured during Final Row b.

Chart Key

o   Chain 1

$\widehat{}_{10}$ 10 Chain

✕   1 single crochet

⊤   1 double crochet

⊗   Securing the loop with a single crochet: Work in a WS row, with loops on the other side (i.e., RS) of the crocheted piece. Insert the hook first into the stitch of the previous row, place the crochet chain loop that is in back on the hook, pull the working yarn through, and finish working the single crochet.

⟶   Bridging: For better orientation, the chart has been drawn with spaces bridged by arrows that do not require any action in the actual crochet work. The row after a loop is always worked continuously without interruption—in this pattern, working single crochet continuously into stitches of row below, skipping the chain loops.

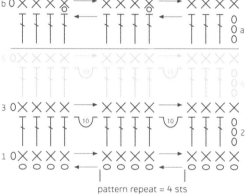

pattern repeat = 4 sts

DOUBLE-LAYER HONEYCOMB GRID

[multiple of 12 + 3 ch + 3 beg-ch]

Work in rows, following the chart; Row 1 is a WS row. Begin with the stitch before the pattern repeat, repeat the marked pattern repeat (12 sts wide) widthwise, and end with the stitches after the pattern repeat. Work Rows 1–5 once, and then repeat Rows 2–5 for pattern.

When working the raised double crochets, after drawing the working yarn through, pull the loop slightly longer until it has the same height as the regular double crochets.

Chart Key

o   Chain 1

⊤   1 double crochet

⌡   Bpdc: 1 back post double crochet

3 raised treble crochets and 3 treble crochets crossed to the right: Skip 3 double crochets of the previous row, and work 1 front post treble crochet around each of the following 3 double crochets of the previous row; then, going back behind the already worked raised double crochets, work 1 treble crochet into each of the 3 skipped stitches. The raised treble crochets located in front lean to the right.

3 treble crochets and 3 raised treble crochets crossed to the left: Skip 3 double crochets of the previous row, and work 1 treble crochet each in the following 3 double crochets of the previous row; then, going back in front of the already worked treble crochets, work 1 front post treble crochet around each of the 3 skipped double crochets. The raised treble crochets located in front lean to the left.

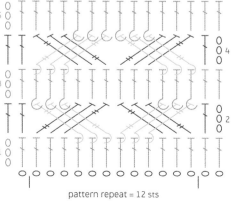

pattern repeat = 12 sts

BROAD BIAS CABLES

[multiple of 16 + 8 ch + 1 beg-ch]

Chart Key

o   Chain 1

✕   1 single crochet

T   1 double crochet

2 groups of 3 treble crochets crossed to the left: Skip 3 stitches of the previous row, and work 1 treble crochet into each of the next 3 stitches of the previous row; then, going back in front of the already worked treble crochets, work 1 treble crochet in each of the 3 skipped stitches so that they end up in front of the background stitches and lean to the left.

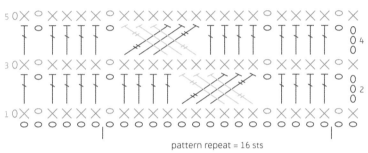

pattern repeat = 16 sts

Work in rows, following the chart; Row 1 is a WS row. Begin with the stitches before the pattern repeat, repeat the marked pattern repeat (16 sts wide) widthwise, and end with the stitches after the pattern repeat. Work Rows 1–5 once, and then repeat Rows 2–5 for pattern.

WAVY CABLE

[multiple of 6 + 3 ch + 3 beg-ch]

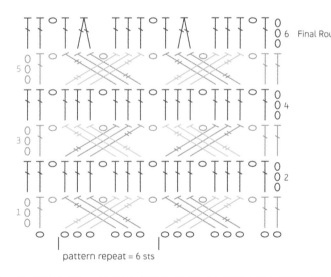

pattern repeat = 6 sts

Chart Key

o   Chain 1

T   1 double crochet

    Dc2tog: Double crochet 2 stitches together

 2 groups of 3 treble crochets cabled to the left with chain 1 between them: Skip 3 double crochets and 1 chain of the previous row, work 1 treble crochet in each of the following 3 double crochets of the previous row, chain 1, and then, going back in front of the already worked treble crochets, work 1 treble crochet in each of the skipped 3 double crochets so that they end up in front of the background stitches and lean to the left.

 2 groups of 3 treble crochets cabled to the right with chain 1 between them: In Row 1 skip 3 chains of the beginning chain, and in Row 5 skip 3 double crochets and 1 chain of the previous row; work 1 treble crochet in each of the following 3 chains of the beginning chain or, in Row 5, work 1 treble crochet in each of the following 3 double crochets of the previous row; then chain 1, and, going back behind the already worked treble crochets, work 1 treble crochet into each of the skipped chains of the beginning chain or into the skipped 3 double crochets. The treble crochets in front lean to the right.

Work in rows, following the chart; Row 1 is a WS row. Begin with the stitches before the pattern repeat, repeat the marked pattern repeat (6 sts wide) widthwise, and end with the stitches after the pattern repeat. In Row 1, owing to the cabled stitches, 2 stitches each are increased in the pattern repeat and in the space between stitches. Work Rows 1–5 once, and then repeat Rows 2–5 for pattern. Finish the crocheted piece by working the final row once, at the same time reducing the cables by crocheting 2 double crochets together atop the treble crochets located in back.

Those treble crochets that are located in front on the RS of the crocheted fabric are shown in color on the chart.

TULIP CABLE

[multiple of 20 + 2 ch + 1 beg-ch]

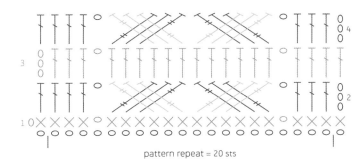

pattern repeat = 20 sts

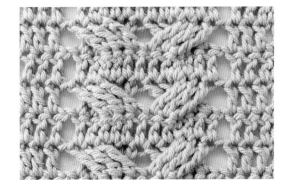

Chart Key

○	Chain 1		
✕	1 single crochet	⊤	1 double crochet

2 groups of 3 treble crochets cabled to the right: Skip 3 stitches of the previous row, and work 1 treble crochet into each of the following 3 stitches of the previous row; then, going back behind the already worked treble crochets, work 1 treble crochet into each of the 3 skipped stitches. The treble crochets in front lean to the right.

2 groups of 3 treble crochets crossed to the left: Skip 3 stitches of the previous row, and work 1 treble crochet into each of the next 3 stitches of the previous row; then, going back in front of the already worked treble crochets, work 1 treble crochet into each of the 3 skipped stitches so that they end up in front of the background stitches and lean to the left.

Work in rows, following the chart; Row 1 is a WS row. Begin with the stitch before the pattern repeat, repeat the marked pattern repeat (20 sts wide) widthwise, and end with the stitch after the pattern repeat. Work Rows 1–4 once, and then repeat Rows 3 and 4 for pattern.

The treble crochets that are located in front on the RS of the crocheted fabric are shown in color on the chart.

STAGGERED TWIN CABLE

[multiple of 20 + 10 ch + 3 beg-ch]

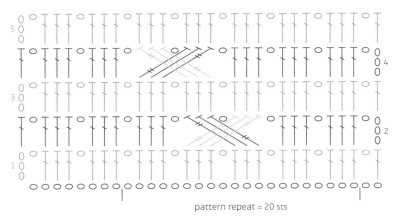

pattern repeat = 20 sts

Chart Key

○	Chain 1	⊤	1 double crochet

2 groups of 3 treble crochets cabled to the right with chain 1 between them: Skip 3 double crochets and 1 chain of the previous row, work 1 treble crochet into each of the following 3 double crochets of the previous row, and chain 1; then, going back behind the already worked treble crochets, work 1 treble crochet into each of the skipped 3 double crochets. The treble crochets in front lean to the right.

2 groups of 3 treble crochets cabled to the left with chain 1 between them: Skip 3 double crochets and 1 chain of the previous row, work 1 treble crochet into each of the following 3 double crochets of the previous row, and chain 1; then, going back in front of the already worked treble crochets, work 1 treble crochet into each of the skipped 3 double crochets so that they end up in front of the background stitches and lean to the left.

Work in rows, following the chart; Row 1 is a WS row. Begin with the stitches before the pattern repeat, repeat the marked pattern repeat (20 sts wide) widthwise, and end with the stitches after the pattern repeat. Work Rows 1–5 once, and then repeat Rows 2–5 for pattern.

Those treble crochets that are located in front on the RS of the crocheted fabric are shown in color on the chart.

328 TWIN LOOP CABLES

[multiple of 6 + 4 ch + 1 beg-ch]

Work in rows, following the chart; Row 1 is a WS row. Repeat the marked pattern repeat (6 sts wide) widthwise, and end with the stitches after the pattern repeat. Work Rows 1–4 once, and then repeat Rows 3 and 4 for pattern. Finish the crocheted piece by adding Final Rows a, b, and c at the end.

Twisting the cable: Start at the bottom edge of the piece. Cross the crocheted chain loops (located side by side and spaced 2 stitches apart from each other) over one another, and then pull the loops above them from back to front through the 2 first loops and toward the top. Cross the passed-through loops again in the same direction, take up the next 2 loops, and pull these through, too, and so on. The chain loops will be secured during Final Row c.

Chart Key

o   Chain 1

⌣12⌣   Chain 12

✕   1 single crochet

T   1 half double crochet

✕̸   Secure the loop with 1 single crochet: Work in a WS row, with loops in back of the crocheted piece. Insert the hook first into the stitch of the previous row, place the crochet chain loop that is in back on the hook, pull the working yarn through, and finish working the single crochet.

→   Bridging: For better orientation, the chart has been drawn with spaces bridged by arrows, which do not require any action in the actual crochet work. The row after a loop is always worked continuously without interruption—in this pattern, working half double crochets in half double crochets (or single crochets in Row 1) of the previous row. This also applies to the beginning chain.

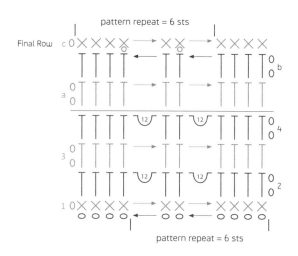

RAISED KNIT-LOOK CABLE

[multiple of 16 + 1 ch + 3 beg-ch; cable width = 8 sts]

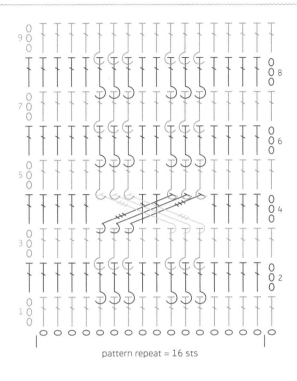

pattern repeat = 16 sts

Work in rows, following the chart; Row 1 is a WS row. Repeat the marked pattern repeat (16 sts wide) widthwise, and end with the stitch after the pattern repeat. Work Rows 1–9 once, and then repeat Rows 4–9 for pattern.

When working the raised double crochets, after drawing the working yarn through, pull the loop slightly longer, to approximately the same height as the regular double crochets.

Chart Key

○   Chain 1   Ⱶ 1 double crochet   Fpdc: 1 front post double crochet   Bpdc: 1 back post double crochet

2 groups of 3 raised double treble crochets crossed to the left with 2 double crochets in between: Skip 5 stitches of the previous row, and work 1 front post double treble crochet around each of the following 3 stitches of the previous row; then, going back behind the already worked raised double treble crochets, work 1 double crochet into each of the skipped 2 stitches immediately before the 3 raised double treble crochets, and, going back in front of the already worked raised double treble crochets, work 1 front post double treble crochet around each of the skipped first, second, and third stitch of the previous row. The front post double crochets located in front lean to the left.

330 BRAIDED CHAINED CABLE

[cable width = 6 base pattern sts]

Work in rows, following the chart. Shown are the cable, and to the right and left of it, 5 stitches each of the main pattern. The background pattern can be worked over any number of stitches widthwise, keeping in mind that per cable, 6 stitches of the background pattern are covered up by the cable (3 stitches before and 3 stitches after the cable).

Cable loops: For each cable, during the first working step, loops are crocheted within the background pattern, each created by starting with a chain, and then working 3 rows of single crochet on top. Work Rows 1–8 once, and then repeat Rows 5–8 for pattern, changing colors after every 4 rows, always at the beginning of a new loop. Finish the crocheted piece by adding Final Rows a, b, c, and d at the end. During the second working step, the loops are braided.

Braiding the cable: Place the crocheted piece loop-side up. Fold the first loop at the bottom edge of the crocheted piece toward the back, as done when turning a collar, so that the bottom edge of the piece is in the back and the tops of the stitches in the last loop row point up.

Now, start braiding. Pull the second loop from back to front through the first loop, and immediately fold it to the back as done for the first loop. Pull the next loop through the second loop, fold it to the back, and so on until the whole cable has been braided. Temporarily secure the last loop with a safety pin; it will be fastened with a single crochet when working the Final Row e or adding an edging, or it can be sewn on.

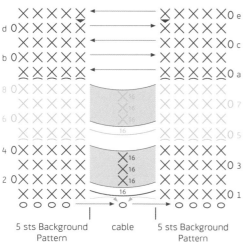

5 sts Background Pattern   cable   5 sts Background Pattern

Chart Key

○	Chain 1	✕	1 single crochet

Work 16 single crochets into the chain of 16, followed by 2 more rows of 16 single crochets each

Fasten the cable loop with a single crochet: Insert the hook first into the stitch of the loop, and then into the stitch of the previous row, pull the working yarn through, and finish working the single crochet.

Bridging: In order to better show the cable loops, the chart has been drawn with spaces bridged by arrows. These spots do not require any action in the actual crochet work (i.e., Rows a–e after the last loop of the crocheted piece are always worked continuously, without interruption). This also applies to the beginning chain.

RIBBON CABLE

[cable width = 6 base pattern sts]

Work separately in individual segments A, B, and C. Work the cable strips (= Segment A) in rows from Chart 1. For a piece with several cable strips, work side strips (= Segments B and C) and any strips in between in rows from Chart 2. The photo shows a cable created by crossing 2 crocheted strips, and to the right and left of it, 5 stitches each of the background pattern.

Cable bands: After Row 1 (WS), work over a total of 6 stitches wide in 2 separate strips of 3 stitches each. Work every strip from its own skein of yarn so that it can be worked to any length. For the first strip, repeat Rows 2 and 3 for pattern; for the second strip, join new working yarn in the middle of Row 1 and repeat Rows a and b for pattern.

Side or in-between panels: The base pattern can be worked over any number of stitches widthwise. Instead of single crochets, any other stitch or pattern can be used as long as it has the same regular rhythm to connect to the cable strip. Join to the cable strips at the beginning of a RS or WS row, always with RS facing, so all joining spots look the same. The strips are joined in every other single crochet row of the base pattern; before every join, strips are crossed. Sew the finished Segment B to the cable strip using the beginning tail.

Chart Key

○ Chain 1
● 1 slip stitch
✕ 1 single crochet
┬ 1 double crochet

C Joining: Remove the crochet hook from the loop, RS of work facing up; on the cable strip, insert the hook from top to bottom in the row of single crochets, take up the loop again, pull it through, chain 1, and continue the row.

Crochet Chart 1

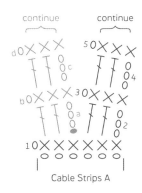

Cable Strips A

Crochet Chart 2

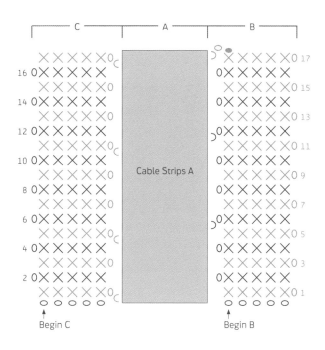

332 CABLED WAVES

[multiple of 7 + 1 ch + 2 beg-ch]

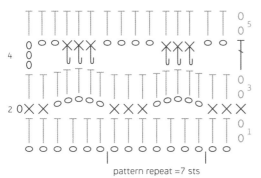

pattern repeat =7 sts

Bands of 1 row of half double crochets are inserted into a background pattern with incorporated slits. This pattern can be used for crocheted pieces worked sideways, so cables run vertically. With horizontally worked cables, the pattern opens up and will look more airy. It can be worked with cable bands either in a contrasting color or all in one color.

Background pattern: Work in rows, following the chart. Begin with the stitches before the pattern repeat, repeat the marked pattern repeat (7 sts wide) widthwise, and end with the stitches after the pattern repeat. Work Rows 1–5 once, and then repeat Rows 2–5 for pattern.

Always work the half double crochets in the back loop of the chain of the previous row.

Bands: Work a row of foundation half double crochets as follows. You will need 10 half double crochets for every pattern repeat of the Background pattern plus 11 half double crochets each for the beginning and the end. Chain 4, yarn over hook once, insert the hook into the first chain worked, draw the working yarn through, and then grasp the working yarn again and pull it through the first loop on the hook. This creates 1 chain, which will be the base of the band. [Pull the yarn through 2 loops on the hook at once] twice to finish the first half double crochet. For the next half double crochet, yarn over hook once, insert the hook at the base of the half double crochet worked before, pull the working yarn through, chain 1, and then finish the half double crochet. Continue this way until the desired length has been reached.

Finishing: Thread each band through the background fabric without twisting it, loosely intertwining the wavy hdc band with the background. Sew on the beginning and end of the band using the yarn tails.

Chart Key

○ Chain 1   ✕ 1 single crochet   ⊤ 1 half double crochet

⑂ 1 single crochet, inserting the hook the following way: Grasp the diagonally located loop of the half double crochet underneath the front loop of the half double crochet with the hook from the bottom to the top, pull the working yarn through, and finish working the single crochet. This places the top loop of the half double crochet on the top.

BRAIDED LOOP CABLE

[cable width = 4 base pattern sts]

Work in rows, following the chart; Row 1 is a WS row. Shown are the cable, and to the right and left of it, 5 stitches of the background pattern. The background pattern can be worked over any number of stitches widthwise, keeping in mind that per cable, 4 stitches of the background pattern are covered up by the cable (2 before and 2 after the cable).

Cable loops: For each cable, during the first working step, loops are crocheted within the background pattern, each created by starting with a chain, and then working 1 row of double crochet. These double crochet loops are worked first in Rows 1 and 2, and then in every following second and third row of the background pattern. Work Rows 1–8 once, and then repeat Rows 3–8 for pattern. Finish the crocheted piece by adding Final Rows a, b, and c at the end. During the second working step, the double crochet loops are braided.

Braiding the cable: Place the crocheted piece loop-side up. Twist the first loop at the bottom edge of the crocheted piece to the right, so that the double crochet bands cross where they emerge. Now, start braiding. Pull the second loop from back to front through the first twisted loop, and immediately twist it to the right. Pull the next loop through the second loop, twist it, and continue until the whole cable has been braided. Temporarily secure the last loop with a safety pin; it will be fastened with a single crochet when you work the final row (see Final Row d) or add an edging, or it can be sewn on.

Chart Key

o	Chain 1	
15	Chain 15 (crochet loosely)	X 1 single crochet ╎ 1 double crochet

Work 15 double crochets into the chain of 15, always working the double crochets around two strands of the beginning chain.

Bridging: In order to better show the cable loops, the chart has been drawn with spaces bridged by arrows. These spots do not require any action in the actual crochet work (i.e., the row after a loop is always worked continuously without interruption). This also applies to the beginning chain.

Fasten the cable loop with a single crochet: Insert the hook first into the stitch of the loop and then into the stitch of the previous row, pull the working yarn through, and finish working the single crochet.

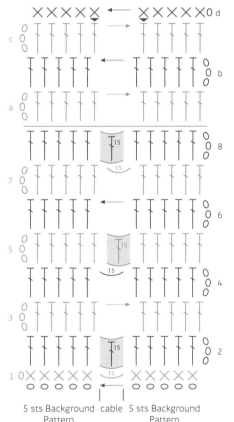

5 sts Background cable 5 sts Background
Pattern   Pattern

RIPPLE AND CHEVRON PATTERNS

334 SHALLOW CHEVRONS WITH EYELETS

[multiple of 12 + 3 beg-ch]

Work in rows, following the chart. Begin every row with the stitches before the pattern repeat, repeat the marked pattern repeat (12 sts wide) widthwise, and end with the stitches after the pattern repeat. Work Rows 1–3 once, and then repeat Rows 2 and 3 for pattern.

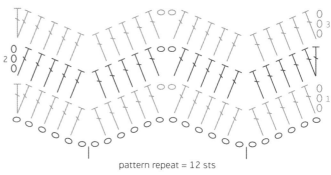

pattern repeat = 12 sts

Chart Key

○ Chain 1   † 1 double crochet   ⋁ Dc2-in-1: 2 double crochets into the same spot

335 RIPPLES WITH CROSSINGS

[multiple of 20 + 1 beg-ch]

Work in rows, following the chart. Begin every row with the stitches before the pattern repeat, repeat the marked pattern repeat (20 sts wide) widthwise, and end with the stitches after the pattern repeat. Work Rows 1–9 once, and then repeat Rows 2–9 for pattern.

Chart Key

○ Chain 1
✕ 1 single crochet
† 1 double crochet

⋉ 2 double crochets crossed to the right: Skip 1 stitch of the previous row, work the first double crochet into the next stitch of the previous row, and work the second double crochet, going back behind the first double crochet into the skipped stitch

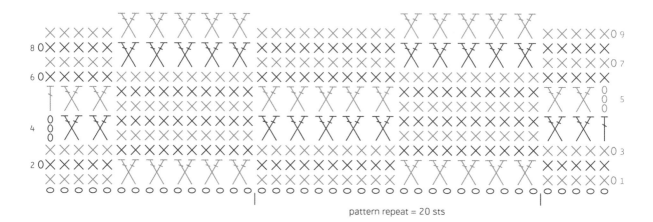

pattern repeat = 20 sts

336 DOUBLE CROCHET CHEVRONS

[multiple of 12 + 3 beg-ch]

Work in rows, following the chart. Begin every row with the stitches before the pattern repeat, repeat the marked pattern repeat (12 sts wide) widthwise, and end with the stitches after the pattern repeat. Work Rows 1–3 once, and then repeat Rows 2 and 3 for pattern.

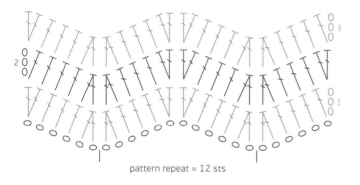

pattern repeat = 12 sts

Chart Key

○ Chain 1

⊤ 1 double crochet

V Dc2-in-1: 2 double crochets into the same stitch

⋀ Dc2tog: Double crochet 2 stitches together

337 WAVES WITH FANS

[multiple of 18 + 1 ch + 1 beg-ch]

Work in rows, following the chart. Begin every row with the stitches before the pattern repeat, repeat the marked pattern repeat (18 sts wide) widthwise, and end with the stitches after the pattern repeat. Work Rows 1–15 once, and then repeat Rows 2–15 for pattern.

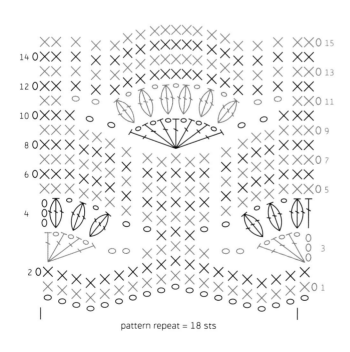

pattern repeat = 18 sts

Chart Key

○ Chain 1

✕ 1 single crochet

⊤ 1 double crochet

Dc3tog-in-1: 3 double crochets into the same stitch and crocheted together

[1 double crochet, chain 1, 1 double crochet, chain 1, 1 double crochet] into the same stitch

[1 double crochet, chain 1] 3 times, 1 double crochet into the same stitch

[1 double crochet, chain 1] 6 times, 1 double crochet into the same stitch

338 UP AND DOWN THE STAIRS

[multiple of 16 + 1 ch + 3 beg-ch]

Chart Key

○   Chain 1

┃   1 double crochet

⅄   Dc2tog: Double crochet 2 stitches together

⅄   Dc3tog: Double crochet 3 stitches together

    Dc5-in-1: 5 double crochets into the same stitch

    Dc5tog: Double crochet 5 stitches together

    1 double crochet, chain 1, 1 double crochet, chain 1, 1 double crochet into the same stitch

Work in rows, following the chart. Begin every row with the stitches before the pattern repeat, repeat the marked pattern repeat (16 sts wide) widthwise, and end with the stitches after the pattern repeat. Work Rows 1–3 once, and then repeat Rows 2 and 3 for pattern.

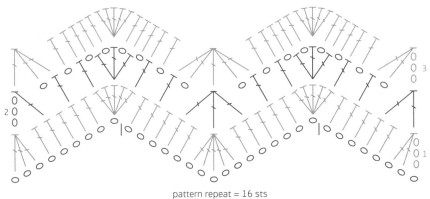

pattern repeat = 16 sts

339 SHALLOW CHEVRONS WITH MESH

[multiple of 16 + 1 ch + 3 beg-ch]

Work in rows, following the chart. Begin every row with the stitches before the pattern repeat, repeat the marked pattern repeat (16 sts wide) widthwise, and end with the stitches after the pattern repeat. Work Rows 1–3 once, and then repeat Rows 2 and 3 for pattern.

Chart Key

○   Chain 1

✕   1 single crochet

┃   1 double crochet

⅄   Dc2tog: Double crochet 2 stitches together

⅄   Dc3tog: Double crochet 3 stitches together

    Dc5-in-1: 5 double crochets into the same stitch

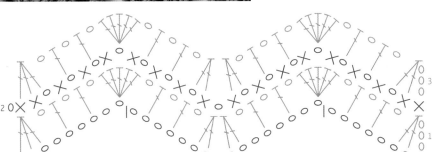

pattern repeat = 16 sts

340 ZIGZAG CORDON

[multiple of 16 + 4 ch + 3 beg-ch]

Work in rows, following the chart. Begin every row with the stitches before the pattern repeat, repeat the marked pattern repeat (16 sts wide) widthwise, and end with the stitches after the pattern repeat. Work Rows 1–3 once, and then repeat Rows 2 and 3 for pattern.

Chart Key

○	Chain 1		Fpdc: 1 front post double crochet
	1 double crochet		Bpdc: 1 back post double crochet
V	Dc2-in-1: 2 double crochets into the same stitch		

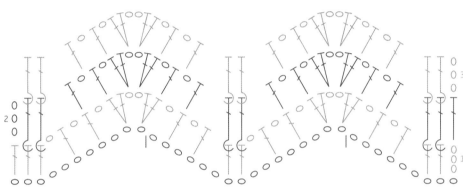

pattern repeat = 16 sts

341 SHALLOW CHEVRONS

[multiple of 12 + 3 beg-ch]

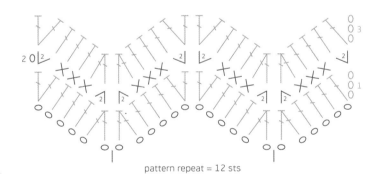

pattern repeat = 12 sts

Chart Key

○	Chain 1	Sc2-in-1: 2 single crochets into the same stitch	Dc2-in-1: 2 double crochets into the same stitch
✕	1 single crochet		
	1 double crochet	Sc2tog: Single crochet 2 stitches together	Dc2tog: Double crochet 2 stitches together

Work in rows, following the chart. Begin every row with the stitches before the pattern repeat, repeat the marked pattern repeat (12 sts wide) widthwise, and end with the stitches after the pattern repeat. Work Rows 1–3 once, and then repeat Rows 2 and 3 for pattern.

342 CHEVRONS WITH RIDGES

[multiple of 10 +1 ch + 3 beg-ch]

pattern repeat = 10 sts

Work in rows, following the chart. Begin every row with the stitches before the pattern repeat, repeat the marked pattern repeat (10 sts wide) widthwise, and end with the stitches after the pattern repeat. Work Rows 1–3 once, and then repeat Rows 2 and 3 for pattern.

Chart Key

○   Chain 1

| 1 double crochet

⊥   Blo-dc: 1 double crochet through the back loop only

⊤   Flo-dc: 1 double crochet through the front loop only

V   Dc2-in-1: 2 double crochets into the same stitch

V̇   [1 double crochet, chain 1, 1 double crochet] into the same stitch

⋀   Dc3tog: Double crochet 3 stitches together

⋀   Blo-dc3tog: Double crochet 3 stitches together through the back loop only

⋀   Flo-dc3tog: Double crochet 3 stitches together through the front loop only

343 NAUTICAL SHELL CHEVRONS

[multiple of 16 + 1 ch + 3 beg-ch]

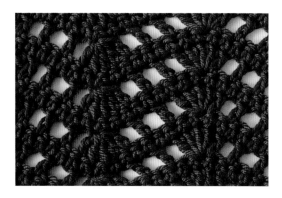

Work in rows, following the chart. Begin every row with the stitches before the pattern repeat, repeat the marked pattern repeat (16 sts wide) widthwise, and end with the stitches after the pattern repeat. Work Rows 1–3 once, and then repeat Rows 2 and 3 for pattern.

Chart Key

○   Chain 1

✕   1 single crochet

| 1 double crochet

⋀   Dc2tog: Double crochet 2 stitches together

⋀   Dc3tog: Double crochet 3 stitches together

⋔   Dc5-in-1: 5 double crochets into the same stitch

⋀   Dc5tog: Double crochet 5 stitches together

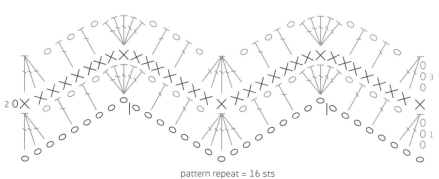

pattern repeat = 16 sts

344 GENTLE WAVES

[multiple of 14 + 2 ch + 1 beg-ch]

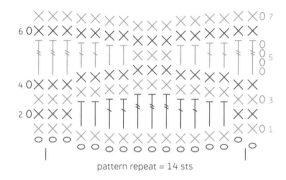

pattern repeat = 14 sts

Chart Key

○ Chain 1

✕ 1 single crochet

⊤ 1 half double crochet

⊤ 1 double crochet

↑ 1 treble crochet

Work in rows, following the chart. Begin every row with the stitches before the pattern repeat, repeat the marked pattern repeat (14 sts wide) widthwise, and end with the stitches after the pattern repeat. Work Rows 1–7 once, and then repeat Rows 2–7 for pattern.

345 MESH-LOOK CHEVRONS

[multiple of 16 + 1 ch + 3 beg-ch]

Work in rows, following the chart. Begin every row with the stitches before the pattern repeat, repeat the marked pattern repeat (16 sts wide) widthwise, and end with the stitches after the pattern repeat. Work Rows 1–3 once, and then repeat Rows 2 and 3 for pattern.

From Row 2 on, always work the groups of [2 double crochets, chain 1, 2 double crochets] into the chain space of the previous row, around the chain.

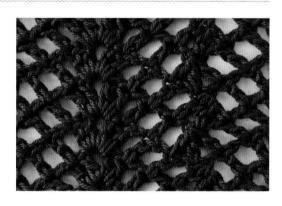

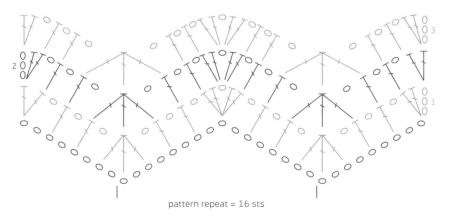

pattern repeat = 16 sts

Chart Key

○ Chain 1

↑ 1 double crochet

 Dc2-in-1: 2 double crochets into the same stitch

Dc3tog: Double crochet 3 stitches together

[2 double crochets, chain 1, 2 double crochets] in the same spot

346 TALL MESH WAVES

[multiple of 16 + 3 ch + 1 beg-ch]

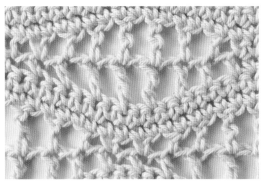

Work in rows, following the chart. Begin every row with the stitches before the pattern repeat, repeat the marked pattern repeat (16 sts wide) widthwise, and end with the stitches after the pattern repeat. Work Rows 1–10 once, and then repeat Rows 3–10 for pattern.

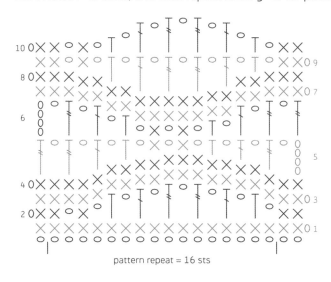

pattern repeat = 16 sts

Chart Key

○ Chain 1

✕ 1 single crochet

T 1 half double crochet

T 1 double crochet

T̸ 1 treble crochet

347 WAVY GRID WITH PICOTS

[multiple of 22 + 7 ch + 1 beg-ch]

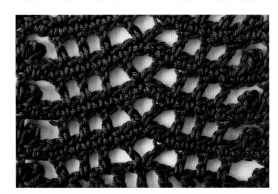

Work in rows, following the chart. Begin every row with the stitches before the pattern repeat, repeat the marked pattern repeat (22 sts wide) widthwise, and end with the stitches after the pattern repeat. Work Rows 1–4 once, and then repeat Rows 3 and 4 for pattern.

Chart Key

○ Chain 1

✕ 1 single crochet

T 1 half double crochet

T 1 double crochet

⟨○○○⟩ [1 double crochet, chain 3, 1 double crochet] into the same stitch

○⊶○ 1 picot of 3: Chain 3, and then join with 1 slip stitch back into the first chain

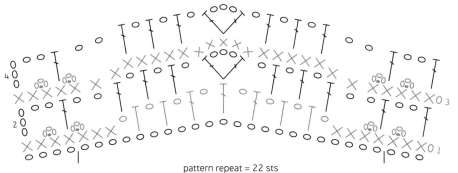

pattern repeat = 22 sts

348 WAVES WITH WHITE CAPS
[multiple of 16 + 3 ch + 1 beg-ch]

Work in rows, following the chart. Begin every row with the stitches before the pattern repeat, repeat the marked pattern repeat (16 sts wide) widthwise, and end with the stitches after the pattern repeat. Work Rows 1–7 once, and then repeat Rows 2–7 for pattern.

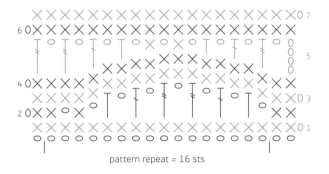

pattern repeat = 16 sts

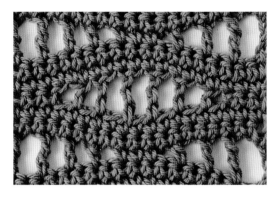

Chart Key
o   Chain 1
X   1 single crochet
T   1 half double crochet
⊤   1 double crochet
⊥   1 treble crochet

349 CHEVRONS WITH A VIEW
[multiple of 18 + 1 ch + 3 beg-ch]

Work in rows, following the chart. Begin every row with the stitches before the pattern repeat, repeat the marked pattern repeat (18 sts wide) widthwise, and end with the stitches after the pattern repeat. Work Rows 1–3 once, and then repeat Rows 2 and 3 for pattern.

Chart Key
o   Chain 1
X   1 single crochet
T   1 double crochet
 Dc2-in-1: 2 double crochets into the same stitch
 Dc3-in-1: 3 double crochets into the same stitch
 [1 double crochet, chain 1, 1 double crochet] into the same stitch
[2 double crochets, chain 1, 2 double crochets] into the same stitch

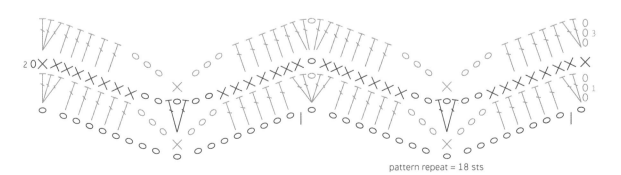

pattern repeat = 18 sts

350 BERRY CHEVRONS

[multiple of 12 + 1 ch + 3 beg-ch]

Work in rows, following the chart; Row 1 is a WS row. Begin every row with the stitches before the pattern repeat, repeat the marked pattern repeat (12 sts wide) widthwise, and end with the stitches after the pattern repeat. Work Rows 1–3 once, and then repeat Rows 2 and 3 for pattern.

From Row 2 on, always work the dc3tog-in-1 into 1 chain of the previous row.

Chart Key

○ Chain 1

 1 double crochet

Dc3tog-in-1: 3 double crochets into the same stitch and crocheted together

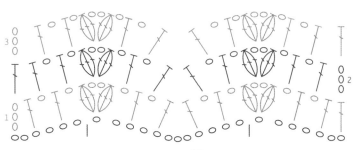

pattern repeat = 12 sts

351 WAVES WITH DOUBLE TREBLE CROCHETS

[multiple of 12 + 1 ch + 5 beg-ch]

Chart Key

○ Chain 1

× 1 single crochet

Sc2tog: Single crochet 2 stitches together

1 double treble crochet

Dtr3tog: Double treble crochet 3 stitches together

[1 double treble crochet, chain 1, 1 double treble crochet] into the same stitch

Dtr4tog: Double treble crochet 4 stitches together

Dtr7tog: Double treble crochet 7 stitches together

Work in rows, following the chart. Begin every row with the stitches before the pattern repeat, repeat the marked pattern repeat (12 sts wide) widthwise, and end with the stitches after the pattern repeat. Work Rows 1–3 once, and then repeat Rows 2 and 3 for pattern.

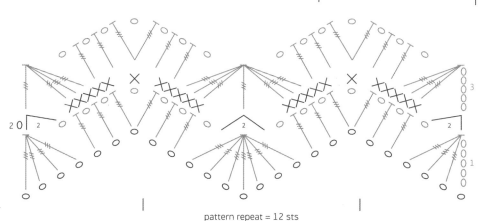

pattern repeat = 12 sts

352 DENSE SMOCKED WAVES

[multiple of 12 + 4 ch + 1 beg-ch]

Work in rows, following the chart. Begin every row with the stitches before the pattern repeat, repeat the marked pattern repeat (12 sts wide) widthwise, and end with the stitches after the pattern repeat. Work Rows 1–15 once, and then repeat Rows 2–15 for pattern.

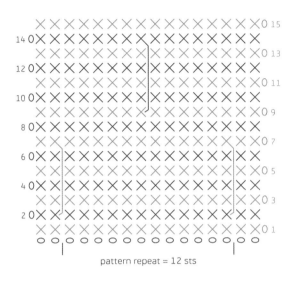

pattern repeat = 12 sts

Chart Key

o Chain 1

✕ 1 single crochet

} 1 spike stitch in single crochet: Insert the hook into the stitch 5 rows below, draw the working yarn through, and lengthen the loop to a height of just above the top edge of the current row. Finish the single crochet.

353 CHEVRONS ON A TRELLIS GROUND

[multiple of 24 + 1 ch + 1 beg-ch]

Work in rows, following the chart. At the beginning of the row, 1 chain of the beginning chain replaces the first single crochet, or 3 chains of the beginning chain replace the first double crochet. Begin every row with the stitches before the pattern repeat, repeat the marked pattern repeat (24 sts wide) widthwise, and end with the stitches after the pattern repeat. Work Rows 1–7 once, and then repeat Rows 4–7 for pattern.

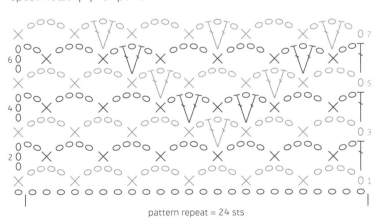

pattern repeat = 24 sts

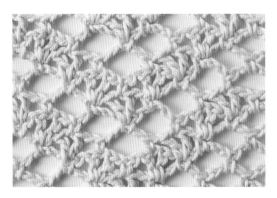

Chart Key

o Chain 1

✕ 1 single crochet

T 1 double crochet

V [1 double crochet, chain 1, 1 double crochet] into the same stitch

354 GENTLE SWELL [multiple of 14 + 3 ch + 3 beg-ch]

Work in rows, following the chart. Begin every row with the stitches before the pattern repeat, repeat the marked pattern repeat (14 sts wide) widthwise, and end with the stitches after the pattern repeat. Work Rows 1–3 once, and then repeat Rows 2 and 3 for pattern.

Chart Key

○ Chain 1

✕ 1 single crochet

† 1 double crochet

Dc2-in-1: 2 double crochets into the same stitch

Dc3-in-1: 3 double crochets into the same stitch

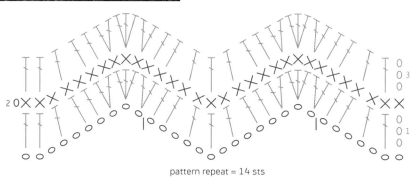

pattern repeat = 14 sts

355 CHEVRON GRID [multiple of 20 + 1 ch + 3 beg-ch]

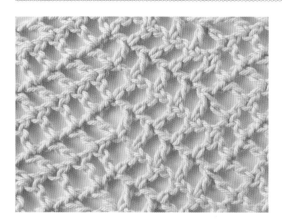

Work in rows, following the chart. Begin every row with the stitches before the pattern repeat, repeat the marked pattern repeat (20 sts wide) widthwise, and end with the stitches after the pattern repeat. Work Rows 1–3 once, and then repeat Rows 2 and 3 for pattern.

Chart Key

○ Chain 1

† 1 double crochet

Dc2tog: Double crochet 2 stitches together

[1 double crochet, chain 1, 1 double crochet] into the same stitch

[1 double crochet, chain 3, 1 double crochet] into the same stitch

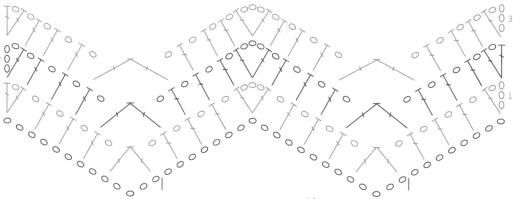

pattern repeat = 20 sts

356 DIAMOND ZIGZAG

[multiple of 10 + 6 ch + 3 beg-ch]

Work in rows, following the chart. Begin every row with the stitches before the pattern repeat, repeat the marked pattern repeat (10 sts wide) widthwise, and end with the stitches after the pattern repeat. Work Rows 1–3 once, and then repeat Rows 2 and 3 for pattern.

Chart Key

o	Chain 1		
X	1 single crochet		

V Dc2-in-1: 2 double crochets into the same stitch

Dc2tog: Double crochet 2 stitches together

Dc5-in-1: 5 double crochets into the same stitch

Dc5tog: Double crochet 5 stitches together

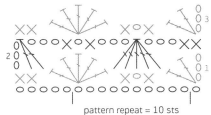

pattern repeat = 10 sts

357 ROLLING WAVES

[multiple of 12 + 1 ch +3 beg-ch]

Work in rows, following the chart; Row 1 is a WS row. Begin every row with the stitches before the pattern repeat, repeat the marked pattern repeat (12 sts wide) widthwise, and end with the stitches after the pattern repeat. Work Rows 1–5 once, and then repeat Rows 2–5 for pattern.

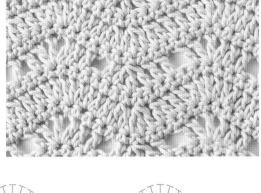

Chart Key

o   Chain 1

X   1 single crochet

| 1 double crochet

Dc2tog: Double crochet 2 stitches together

Dc3tog: Double crochet 3 stitches together

Dc2-in-1: 2 double crochets into the same stitch

Dc3-in-1: 3 double crochets into the same stitch

[1 double crochet, chain 1, 1 double crochet, chain 1, 1 double crochet] into the same stitch

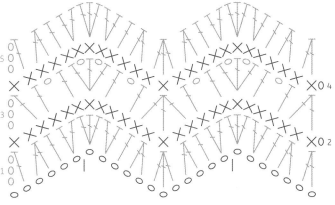

pattern repeat = 12 sts

358 CHEVRONS WITH RAKED WINDOWS

[multiple of 9 + 2 beg-ch]

Work in rows, following the chart; Row 1 is a WS row. Begin every row with the stitches before the pattern repeat, repeat the marked pattern repeat (9 sts wide) widthwise, and end with the stitches after the pattern repeat. Work Rows 1–5 once, and then repeat Rows 2–5 for pattern.

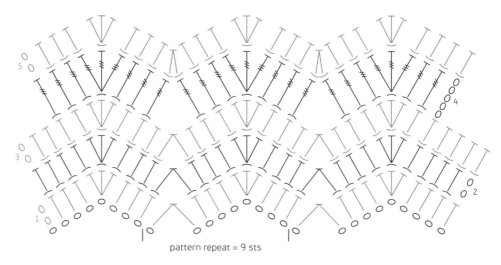

pattern repeat = 9 sts

Chart Key

○ Chain 1

⊺ 1 half double crochet

Blo-hdc: 1 half double crochet through the back loop only

Flo-hdc: 1 half double crochet through the front loop only

Hdc2tog: Half double crochet 2 stitches together

Flo-hdc2tog: Half double crochet 2 stitches together through the front loop only

Blo-hdc2tog: Half double crochet 2 stitches together through the back loop only

Flo-hDc3-in-1: 3 half double crochets through the front loop only into the same stitch

Blo-hDc3-in-1: 3 half double crochets through the back loop only into the same stitch

Blo-dtr: 1 double treble crochet through the back loop only

Blo-dtr3-in-1: 3 double treble crochets through the back loop only into the same stitch

359 DOUBLE CROCHET IN GENTLE WAVES

[multiple of 17 + 3 beg-ch]

Work in rows, following the chart. At the beginning of the row, 3 beginning chains replace the first double crochet. Begin every row with the stitches before the pattern repeat, repeat the marked pattern repeat (17 sts wide) widthwise, and end with the stitches after the pattern repeat. Work Rows 1–3 once, and then repeat Rows 2 and 3 for pattern.

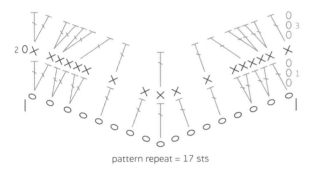

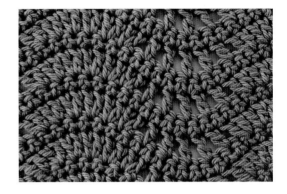

pattern repeat = 17 sts

Chart Key

o Chain 1

⊤ 1 double crochet

✕ 1 single crochet

∨ Dc2-in-1: 2 double crochets into the same stitch

360 ALTERNATING WAVES

[multiple of 16 + 3 beg-ch]

Chart Key

o Chain 1

✕ 1 single crochet

⊤ 1 double crochet

⋀ Dc2tog: Double crochet 2 stitches together

⋀ Dc3tog: Double crochet 3 stitches together

Dc5-in-1: 5 double crochets into the same stitch

Dc5tog: Double crochet 5 stitches together

Work in rows, following the chart. Begin every row with the stitches before the pattern repeat, repeat the marked pattern repeat (16 sts wide) widthwise, and end with the stitches after the pattern repeat. Work Rows 1–7 once, and then repeat Rows 2–7 for pattern.

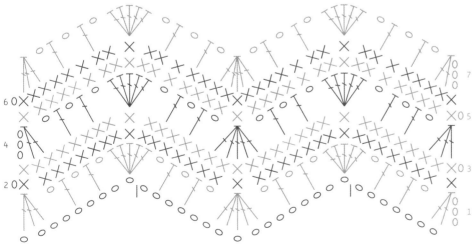

pattern repeat = 16 sts

361 UP AND DOWN WITH DOUBLE CROCHETS [multiple of 14 + 2 ch + 3 beg-ch]

Work in rows, following the chart. Begin every row with the stitches before the pattern repeat, repeat the marked pattern repeat (14 sts wide) widthwise, and end with the stitches after the pattern repeat. Work Rows 1–3 once, and then repeat Rows 2 and 3 for pattern.

From Row 2 on, always work the double crochets into the chain space of the previous row, around the chain, except for the double crochet at the end of the row, which is worked into the top chain of the beg-ch.

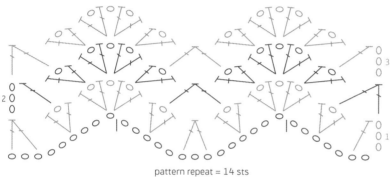

pattern repeat = 14 sts

Chart Key

○	Chain 1
†	1 double crochet
V	[1 double crochet, chain 1, 1 double crochet] in the same spot
X	Dc2tog: Double crochet 2 stitches together

362 GRANNY CHEVRONS [multiple of 22 + 3 beg-ch]

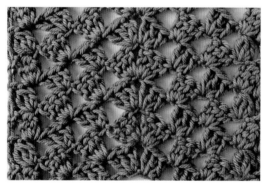

Work in rows, following the chart. Begin every row with the stitches before the pattern repeat, repeat the marked pattern repeat (22 sts wide) widthwise, and end with the stitches after the pattern repeat. Work Rows 1–3 once, and then repeat Rows 2 and 3 for pattern.

Chart Key

○	Chain 1
†	1 double crochet
V	Dc3-in-1: 3 double crochets into the same stitch
⬦	Dc3tog-in-1: 3 double crochets into the same stitch and crocheted together

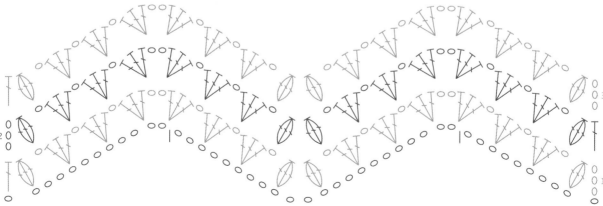

pattern repeat = 22 sts

363 FEATHER-AND-FAN

[multiple of 19 + 3 beg-ch]

Work in rows, following the chart. Begin every row with the stitches before the pattern repeat, repeat the marked pattern repeat (19 sts wide) widthwise, and end with the stitches after the pattern repeat. Work Rows 1–7 once, and then repeat Rows 2–7 for pattern.

Chart Key

○ Chain 1

✕ 1 single crochet

┬ 1 double crochet

┬ 1 double treble crochet

Dc5-in-1: 5 double crochets into the same stitch

[1 double treble crochet, chain 1] 3 times, 1 double treble crochet into the same stitch

[1 double treble crochet, chain 1] twice, 1 double treble crochet into the same stitch

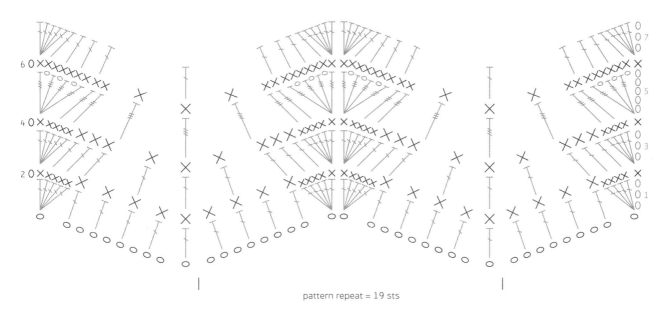

pattern repeat = 19 sts

364 RIPPLE-AND-GROOVE PATTERN

[multiple of 19 + 1 ch + 2 beg-ch]

Work in rows, following the chart. At the beginning of the row, 2 chains of the beginning chain replace the first half double crochet, 3 chains replace the first double crochet, 4 chains replace the first treble crochet, and 5 chains replace the first double treble crochet. Begin every row with the stitches before the pattern repeat, repeat the marked pattern repeat (19 sts wide) widthwise, and end with the stitches after the pattern repeat. Work Rows 1–8 once, and then repeat Rows 3–8 for pattern.

Chart Key

o	Chain 1
✕	1 single crochet
Č	Bpsc: 1 back post single crochet
⊤	1 half double crochet
⊤	1 double crochet
⊤	1 treble crochet
⊤	1 double treble crochet
⊼	Dc5-in-1: 5 double crochets into the same stitch
⊼	Tr5-in-1: 5 treble crochets into the same stitch

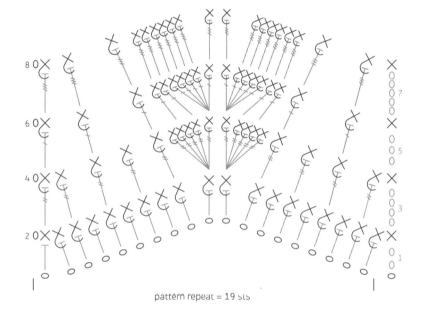

pattern repeat = 19 sts

365 SHELL WAVES

[multiple of 19 + 3 beg-ch]

Work in rows, following the chart. Begin every row with the stitches before the pattern repeat, repeat the marked pattern repeat (19 sts wide) widthwise, and end with the stitches after the pattern repeat. Work Rows 1–3 once, and then repeat Rows 2 and 3 for pattern.

Chart Key

 o Chain 1 ⊤ 1 double crochet Dc5-in-1: 5 double crochets into the same stitch

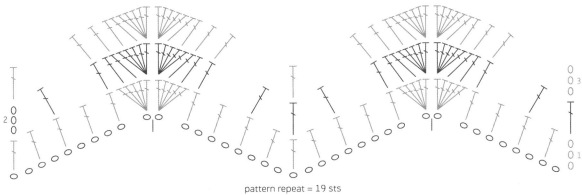

pattern repeat = 19 sts

366 EMPHASIZED WAVES

[multiple of 19 + 3 beg-ch]

Work in rows, following the chart; Row 1 is a WS row. Begin every row with the stitches before the pattern repeat, repeat the marked pattern repeat (19 sts wide) widthwise, and end with the stitches after the repeat. Work Rows 1–3 once, and then repeat Rows 2 and 3 for pattern.

Chart Key

o Chain 1

⊤ 1 double crochet

✕ Fpsc: 1 front post single crochet

Dc4-in-1: 4 double crochets into the same stitch

Dc5-in-1: 5 double crochets into the same stitch

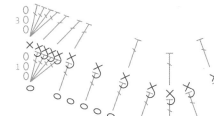 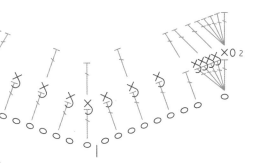

pattern repeat = 19 sts

367 GRANNY WAVES

[multiple of 27 + 1 ch + 3 beg-ch]

Work in rows, following the chart. Begin every row with the stitches before the pattern repeat, repeat the marked pattern repeat (27 sts wide) widthwise, and end with the stitches after the pattern repeat. Work Rows 1–3 once, and then repeat Rows 2 and 3 for pattern.

From Row 2 on, the stitch groups of 3 double crochets into the same stitch or [3 double crochets, chain 1, 3 double crochets] into the same stitch are always placed between the groups of double crochet of the previous row.

Chart Key

 o   Chain 1

    1 double crochet

    Dc3-in-1: 3 double crochets into the same stitch

    [3 double crochets, chain 1, 3 double crochets] into the same stitch

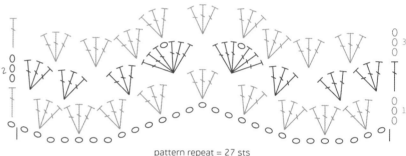

pattern repeat = 27 sts

368 LATTICE STRUTS

[multiple of 20 + 3 beg-ch]

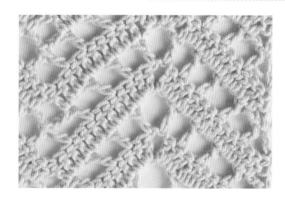

Work in rows, following the chart. Begin every row with the stitches before the pattern repeat, repeat the marked pattern repeat (20 sts wide) widthwise, and end with the stitches after the pattern repeat. Work Rows 1–3 once, and then repeat Rows 2 and 3 for pattern.

Chart Key

o Chain 1

    1 double crochet

    Dc2tog: Double crochet 2 stitches together

    Dc2-in-1: 2 double crochets into the same stitch

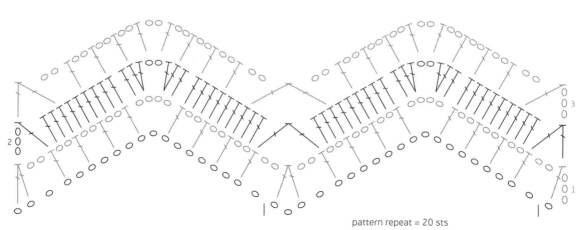

pattern repeat = 20 sts

369 ZIGZAGS WITH MESH ROWS

[multiple of 14 + 1 ch + 3 beg-ch]

Work in rows, following the chart. Begin every row with the stitches before the pattern repeat, repeat the marked pattern repeat (14 sts wide) widthwise, and end with the stitches after the pattern repeat. Work Rows 1–5 once, and then repeat Rows 2–5 for pattern.

In Row 3, work the center group of [Dc2tog-in-1, ch4, Dc2tog-in-1] into the chain space of the previous row, around the chain. In Row 4, always work the single crochet into the chain space of the previous row, around the chain.

Chart Key

○	Chain 1
✕	1 single crochet
⩓	Dc2tog: Double crochet 2 stitches together
	Dc2tog-in-1: 2 double crochets into the same stitch and crocheted together

⊤	1 double crochet
⋁	Dc2-in-1: 2 double crochets into the same stitch
	4 double crochets with 2 different bases crocheted together: Work the first and second double crochet together into the same double crochet of the previous row, skip the next stitch of the previous row, and work the third and fourth double crochet into the next double crochet of the previous row.

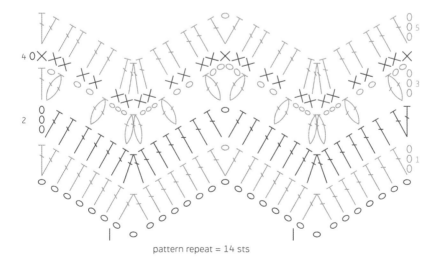

pattern repeat = 14 sts

370 RAISED WAVES

Work in rows, following the chart. Begin every row with the stitches before the pattern repeat, repeat the marked pattern repeat (19 sts wide) widthwise, and end with the stitches after the pattern repeat. Work Rows 1–8 once, and then repeat Rows 3–8 for pattern.

Chart Key

o Chain 1

╳ 1 single crochet

╳ Bpsc: 1 back post single crochet

| 1 half double crochet

† 1 double crochet

⊤ 1 double treble crochet

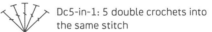 Dc5-in-1: 5 double crochets into the same stitch

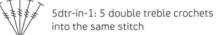 5dtr-in-1: 5 double treble crochets into the same stitch

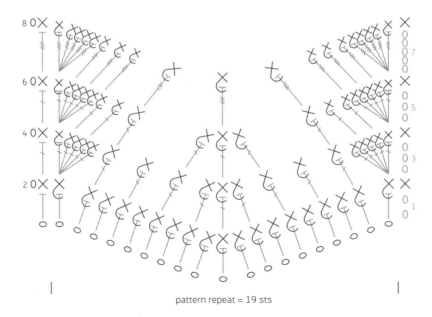

pattern repeat = 19 sts

371 RAISED SPIKES

[multiple of 16 + 1 ch + 3 beg-ch]

Chart Key

○ Chain 1

⊤ 1 double crochet

⊤ Bpdc: 1 back post double crochet

⊤ Fpdc: 1 front post double crochet

 Dc2-in-1: 2 double crochets into the same spot

 Dc3-in-1: 3 double crochets into the same spot

 [2 double crochets, chain 1, 2 double crochets] into the same stitch

Dc5tog: Double crochet 5 stitches together

Fpdc5-tog: Front post double crochet 5 stitches together

Bpdc5-tog: Back post double crochet 5 stitches together

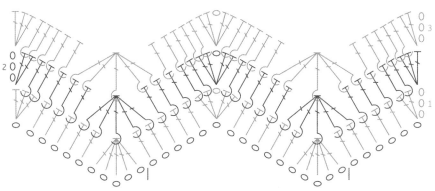

pattern repeat = 16 sts

Work in rows, following the chart. Begin every row with the stitches before the pattern repeat, repeat the marked pattern repeat (16 sts wide) widthwise, and end with the stitches after the pattern repeat. Work Rows 1–3 once, and then repeat Rows 2 and 3 for pattern.

From Row 2 on, work the 2 or 3 double crochets into the chain space of the previous row, around the chain.

372 DENSE CHEVRONS WITH CLUSTERS

[multiple of 21 + 11 ch + 1 beg-ch]

Chart Key

○ Chain 1

✕ 1 single crochet

 Sc2-in-1: 2 single crochets into the same stitch

 Sc3-in-1: 3 single crochets into the same stitch

Sc2tog: Single crochet 2 stitches together

Dc2tog-in-1: 2 double crochets into the same stitch and crocheted together

Dc3tog-in-1: 3 double crochets into the same stitch and crocheted together

 6 double crochets with 2 different bases crocheted together: Work 3 double crochets into the same single crochet of the previous row, skip the next 2 single crochets of the previous row, and work 3 double crochets into the next single crochet of the previous row. Now, crochet all 6 double crochets together.

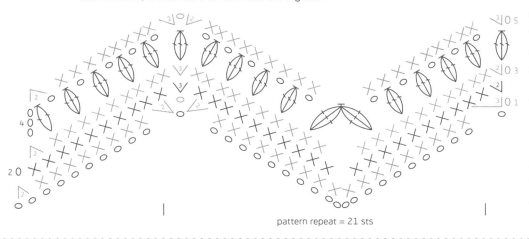

pattern repeat = 21 sts

Work in rows, following the chart. Begin every row with the stitches before the pattern repeat, repeat the marked pattern repeat (21 sts wide) widthwise, and end with the stitches after the pattern repeat. Work Rows 1–5 once, and then repeat Rows 2–5 for pattern.

EDGINGS AND BORDERS

373 PICOT EDGING

[multiple of 4 + 2 ch + 1 beg-ch]

Work in rows, following the chart. If the edging is crocheted directly onto the main piece, the selvedge stitches of the crocheted or knitted main piece replace the beginning chain. Begin every row with the stitches before the pattern repeat, repeat the marked pattern repeat (4 sts wide) widthwise, and end with the stitches after the pattern repeat. Work Rows 1–3 once.

Chart Key

○ Chain 1   ✕ 1 single crochet

⊤ 1 double crochet

₀⅗₀ 1 picot of 3: Chain 3, and then join with 1 slip stitch back into the first chain

✕ 2 crossed double crochets: Skip 1 single crochet, work the first double crochet into the next single crochet of the previous row, and then work the second double crochet, going back into the skipped single crochet

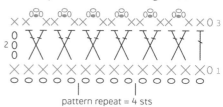

pattern repeat = 4 sts

374 OPEN-SHELL-AND-PICOT EDGING

[multiple of 10 + 1 ch + 3 beg-ch]

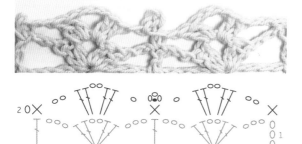

pattern repeat = 10 sts

Work in rows, following the chart. If the edging is crocheted directly onto the main piece, the selvedge stitches of the crocheted or knitted main piece replace the beginning chain. Begin every row with the stitches before the pattern repeat, repeat the marked pattern repeat (10 sts wide) widthwise, and end with the stitches after the pattern repeat. Work Rows 1 and 2 once.

In Row 2, always work the groups of [2 double crochets, chain 2, 2 double crochets] into the chain space of the previous row, around the chain.

This edging may be worked larger by repeating Row 2 as often as desired.

Chart Key

○ Chain 1

✕ 1 single crochet

⊤ 1 double crochet

⋎ [2 double crochets, chain 2, 2 double crochets] in the same spot

₀⅗₀ 1 picot of 3: Chain 3, and then join with 1 slip stitch back into the first chain

375 SHELL EDGING WITH CROSSINGS

[multiple of 6 + 5 ch + 1 beg-ch]

Work in rows, following the chart; Row 1 is a WS row. If the edging is crocheted directly onto the main piece, the selvedge stitches of the crocheted or knitted main piece replace the beginning chain. Begin every row with the stitches before the pattern repeat, repeat the marked pattern repeat (6 sts wide) widthwise, and end with the stitches after the pattern repeat. Work Rows 1–4 once.

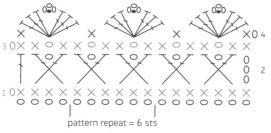

pattern repeat = 6 sts

Chart Key

○ Chain 1

✕ 1 single crochet

⊤ 1 double crochet

₀⅗₀ 1 picot of 3: Chain 3, and then join with 1 slip stitch back into the first chain

 2 crossed double crochets with chain 1 between them: Skip 2 single crochets, work the first double crochet into the next single crochet of the previous row, chain 1, work the second double crochet, going back behind the first double crochet, into the first one of the 2 skipped single crochets

 [3 double crochets, 1 picot, 3 double crochets] in the same spot

MULTI-STRAND CHAINS

[multiple of 16 + 11 ch + 1 beg-ch]

Work in rows, following the chart. If the edging is crocheted directly onto the main piece, the selvedge stitches of the crocheted or knitted main piece replace the beginning chain. Begin every row with the stitches before the pattern repeat, repeat the marked pattern repeat (16 sts wide) widthwise, ending either with a complete repeat or with the stitches after the repeat. Work Rows 1–4 once.

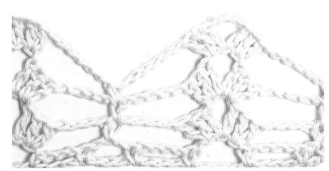

Chart Key

o Chain 1

✕ 1 single crochet

T 1 double crochet

Dc2-in-1: 2 double crochets into the same stitch

[1 double crochet, chain 3, 1 double crochet] into the same stitch

[1 double crochet, chain 4, 1 double crochet] into the same stitch

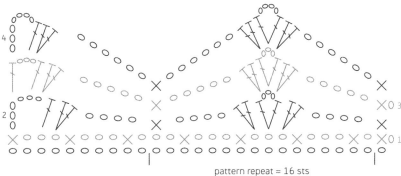

pattern repeat = 16 sts

ARCED EDGING WITH PICOT CHAINS

[multiple of 10 + 1 ch + 1 beg-ch]

Work in rows, following the chart. Begin every row with the stitches before the pattern repeat, repeat the marked pattern repeat (10 sts wide) widthwise, and end with the stitches after the pattern repeat. Work Rows 1–4 once.

In Row 2, work the dc2tog into the chain space of the previous row, around the chain.

After having completed Row 3, move to the start of the beginning chain by working [chain 1, 5 slip stitches], and then work into the unused stitches on the other side of the beginning chain for Row 4 as shown.

Join the edging at the picots to the crocheted or knitted main piece.

Chart Key

o Chain 1

• 1 slip stitch

✕ 1 single crochet

T 1 double crochet

T 1 treble crochet

1 picot of 3: Chain 3, and then join with 1 slip stitch back into the first chain

2 crossed double crochets with chain 1 between them: Skip 2 chains of the previous row, work the first double crochet into the next chain, chain 1, work the second double crochet, going back behind the first double crochet, into the first one of the 2 skipped chains

Dc2tog: Double crochet 2 stitches together

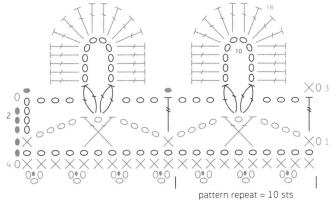

pattern repeat = 10 sts

CROSS-AND-SHELL EDGING

[multiple of 6 + 4 ch + 4 beg-ch]

Work in rows, following the chart. If the edging is crocheted directly onto the main piece, the selvedge stitches of the crocheted or knitted main piece replace the beginning chain. Begin every row with the stitches before the pattern repeat, repeat the marked pattern repeat (6 sts wide) widthwise, and end with the stitches after the pattern repeat. Work Rows 1–3 once.

In Row 3, always work the sequence of [3 double crochets, 1 picot, 3 double crochets] into the chain space of the previous row, around the chain.

Chart Key

o   Chain 1

X   1 single crochet

 1 picot of 3: Chain 3, and then join with 1 slip stitch back into the first chain

| 1 treble crochet

2 crossed treble crochets with chain 1 between them: Skip 2 chains of the previous row, work the first treble crochet into the next chain, chain 1, and then work the second treble crochet, going back behind the first treble crochet, into the first one of the 2 skipped chains

 [3 double crochets, 1 picot, 3 double crochets] in the same chain space

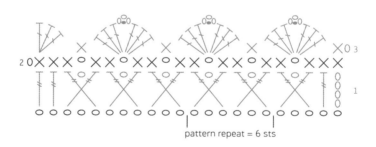

pattern repeat = 6 sts

FLORAL LACE EDGING

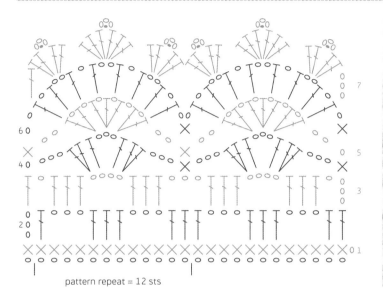

pattern repeat = 12 sts

Chart Key

○ Chain 1

╳ 1 single crochet

┬ 1 double crochet

V Dc2-in-1: 2 double crochets into the same stitch

1 picot of 3: Chain 3, and then join with 1 slip stitch back into the first chain

[1 double crochet, chain 1, 1 double crochet] into the same stitch

[1 double crochet, chain 1, 1 double crochet, chain 1, 1 double crochet] into the same stitch

Work in rows, following the chart. If the edging is crocheted directly onto the main piece, the selvedge stitches of the crocheted or knitted main piece replace the beginning chain. Begin every row with the stitches before the pattern repeat, repeat the marked pattern repeat (12 sts wide) widthwise, and end with the stitches after the pattern repeat. Work Rows 1–7 once.

In Row 6 work the individual double crochets, and in Row 7 work the groups of double crochets into the chain space of the previous row, around the chain.

OPEN PICOT FAN EDGING

Work in rows, following the chart. If the edging is crocheted directly onto the main piece, the selvedge stitches of the crocheted or knitted main piece replace the beginning chain. Begin every row with the stitches before the pattern repeat, repeat the marked pattern repeat (8 sts wide) widthwise, and end with the stitches after the pattern repeat. Work Rows 1–3 once.

Chart Key

○ Chain 1

╳ 1 single crochet

┬ 1 double crochet

[1 double crochet, 1 picot, chain 1, 1 double crochet, 1 picot, chain 1, 1 double crochet, 1 picot, chain 1, 1 double crochet] into the same stitch

1 picot of 3: Chain 3, and then join with 1 slip stitch back into the first chain

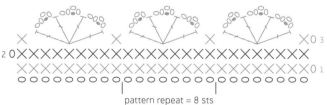

pattern repeat = 8 sts

381 DIAMOND EDGING

[multiple of 20 + 11 ch + 5 beg-ch]

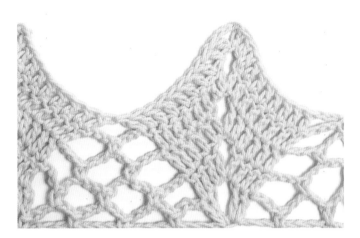

Work in rows, following the chart; Row 1 is a WS row. If the edging is crocheted directly onto the main piece, the selvedge stitches of the crocheted or knitted main piece replace the beginning chain. Begin every row with the stitches before the pattern repeat, repeat the marked pattern repeat (20 sts wide) widthwise, ending either with a complete repeat or with the stitches after the repeat. Depending on the desired length of the edging, you may end up working only half a pattern repeat widthwise. Work Rows 1–5 once.

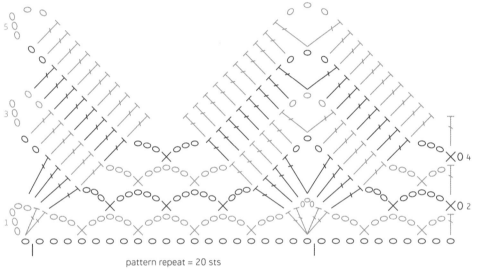

pattern repeat = 20 sts

Chart Key

○   Chain 1

✕   1 single crochet

↑   1 double crochet

⋁   Dc2-in-1: 2 double crochets into the same stitch

     [2 double crochets, chain 3, 2 double crochets] into the same stitch

     [1 double crochet, chain 3, 1 double crochet] into the same stitch

382 STAR FLOWERS

[multiple of 6 + 1 ch + 1 beg-ch]

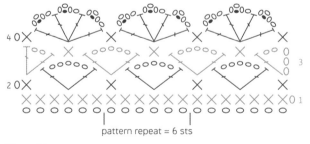

pattern repeat = 6 sts

Work in rows, following the chart. If the edging is crocheted directly onto the main piece, the selvedge stitches of the crocheted or knitted main piece replace the beginning chain. Begin every row with the stitches before the pattern repeat, repeat the marked pattern repeat (6 sts wide) widthwise, and end with the stitches after the pattern repeat. Work Rows 1–4 once.

Chart Key

○   Chain 1

✕   1 single crochet

↑   1 double crochet

    1 picot of 3: Chain 3, and then join with 1 slip stitch back into the first chain

     [1 double crochet, chain 5, 1 double crochet] into the same stitch

     [1 double crochet, chain 2, 1 double crochet] into the same stitch

    [1 double crochet, 1 picot, chain 1, 1 double crochet, 1 picot, chain 1, 1 double crochet] into the same stitch

FLOWER TRIM
[multiple of 9 + 1 ch + 2 beg-ch]

Work in rows, following the chart. Begin every row with the stitches before the pattern repeat, repeat the marked pattern repeat (9 sts wide) widthwise, and end with the stitches after the pattern repeat. Work Rows 1–3 once.

After completing Row 2, move to the beginning chain by working [chain 1, 3 slip stitches], and then work into the unused stitches on the other side of the beginning chain for Row 3 as shown.

In Rows 2 and 3, always work the 5 double crochets crocheted together into the chain space of the previous row, around the chain.

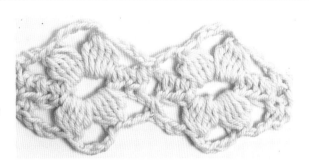

Chart Key

o	Chain 1	●	1 slip stitch
✕	1 single crochet	T	1 half double crochet

 Dc5tog: Double crochet 5 stitches together

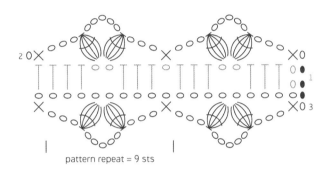

pattern repeat = 9 sts

FLOWER EDGING
[multiple of 8 + 1 ch + 1 beg-ch]

Work in rows, following the chart. If the edging is crocheted directly onto the main piece, the selvedge stitches of the crocheted or knitted main piece replace the beginning chain. Begin every row with the stitches before the pattern repeat, repeat the marked pattern repeat (8 sts wide) widthwise, and end with the stitches after the pattern repeat. Work Rows 1 and 2 once.

In Row 2, for the flower motifs, follow the direction of the arrows. After having worked the first petal (= 3 double crochets into the same stitch and crocheted together), chain 5, and join into the round with 1 slip stitch. Rotate this chain ring so that the working loop is located to the right of the ring. Now, continue from the chart, working the next petal into the chain space of the chain ring, and so on.

Chart Key

o	Chain 1		Dc2tog: Double crochet 2 stitches together
●	1 slip stitch		
✕	1 single crochet		Dc3tog: Double crochet 3 stitches together
T	1 double crochet		

 Dc3tog-in-1: 3 double crochets into the same stitch and crocheted together

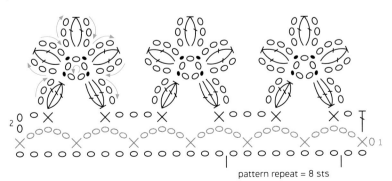

pattern repeat = 8 sts

216

385 EDGING WITH CROSSED DOUBLE CROCHETS [multiple of 3 + 2 ch + 1 beg-ch]

Work in rows, following the chart. If the edging is crocheted directly onto the main piece, the selvedge stitches of the crocheted or knitted main piece replace the beginning chain. Begin every row with the stitches before the pattern repeat, repeat the marked pattern repeat (3 sts wide) widthwise, and end with the stitches after the pattern repeat. Work Rows 1–4 once.

Chart Key

- o Chain 1
- X 1 single crochet
- 1 double crochet

2 crossed double crochets with chain 1 between them: Skip 2 single crochets, work the first double crochet into the next single crochet of the previous row, chain 1, work the second double crochet, going back behind the already worked double crochet, into the first one of the 2 skipped single crochets

pattern repeat = 3 sts

386 SLANTED BOBBLE BORDER [multiple of 4 + 1 ch + 1 beg-ch]

Work in rows, following the chart. If the edging is crocheted directly onto the main piece, the selvedge stitches of the crocheted or knitted main piece replace the beginning chain. Begin every row with the stitches before the pattern repeat, repeat the marked pattern repeat (4 sts wide) widthwise, and end with the stitches after the pattern repeat. Work Rows 1–3 once.

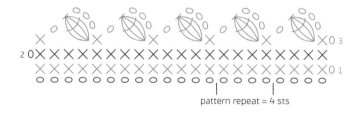

Chart Key

- o Chain 1
- X 1 single crochet

1 group of stitches: [1 single crochet, chain 3, 4 double crochets] into the single crochet worked last, and crocheted together

pattern repeat = 4 sts

387 EDGING WITH TRIPLE PICOTS IN ARCS [multiple of 6 + 1 ch + 2 beg-ch]

Work in rows, following the chart. If the edging is crocheted directly onto the main piece, the selvedge stitches of the crocheted or knitted main piece replace the beginning chain. Begin every row with the stitches before the pattern repeat, repeat the marked pattern repeat (6 sts wide) widthwise, and end with the stitches after the pattern repeat. Work Rows 1–3 once.

In Row 3, always work the 12 single crochets into the chain space of the previous row, around the chain.

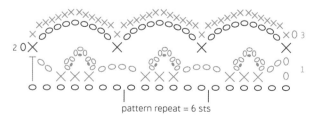

Chart Key

- o Chain 1
- X 1 single crochet
- 1 half double crochet
- 1 picot of 3: Chain 3, and then join with 1 slip stitch back into the first chain

pattern repeat = 6 sts

SHELL UPON SHELL

[multiple of 6 + 1 ch + 1 beg-ch]

Work in rows, following the chart. If the edging is crocheted directly onto the main piece, the selvedge stitches of the crocheted or knitted main piece replace the beginning chain. Begin every row with the stitches before the pattern repeat, repeat the marked pattern repeat (6 sts wide) widthwise, and end with the stitches after the pattern repeat. Work Rows 1–5 once.

In Row 5, always work the sequence of [2 double crochets, chain 1, 2 double crochets, chain 1, 2 double crochets] into the chain space of the previous row, around the chain.

Chart Key

o   Chain 1

✕   1 single crochet

 [1 double crochet, chain 1, 1 double crochet] into the same stitch

 [1 double crochet, chain 1, 2 double crochets] into the same stitch

[2 double crochets, chain 1, 2 double crochets, chain 1, 2 double crochets] into the same stitch

[2 double crochets, chain 1, 2 double crochets] into the same stitch

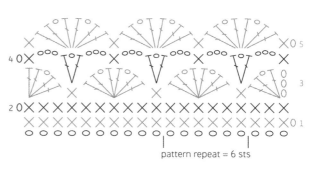

pattern repeat = 6 sts

NARROW SHELL BORDER

[multiple of 6 + 1 ch + 1 beg-ch]

Work in rows, following the chart. If the edging is crocheted directly onto the main piece, the selvedge stitches of the crocheted or knitted main piece replace the beginning chain. Begin every row with the stitches before the pattern repeat, repeat the marked pattern repeat (6 sts wide) widthwise, and end with the stitches after the pattern repeat. Work Rows 1–3 once.

Chart Key

o   Chain 1

✕   1 single crochet

 Dc2-in-1: 2 double crochets into the same stitch

 [1 double crochet, chain 3, 1 double crochet] into the same stitch

Dc3-in-1: 3 double crochets into the same stitch

Dc5-in-1: 5 double crochets into the same stitch

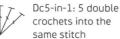

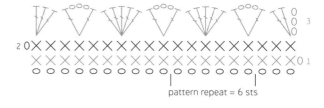

pattern repeat = 6 sts

390 ARCED EDGING WITH PICOTS [multiple of 9 + 3 beg-ch]

Work in rows, following the chart; Row 1 is a WS row. If the edging is crocheted directly onto the main piece, the selvedge stitches of the crocheted or knitted main piece replace the beginning chain. Begin every row with the stitches before the pattern repeat, repeat the marked pattern repeat (9 sts wide) widthwise, and end with the stitches after the pattern repeat. Work Rows 1 and 2 once.

Chart Key

○ Chain 1

● 1 slip stitch

✕ 1 single crochet

T 1 double crochet

o●o 1 picot of 3: Chain 3, and then join with 1 slip stitch back into the first chain

o●o 1 picot of 5: Chain 5, and then join with 1 slip stitch back into the first chain

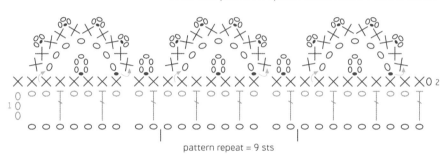

pattern repeat = 9 sts

391 TRELLIS FINS [multiple of 16 + 1 ch + 1 beg-ch]

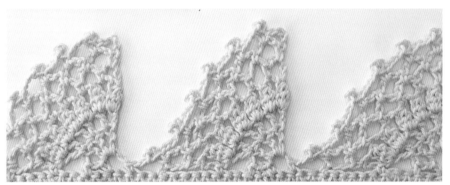

Work in rows, following the chart; Row 1 is a WS row. If the edging is crocheted directly onto the main piece, the selvedge stitches of the crocheted or knitted main piece replace the beginning chain. Begin with the stitches before the pattern repeat, repeat the marked pattern repeat (16 sts wide) widthwise, ending with a full repeat. Work Rows 1–8 once, and then repeat Rows 2–8 for pattern.

Chart Key

○ Chain 1

✕ 1 single crochet

T 1 double crochet

V [1 double crochet, chain 1, 1 double crochet] into the same stitch

Dc3tog-in-1: 3 double crochets into the same stitch and crocheted together

o●o 1 picot of 3: Chain 3, and then join with 1 slip stitch back into the first chain

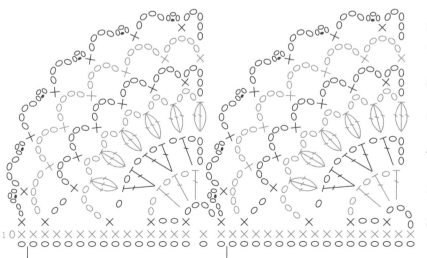

pattern repeat = 16 sts

PICOT FAN EDGING

[multiple of 9 + 3 ch + 1 beg-ch]

Work in rows, following the chart. If the edging is crocheted directly onto the main piece, the selvedge stitches
of the crocheted or knitted main piece replace the beginning chain. Begin every row with the stitches before the
pattern repeat, repeat the marked pattern repeat (9 sts
wide) widthwise, and end with the stitches after the pattern repeat. Work Rows 1–4 once.

In Row 3, always work the 3 groups of double crochets
stitched together into the same spot (into the joined top
of the double crochet together) of the previous row.

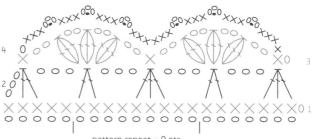

pattern repeat = 9 sts

Chart Key

o	Chain 1		Dc2tog: Double crochet 2 stitches together
✕	1 single crochet		Dc3tog: Double crochet 3 stitches together
	1 double crochet		Dc3tog-in-1: 3 double crochets into the same stitch and crocheted to- gether
o⦿o	1 picot of 3: Chain 3, and then join with 1 slip stitch back into the first chain		

DIAMOND EDGING WITH PICOTS

[multiple of 4 + 1 ch + 3 beg-ch]

Work in rows, following the chart. If the edging is crocheted directly onto the main piece, the selvedge stitches
of the crocheted or knitted main piece replace the beginning chain. Begin every row with the stitches before the
pattern repeat, repeat the marked pattern repeat (4 sts
wide) widthwise, and end with the stitches after the pattern repeat. Work Rows 1–3 once.

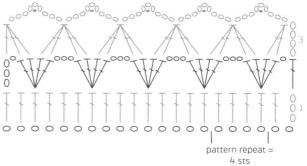

pattern repeat =
4 sts

Chart Key

o	Chain 1		Dc4-in-1: 4 double crochets into the same stitch
	1 double crochet		Dc2tog: Double crochet 2 stitches together
o⦿o	1 picot of 3: Chain 3, and then join with 1 slip stitch back into the first chain		

 Dc4tog: Double crochet 4 stitches together, working the
first 2 double crochets into the last 2 double crochets
of the group of double crochets of the previous row,
skip the chain arc, work the next 2 double crochets into
the first 2 double crochets of the following group of
double crochets of the previous row

 Dc3tog: Double crochet 3 stitches together, working the
first 2 double crochets into the last 2 double crochets of
the last group of double crochets of the previous row,
skip 1 chain, work the last double crochet into the top
chain of the turning chain of the previous row

394 TRELLIS EDGING WITH BUDS [multiple of 6 + 1 beg-ch]

Work in rows, following the chart. If the edging is crocheted directly onto the main piece, the selvedge stitches of the crocheted or knitted main piece replace the beginning chain. Begin every row with the stitches before the pattern repeat, repeat the marked pattern repeat (6 sts wide) widthwise, and end with the stitches after the pattern repeat. Work Rows 1–5 once.

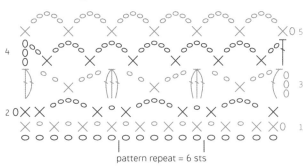

pattern repeat = 6 sts

Chart Key

○ Chain 1

✕ 1 single crochet

┬ 1 double crochet

 Dc3tog: Double crochet 3 stitches together

Dc2tog-in-1: 2 double crochets into the same stitch and crocheted together

395 ARCED EDGING WITH SPIKES [multiple of 3 + 1 ch + 1 beg-ch]

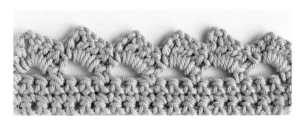

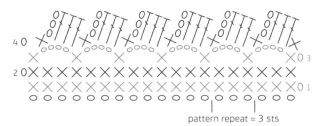

pattern repeat = 3 sts

Work in rows, following the chart. If the edging is crocheted directly onto the main piece, the selvedge stitches of the crocheted or knitted main piece replace the beginning chain. Begin every row with the stitches before the pattern repeat, repeat the marked pattern repeat (3 sts wide) widthwise, and end with the stitches after the pattern repeat. Work Rows 1–4 once.

In Row 4, always work the 1 single crochet into the first chain of the chain arc, and the 3 double crochets into the chain space, around the chain.

Chart Key

○ Chain 1

✕ 1 single crochet

┬ 1 double crochet

396 OPENWORK EDGING [multiple of 3 + 1 ch + 1 beg-ch]

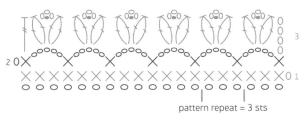

pattern repeat = 3 sts

Work in rows, following the chart. If the edging is crocheted directly onto the main piece, the selvedge stitches of the crocheted or knitted main piece replace the beginning chain. Begin every row with the stitches before the pattern repeat, repeat the marked pattern repeat (3 sts wide) widthwise, and end with the stitches after the pattern repeat. Work Rows 1–3 once.

In Row 3, always work the sequence of [double crochet 2 stitches together, 1 picot of 3, double crochet 2 stitches together] into the chain space, around the chain.

Chart Key

○ Chain 1

✕ 1 single crochet

 1 picot of 3: Chain 3, and then join with 1 slip stitch back into the first chain

┬ 1 treble crochet

Dc2tog: Double crochet 2 stitches together

SHELLS UNDER THE ROOF

[multiple of 7 + 2 ch + 1 beg-ch]

Work in rows, following the chart. If the edging is crocheted directly onto the main piece, the selvedge stitches of the crocheted or knitted main piece replace the beginning chain. Begin every row with the stitches before the pattern repeat, repeat the marked pattern repeat (7 sts wide) widthwise, and end with the stitches after the pattern repeat. Work Rows 1 and 2 once.

Chart Key

○ Chain 1

✕ 1 single crochet

 Dc7-in-1: 7 double crochets into the same stitch

pattern repeat = 7 sts

TRIM WITH SCALLOPED EDGING

[multiple of 16 + 14 ch + 3 beg-ch]

Work in rows, following the chart. If the edging is crocheted directly onto the main piece, the selvedge stitches of the crocheted or knitted main piece replace the beginning chain. Begin every row with the stitches before the pattern repeat, repeat the marked pattern repeat (16 sts wide) widthwise, and end with the stitches after the pattern repeat. Work Rows 1–3 once.

In Row 2, always work the groups of 4 double crochet into the chain space of the previous row, around the chain, and crochet them off together.

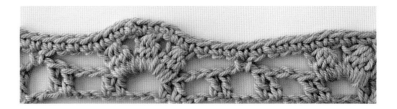

Chart Key

○ Chain 1

T 1 double crochet

✕ 1 single crochet

Dc4tog: Double crochet 4 stitches together

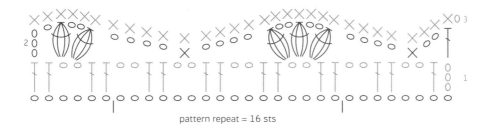

pattern repeat = 16 sts

SPIKY BORDER [multiple of 4 + 1 ch + 1 beg-ch]

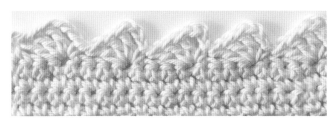

Work in rows, following the chart. If the edging is crocheted directly onto the main piece, the selvedge stitches of the crocheted or knitted main piece replace the beginning chain. Begin every row with the stitches before the pattern repeat, repeat the marked pattern repeat (4 sts wide) widthwise, and end with the stitches after the pattern repeat. Work Rows 1–3 once.

pattern repeat = 4 sts

Chart Key

o Chain 1

X 1 single crochet

1 group of stitches: [1 single crochet, chain 3, 3 double crochets] into the same single crochet

SCALLOPED-ARC EDGING [multiple of 6 + 4 ch + 1 beg-ch]

pattern repeat = 6 sts

Work in rows, following the chart. If the edging is crocheted directly onto the main piece, the selvedge stitches of the crocheted or knitted main piece replace the beginning chain. Begin every row with the stitches before the pattern repeat, repeat the marked pattern repeat (6 sts wide) widthwise, and end with the stitches after the pattern repeat. Work Rows 1–3 once.

In Row 3, always work the single crochets into the chain space of the previous row, around the chain.

Chart Key

o Chain 1

X 1 single crochet

T 1 double crochet

POMPOUS TRIM

[multiple of 10 + 1 ch + 1 beg-ch]

Chart Key

○   Chain 1

●   1 slip stitch

✕   1 single crochet

T   1 double crochet

‡   1 treble crochet

1 picot of 3: Chain 3, and then join with 1 slip stitch back into the first chain

1 group of stitches: 2 treble crochets into the same stitch with chain 6 and 1 double crochet in between: Work 1 treble crochet into the single crochet of the previous row, chain 6, 1 double crochet into the treble crochet worked last, 1 treble crochet into the same single crochet as the first treble crochet

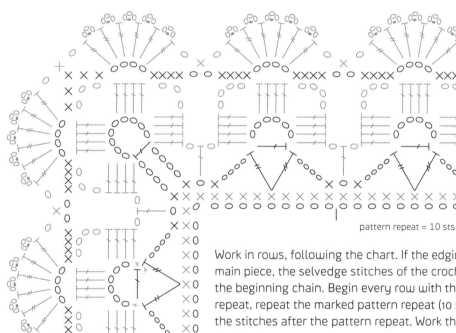

pattern repeat = 10 sts

Work in rows, following the chart. If the edging is crocheted directly onto the main piece, the selvedge stitches of the crocheted or knitted main piece replace the beginning chain. Begin every row with the stitches before the pattern repeat, repeat the marked pattern repeat (10 sts wide) widthwise, and end with the stitches after the pattern repeat. Work the corners as shown. Work Rows 1–5 once.

In Rows 3, 4, and 5, always work the stitches into the chain space of the previous row, around the chain.

PRINCESS TRELLIS

[multiple of 8 + 5 ch + 1 beg-ch]

Work in rows, following the chart. If the edging is crocheted directly onto the main piece, the selvedge stitches of the crocheted or knitted main piece replace the beginning chain. Begin every row with the stitches before the pattern repeat, repeat the marked pattern repeat (8 sts wide) widthwise, and end with the stitches after the pattern repeat. Work Rows 1–4 once.

In Row 4, always work the single crochet into the chain space of the previous row, around the chain.

Chart Key

○ Chain 1

✕ 1 single crochet

╎ 1 double crochet

○○○ 1 picot of 5: Chain 5, and then join with 1 slip stitch back into the first chain

pattern repeat = 8 sts

BLOSSOM EDGING

[multiple of 3 + 1 ch + 1 beg-ch]

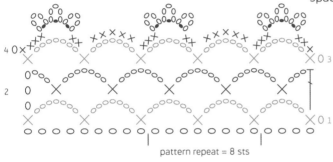

Work in rows, following the chart. If the edging is crocheted directly onto the main piece, the selvedge stitches of the crocheted or knitted main piece replace the beginning chain. Begin every row with the stitches before the pattern repeat, repeat the marked pattern repeat (3 sts wide) widthwise, and end with the stitches after the pattern repeat. Work Rows 1 and 2 once.

pattern repeat = 3 sts

Chart Key

○ Chain 1

✕ 1 single crochet

╎ 1 double crochet

◇ Dc2tog-in-1: 2 double crochets into the same stitch and crocheted together

LACE TRIM WITH SHELL EDGE

[multiple of 6 + 1 ch + 3 beg-ch]

Work in rows, following the chart. If the edging is crocheted directly onto the main piece, the selvedge stitches of the crocheted or knitted main piece replace the beginning chain. Begin every row with the stitches before the pattern repeat, repeat the marked pattern repeat (6 sts wide) widthwise, and end with the stitches after the pattern repeat. Work Rows 1–3 once.

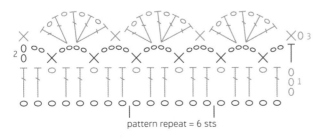

pattern repeat = 6 sts

Chart Key

○ Chain 1

✕ 1 single crochet

╎ 1 double crochet

 [1 double crochet, chain 1, 1 double crochet, chain 1, 1 double crochet] into the same stitch

 [1 double crochet, chain 1, 1 double crochet] into the same stitch

WINDOW EDGING

[multiple of 12 + 1 ch + 3 beg-ch]

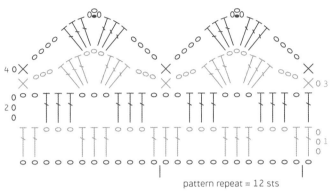

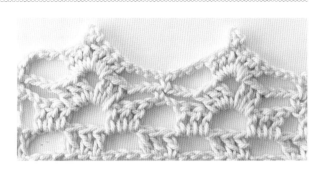

pattern repeat = 12 sts

Chart Key

○ Chain 1

✕ 1 single crochet

┬ 1 double crochet

○○○ 1 picot of 3: Chain 3, and then join with 1 slip stitch back into the first chain

Work in rows, following the chart. If the edging is crocheted directly onto the main piece, the selvedge stitches of the crocheted or knitted main piece replace the beginning chain. Begin every row with the stitches before the pattern repeat, repeat the marked pattern repeat (12 sts wide) widthwise, ending with a full repeat. Work Rows 1–4 once.

From Row 2 on, always work the double crochets into the chain space of the previous row, around the chain.

PICOT SHELL EDGING

[multiple of 8 + 2 ch + 7 sts per corner + 1 beg-ch]

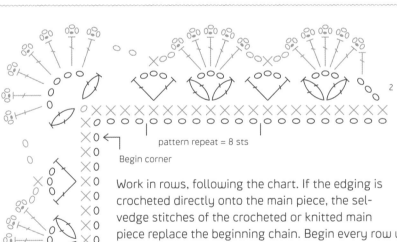

pattern repeat = 8 sts

Begin corner

Work in rows, following the chart. If the edging is crocheted directly onto the main piece, the sel-vedge stitches of the crocheted or knitted main piece replace the beginning chain. Begin every row with the stitches before the pattern repeat, repeat the marked pattern repeat (8 sts wide) widthwise, and end with the stitches after the pattern repeat. Work the corners as shown. Work Rows 1–3 once.

In Row 2, always work the groups of [2 double crochets into the same stitch and crocheted together, chain 3, 2 double crochets into the same stitch and crocheted together] into the same stitch (= 1 single crochet); at the corners, work the sequence of [2 double crochets into the same stitch and crocheted together, chain 5, 2 double crochets into the same stitch and crocheted together] into the chain.

In Row 3, always work the double crochets and single crochets into the chain space of the previous row, around the chain.

Chart Key

○ Chain 1

✕ 1 single crochet

┬ 1 half double crochet

┬ 1 double crochet

◊ Dc2tog-in-1: 2 double crochets into the same stitch and crocheted together

 1 picot of 3: Chain 3, and then join with 1 slip stitch back into the first chain

 [1 double crochet, chain 3, 1 double crochet] into the same stitch

CLOVER LEAVES

[start with 3 ch + 3 beg-ch]

Work in rows, following the chart. Work Rows 1–4 once, following the direction of the arrows. Repeat Rows 3 and 4 for pattern, until the desired length has been reached.

From Row 2 on, always work the stitches into the chain space of the previous row, around the chain.

Chart Key

o   Chain 1

●   1 slip stitch

✗   1 single crochet

⊤   1 half double crochet

⊤   1 double crochet

⨍   1 treble crochet

[1 double crochet, chain 3, 1 double crochet] into the same spot

[1 double crochet, chain 3, 1 double crochet, chain 3, 1 double crochet, chain 3, 1 double crochet] into the same stitch

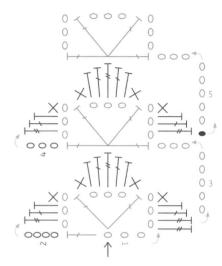

OPEN-FAN LACE EDGING

[multiple of 8 + 1 ch + 1 beg-ch]

Work in rows, following the chart. If the edging is crocheted directly onto the main piece, the selvedge stitches of the crocheted or knitted main piece replace the beginning chain. Begin every row with the stitches before the pattern repeat, repeat the marked pattern repeat (8 sts wide) widthwise, ending with a full repeat. Work Rows 1–4 once.

In Rows 2 and 3, always work the single crochet into the chain space of the chain or chain arc of the previous row.

Chart Key

o   Chain 1

✗   1 single crochet

⊤   1 double crochet

⊤   1 half double crochet

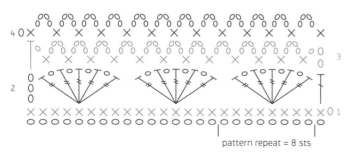

pattern repeat = 8 sts

[1 treble crochet, chain 1, 1 treble crochet, chain 1, 1 treble crochet, chain 1, 1 treble crochet, chain 1, 1 treble crochet] into the same stitch

SHELL EDGING

[multiple of 6 + 3 beg-ch]

Work in rows, following the chart. If the edging is crocheted directly onto the main piece, the selvedge stitches of the crocheted or knitted main piece replace the beginning chain. Begin every row with the stitches before the pattern repeat, repeat the marked pattern repeat (6 sts wide) widthwise, and end with the stitches after the pattern repeat. Work Rows 1–4 once.

Chart Key

○   Chain 1

✕   1 single crochet

 1 double crochet

Dc3-in-1: 3 double crochets into the same stitch

Dc4-in-1: 4 double crochets into the same stitch

Dc7-in-1: 7 double crochets into the same stitch

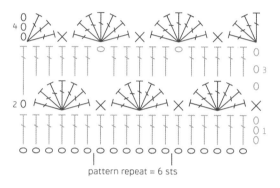

pattern repeat = 6 sts

PETAL FAN EDGING

[multiple of 18 + 3 ch + 3 beg-ch]

Chart Key

○ Chain 1   ✕ 1 single crochet

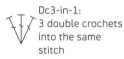 1 half double crochet

 1 double crochet

1 treble crochet

Work in rows, following the chart. If the edging is crocheted directly onto the main piece, the selvedge stitches of the crocheted or knitted main piece replace the beginning chain. Begin every row with the stitches before the pattern repeat, repeat the marked pattern repeat (18 sts wide) widthwise, and end with the stitches after the pattern repeat. Work Rows 1–5 once.

In Row 4, always work the treble crochets, and in Row 5, the groups of double crochet and single crochet, into the chain space of the previous row, around the chain.

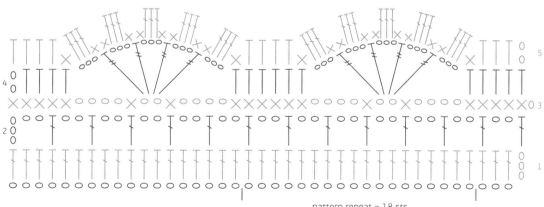

pattern repeat = 18 sts

AIRY SHELL EDGING

[multiple of 6 + 1 ch + 2 sts per corner + 1 beg-ch]

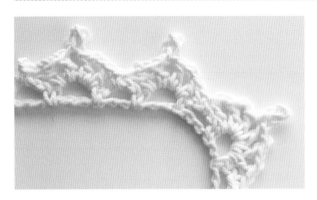

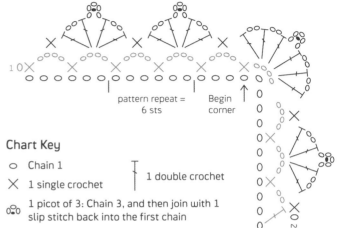

pattern repeat = 6 sts

Begin corner

Chart Key

o Chain 1

✕ 1 single crochet

⌐ 1 double crochet

1 picot of 3: Chain 3, and then join with 1 slip stitch back into the first chain

Work in rows, following the chart; Row 1 is a WS row. If the edging is crocheted directly onto the main piece, the selvedge stitches of the crocheted or knitted main piece replace the beginning chain. Begin every row with the stitches before the pattern repeat, repeat the marked pattern repeat (6 sts wide) widthwise, and end with the stitches after the pattern repeat. Work the corners as shown. Work Rows 1 and 2 once.

In Row 2, begin with 1 single crochet in the next chain space. The double crochets in Row 2 are always worked into the chain space of the previous row, around the chain.

CROWNED ARCED EDGING

[multiple of 4 + 1 ch + 2 sts per corner + 1 beg-ch]

Work in rows, following the chart. If the edging is crocheted directly onto the main piece, the selvedge stitches of the crocheted or knitted main piece replace the beginning chain. Begin every row with the stitches before the pattern repeat, repeat the marked pattern repeat (4 sts wide) widthwise, and end with the stitches after the pattern repeat. Work the corners as shown. Work Rows 1 and 2 once.

In Row 2, work the single crochets into the chain space, around the chain.

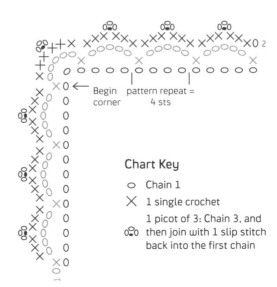

Begin corner

pattern repeat = 4 sts

Chart Key

o Chain 1

✕ 1 single crochet

1 picot of 3: Chain 3, and then join with 1 slip stitch back into the first chain

WAVE BORDER
[multiple of 4 + 1 ch + 3 beg-ch]

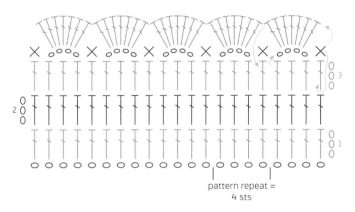

pattern repeat =
4 sts

Chart Key

o Chain 1   X 1 single crochet   ↑ 1 double crochet

Work in rows, following the chart. If the edging is cro-cheted directly onto the main piece, the selvedge stitches of the crocheted or knitted main piece replace the beginning chain. Begin every row with the stitches before the pattern repeat, repeat the marked pattern repeat (4 sts wide) widthwise, and end with the stitches after the pattern repeat. Work Rows 1–3 once.

In Row 3, follow the direction of the arrows: Atop the double crochets of the previous row, always work *[4 double crochets, chain 4], join from the back with 1 single crochet into the base of the first double crochet, work 7 double crochets into the chain space of the chain arc, and then repeat from * for pattern.

POINTY ON BOTH SIDES
[multiple of 8 + 6 sts per corner + 1 beg-ch]

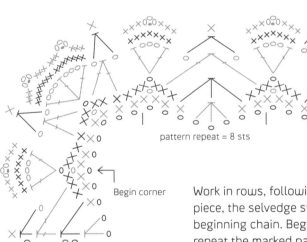

pattern repeat = 8 sts

Begin corner

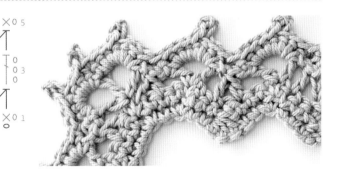

Work in rows, following the chart. If the edging is crocheted directly onto the main piece, the selvedge stitches of the crocheted or knitted main piece replace the beginning chain. Begin every row with the stitches before the pattern repeat, repeat the marked pattern repeat (8 sts wide) widthwise, and end with the stitches after the pattern repeat. Work the corners as shown. Work Rows 1–5 once.

In Row 4, always work the single crochets into the chain space of the previous row, around the chain.

Chart Key

o Chain 1

X 1 single crochet

o°o 1 picot of 3: Chain 3, and then join with 1 slip stitch back into the first chain

↑ 1 double crochet

Λ Hdc2tog: Half double crochet 2 stitches together

Λ Hdc3tog: Half double crochet 3 stitches together

Λ Dc2tog: Double crochet 2 stitches together

 [1 double crochet, chain 3, 1 double crochet] into the same stitch

 [1 double crochet, chain 3, 1 double crochet, chain 3, 1 double crochet] into the same stitch

415 RUFFLE TRIM

[multiple of 16 + 4 ch + 3 beg-ch]

Work in rows, following the chart. If the edging is crocheted directly onto the main piece, the selvedge stitches of the crocheted or knitted main piece replace the beginning chain. Begin every row with the stitches before the pattern repeat, repeat the marked pattern repeat (16 sts wide) widthwise, ending either with a complete repeat or with the stitches after the repeat. Work Rows 1–8 once.

From Row 2 on, always work the double crochets into the chain space of the previous row, around the chain.

This border can be used as edging with flounce effect.

Chart Key

o   Chain 1

⊤   1 double crochet

   Dc3tog: Double crochet 3 stitches together

   Dc2tog: Double crochet 2 stitches together

⋀   2 double crochets crocheted together: Work the first double crochet in the chain space of the previous row, but don't complete the last step yet; skip 1 double crochet of the previous row. Now work the second double crochet into the next chain arc, and crochet both double crochets together.

pattern repeat = 16 sts

PINEAPPLE EDGING

[multiple of 23 + 2 beg-ch]

Work in rows, following the chart. If the edging is crocheted directly onto the main piece, the selvedge stitches of the crocheted or knitted main piece replace the beginning chain. Begin every row with the stitches before the pattern repeat, repeat the marked pattern repeat (23 sts wide) widthwise, and end with the stitches after the pattern repeat. Work Rows 1–11 once.

In Rows 4–11, work the double crochets in the chain space of the previous row, around the chain.

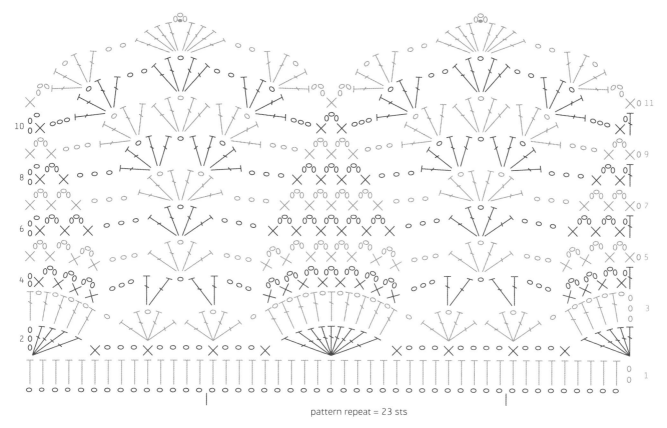

pattern repeat = 23 sts

Chart Key

○ Chain 1

✕ 1 single crochet

⊤ 1 half double crochet

⊤ 1 double crochet

 1 picot of 3: Chain 3, and then join with 1 slip stitch back into the first chain

Dc5-in-1: 5 double crochets into the same stitch

Dc4-in-1: 4 double crochets into the same stitch

[2 double crochets, chain 1, 2 double crochets, chain 1, 2 double crochets] into the same stitch

Dc9-in-1: 9 double crochets into the same stitch

GRANNY SQUARES

417 RETRO SQUARE

Begin the square by working a magic ring plus 3 beginning chains, and then work in rounds, following the chart. Work Rounds 1–4 once, changing color after every round.

In Rounds 3 and 4, always work the double crochets in the chain space of the chain or chain arc of the previous round.

Chart Key

○ 1 adjustable magic ring

o Chain 1

● 1 slip stitch

T 1 double crochet

Dc2tog-in-1: 2 double crochets into the same stitch and crocheted together

◄ The arrow indicates where to join the working yarn: After Rounds 2 and 3, the end of the round and the color change are no longer in the same spot; the working yarn is joined in a new spot with a slip stitch.

418 FOLIAGE

Begin the square with a 6-chain ring plus 3 beginning chains. To make the chain ring, begin with a chain of 6 and join into the round with a slip stitch. Work in rounds, following the chart. Work Rounds 1–6 once.

Instead of using a slip stitch, in Round 4, join with 1 half double crochet into the top chain of the beginning chain.

In Round 1, work the double crochets in the chain space of the ring; in Rounds 2–6, work the double crochets in the chain space of the chain or chain arc.

Chart Key

⬭	Chain 1
●	1 slip stitch
⊤	1 half double crochet
╪	1 double crochet
⋀	Dc3tog: Double crochet 3 stitches together
⋀	Dc4tog: Double crochet 4 stitches together

419 CLASSIC SQUARE

Begin the square by working a magic ring plus 3 beginning chains, and then work in rounds, following the chart. Work Rounds 1–4 once, changing colors after Rounds 2 and 3.

Always work the double crochet in the chain space of the chain or chain arc of the previous round.

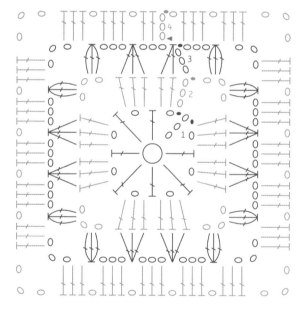

Chart Key

○   1 adjustable magic ring

○   Chain 1

●   1 slip stitch

┬   1 double crochet

⋀   Dc3tog: Double crochet 3 stitches together

◄   The arrow indicates where to join the working yarn: After Round 3, the end of the round and the color change are no longer in the same spot; the working yarn is joined in a new spot with a slip stitch.

420 TRELLIS SQUARE WITH FLOWER CENTER

Begin the square by working a magic ring plus 3 beginning chains, and then work in rounds, following the chart. Work Rounds 1–5 once, changing color after Round 1.

Instead of joining Rounds 2, 3, and 4 with 1 slip stitch, use a double crochet: At the end of Round 2, work the double crochet into the joined top of the double crochet 2 stitches together from the beginning of the round; at the end of Rounds 3 and 4, work the double crochet into the first single crochet of the round.

In Round 5, work the single crochets and double crochets in the chain spaces of the previous round; at the beginning of the round, work the 2 double crochets around the double crochet of the previous round.

Chart Key

◯ 1 adjustable magic ring

o Chain 1

• 1 slip stitch

✕ 1 single crochet

† 1 double crochet

Dc2tog: Double crochet 2 stitches together

Dc3tog: Double crochet 3 stitches together

The arrow indicates where to join the working yarn: After Round 1, the end of the round and the color change are no longer in the same spot; the working yarn is joined in a new spot with a slip stitch.

421. FLORAL TRIANGLE

Begin the triangle with a chain ring plus 3 beginning chains. To make the chain ring, begin with a chain of 5 and join into the round with a slip stitch. Work in rounds, following the chart. Work Rounds 1–4 once.

In Round 1, work the double crochets in the chain space of the chain ring, around the chain. In Rounds 2 and 4, always work the 3 double or treble crochets crocheted together directly into the chain; in Round 3, always work the double crochets in the chain space, around the chain.

Chart Key

o	Chain 1
●	1 slip stitch
✕	1 single crochet
┬	1 double crochet
	Dc2tog: Double crochet 2 stitches together
	Dc3tog: Double crochet 3 stitches together
	Dc3tog-in-1: 3 double crochets into the same stitch and crocheted together
	Tr3tog-in-1: 3 treble crochets into the same stitch and crocheted together
o₀o	1 picot of 3: Chain 3, and then join with 1 slip stitch back into the first chain

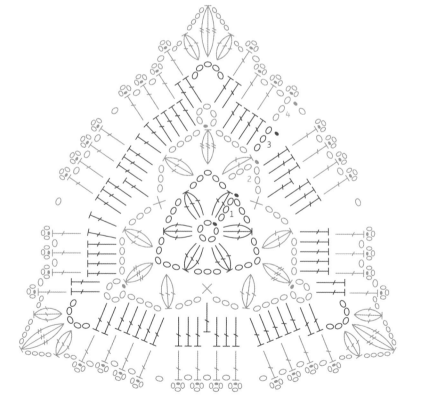

422 SQUARE WITH EYELET DIAGONALS

Begin the square with an adjustable magic ring + 3 beginning chains, and work in the round, following the chart. Work Rounds 1–6 once.

Chart Key

◯   1 adjustable magic ring

○   Chain 1

●   1 slip stitch

⊤   1 double crochet

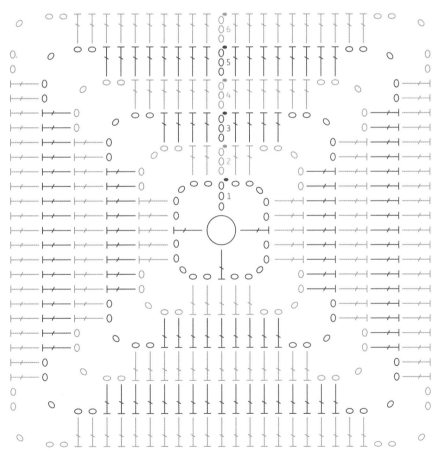

423 FLOWER IN THE GARDEN

Begin the square with a chain ring plus 3 beginning chains. To make the chain ring, chain 4 and join into the round with a slip stitch. Work in rounds, following the chart. Work Rounds 1–5 once, changing colors after Rounds 1, 2, and 3.

In Round 1, work the double crochets in the chain space of the chain ring, and in Rounds 3 and 4, always work the double crochets in the chain space, around the chain.

Chart Key

○   Chain 1

●   1 slip stitch

✕   1 single crochet

┬   1 double crochet

Dc2tog-in-1: 2 double crochets into the same stitch and crocheted together

Dc3tog-in-1: 3 double crochets into the same stitch and crocheted together

◄   The arrow indicates where to join the working yarn: After Round 3, the end of the round and the color change are no longer in the same spot; the working yarn is joined in a new spot with a slip stitch.

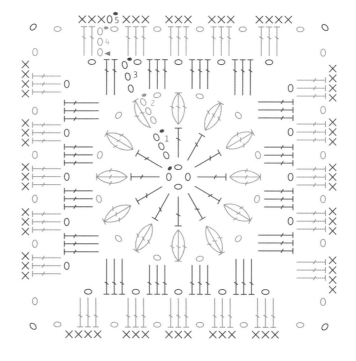

424 PETALS IN A SQUARE

Begin the square by working an adjustable magic ring plus 3
beginning chains, and then work in rounds, following the chart.
Work Rounds 1–4 once, changing color after Round 1.

In Round 3, always work the double crochets in the chain
space of the previous round.

Chart Key

◯ 1 adjustable magic ring

o Chain 1

● 1 slip stitch

| 1 double crochet

 Dc4tog-in-1: 4 double crochets
into the same stitch and crocheted together

 Dc5tog-in-1: 5 double crochets
into the same stitch and crocheted together

 Dc2-in-1: 2 double crochets into
the same stitch

 Dc5-in-1: 5 double crochets into
the same stitch

425 TREBLE CROCHET SQUARE

Begin the square with a chain ring plus 1 beginning chain. To make the chain ring, begin with a chain of 6 and join into the round with a slip stitch. Work in rounds, following the chart. Work Rounds 1–6 once, changing colors after Rounds 2, 3, and 4.

In Round 1, work the single crochets in the chain space of the chain ring.

Chart Key

- ○ Chain 1
- ● 1 slip stitch
- ✕ 1 single crochet
- ⊤ 1 half double crochet
- ⊤ 1 double crochet
- ⊤ 1 treble crochet
- ⊤✕ [1 single crochet and 1 half double crochet] into the same stitch
- ✕⊤ [1 half double crochet and 1 single crochet] into the same stitch
- ⊤⊤ [1 double crochet and 1 treble crochet] into the same stitch
- ◄ The arrow indicates where to join the working yarn: After Rounds 2, 3, and 4, the end of the round and the color change are no longer in the same spot; the working yarn is joined in a new spot with a slip stitch.

426 SHIP'S WHEEL

Begin the square with a chain ring plus 3 beginning chains. To make the chain ring, chain 4 and join into the round with a slip stitch. Work in rounds, following the chart. Work Rounds 1–6 once.

In Round 1, work the double crochets in the chain space of the chain ring, around the chain.

Chart Key

○   Chain 1

●   1 slip stitch

✕   1 single crochet

ǂ   1 double crochet

V   Dc2-in-1: 2 double crochets into the same stitch

427 RAISED FLOWER IN A SQUARE

Chart Key

○	Chain 1	●	1 slip stitch
✕	1 single crochet	│	1 half double crochet
┼	1 double crochet	⌡	1 bpsc worked below: Back post single crochet around the double crochet or bpsc of the next-to-last round
	Tr3tog-in-1: 3 treble crochets into the same stitch and crocheted together		Dtr3tog-in-1: 3 double treble crochets into the same stitch and crocheted together
	[3 double crochets, chain 3, 3 double crochets] into the same stitch		

Begin the square with a chain ring plus 3 beginning chains. To make the chain ring, begin with a chain of 6 and join into the round with a slip stitch. Work in rounds, following the chart. Work Rounds 1–8 once.

In Round 1, work the double crochets in the chain space of the chain ring, around the chain; in Rounds 2–6, work all stitches in the chain space of the previous round, around the chain. In Round 8, work the double crochets directly into the chain.

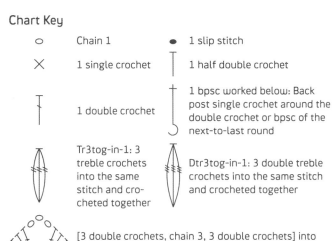

428 FLOWER IN A SQUARE

Begin the square with a chain ring plus 1 beginning chain. To make the chain ring, begin with a chain of 8 and join into the round with a slip stitch. Work in rounds, following the chart. Work Rounds 1–7 once, changing colors after Round 3.

In Round 1, work the single crochets in the chain space of the chain ring; in Round 3, work the stitches in the chain space, around the chain.

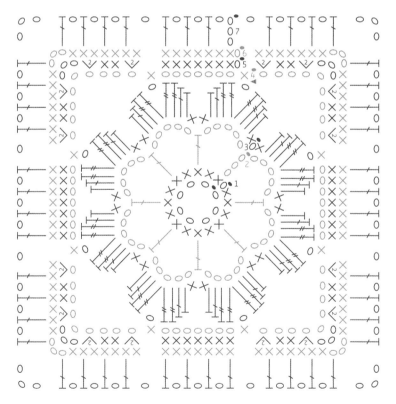

Chart Key

○	Chain 1
●	1 slip stitch
✕	1 single crochet
⊤	1 half double crochet
⊤	1 double crochet
⊤	1 treble crochet
⋁	Sc2-in-1: 2 single crochets into the same stitch

The arrow indicates where to join the working yarn: After Round 3, the end of the round and the color change are no longer in the same spot; the working yarn is joined in a new spot with a slip stitch.

429 PINWHEEL

Begin the square with an adjustable magic ring plus 1 beginning chain, and then work in rounds, following the chart. Work Rounds 1–9 once, changing colors after Rounds 4, 5, 6, and 7.

Chart Key

○   1 adjustable magic ring

o   Chain 1

●   1 slip stitch

✕   1 single crochet

⊤   1 half double crochet

⸗   1 treble crochet

[1 double crochet, chain 3, 1 double crochet] into the same stitch

1 double crochet

The arrow indicates where to join the working yarn: After Rounds 4, 5, 6, and 7, the end of the round and the color change are no longer in the same spot; the working yarn is joined in a new spot with a slip stitch.

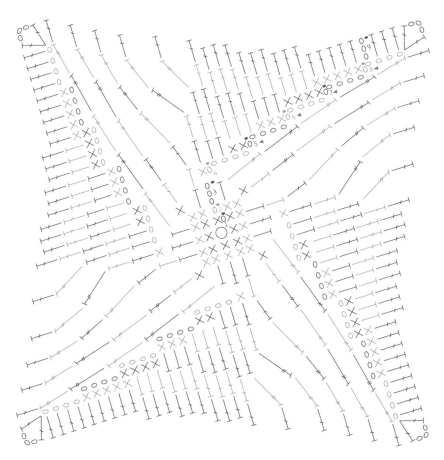

430 FLAME FLOWER

Begin the square by working an adjustable magic ring plus 3 beginning chains, and then work in rounds, following the chart. Work Rounds 1–5 once, changing colors after Rounds 2, 3, and 4.

Always work the double crochet or half double crochet in the chain space of the chain or chain arc of the previous round.

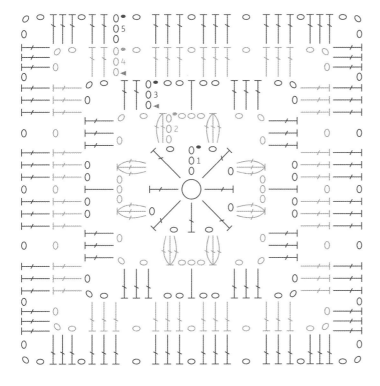

Chart Key

◯   1 adjustable magic ring

○   Chain 1

●   1 slip stitch

│   1 half double crochet

┤   1 double crochet

⋀   Dc2tog: Double crochet 2 stitches together

⋔   Dc3tog: Double crochet 3 stitches together

◄   The arrow indicates where to join the working yarn: After Rounds 2 and 3, the end of the round and the color change are no longer in the same spot; the working yarn is joined in a new spot with a slip stitch.

431 LACE SQUARE

Begin the square with a chain ring plus 3 beginning chains. To make the chain ring, begin with a chain of 8 and join into the round with a slip stitch. Work in rounds, following the chart. Work Rounds 1–5 once.

Instead of joining Round 2 with a slip stitch, work 1 double crochet into the beginning chain.

In Round 1, work the double crochets in the chain space of the chain ring, around the chain. In Round 3, work the treble crochet 2 stitches together or the treble crochet 3 stitches together always in the chain space of the previous round, around the chain (at the beginning and at the end of Round 3, around the arc of double crochet and chain).

Chart Key

○	Chain 1
●	1 slip stitch
✕	1 single crochet
†	1 double crochet
⟋⟍	Tr2tog: Treble crochet 2 stitches together
⟋⟍	Tr3tog: Treble crochet 3 stitches together
⊻	[1 double crochet, chain 1, 1 double crochet] into the same stitch

432 STARBURST SQUARE

Begin the square with a chain ring plus 1 beginning chain. To make the chain ring, begin with a chain of 6 and join into the round with a slip stitch. Work in rounds, following the chart. Work Rounds 1–4 once, changing colors after Round 2.

In Round 1, work the single crochets in the chain space of the chain ring. In Rounds 3 and 4, work the double crochet 2 stitches together or the double crochet 3 stitches together and the single crochets in the chain space of the previous round. In Round 3, work the single crochet into the middle (8th) chain of the chain arc of 15.

Chart Key

○	Chain 1
●	1 slip stitch
✕	1 single crochet
⑂	Dc2tog: Double crochet 2 stitches together
⑃	Dc3tog: Double crochet 3 stitches together
(15	Chain arc of 15 chains

◄ The arrow indicates where to join the working yarn: After Round 2, the end of the round and the color change are no longer in the same spot; the working yarn is joined in a new spot with a slip stitch.

433 FLORAL CROSS MOTIF

Begin the square with a chain ring plus 3 beginning chains. To make the chain ring, begin with a chain of 6 and join into the round with a slip stitch. Work in rounds, following the chart. Work Rounds 1–6 once, working in turned rounds beginning with Round 2, changing the direction of the round at the end of every round (see arrows).

In Round 1, work the double crochets in the chain space of the chain ring, around the chain.

Chart Key

○ Chain 1

● 1 slip stitch

┬ 1 double crochet

⋔ Dc2tog-in-1: 2 double crochets into the same stitch and crocheted together

⬙ Dc3tog-in-1: 3 double crochets into the same stitch and crocheted together

⋎ [1 double crochet, chain 1, 1 double crochet] into the same stitch

⋎ [1 treble crochet, chain 4, 1 treble crochet] into the same stitch

434 ITALIAN SQUARE

Begin the square with a chain ring plus 3 beginning chains. To make the chain ring, begin with a chain of 8 and join into the round with a slip stitch. Work in rounds, following the chart. Work Rounds 1–4 once.

In Round 1, work 2 double crochets into the same stitch and crocheted together or 3 double crochets into the same stitch and crocheted together in the chain space of the chain ring.

Chart Key

○   Chain 1

●   1 slip stitch

╫   1 double crochet

Dc2tog-in-1: 2 double crochets into the same stitch and crocheted together

Dc3tog-in-1: 3 double crochets into the same stitch and crocheted together

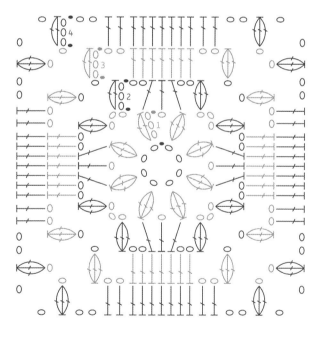

435 TRIANGLE WITH BLOSSOM CENTER

Begin the triangle with a chain ring plus 4 beginning chains. To make the chain ring, begin with a chain of 8 and join into the round with a slip stitch. Work in rounds, following the chart. Work Rounds 1–5 once, changing colors after Rounds 1 and 2.

In Round 1, double crochet 2 stitches together, triple crochet 2 stitches together, and triple crochet 3 stitches together into the chain space of the chain ring. In Rounds 3–5, always work the corner double crochets into the chain space of the previous round.

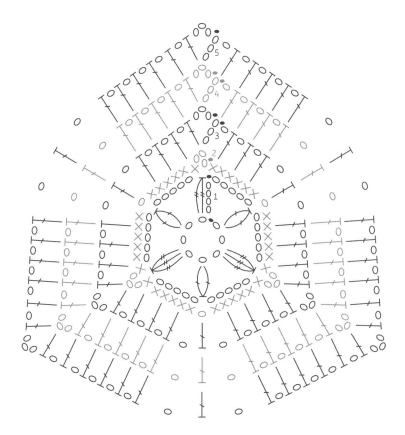

Chart Key

◯	Chain 1
●	1 slip stitch
⊤	1 double crochet
⋀	Dc2tog: Double crochet 2 stitches together
⋀	Tr2tog: Treble crochet 2 stitches together
⋀	Tr3tog: Treble crochet 3 stitches together

436 PUFF STITCH SQUARE

Begin the square with a chain ring plus 3 beginning chains. To make the chain ring, chain 4 and join into the round with a slip stitch. Work in rounds, following the chart. Work Rounds 1–4 once.

In Round 1, work the double crochets in the chain space of the chain ring, around the chain.

Chart Key

○	Chain 1
●	1 slip stitch
	1 double crochet
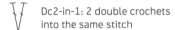	Dc2-in-1: 2 double crochets into the same stitch
	Dc3-in-1: 3 double crochets into the same stitch
	1 puff stitch at the beginning of the round: [Yarn over hook once, insert the hook into the chain of the previous round, pull the working yarn through] 3 times, slightly lengthen the loops, draw the working yarn through all 7 loops on the hook at once
	1 puff stitch: [Yarn over hook once, insert the hook into the chain of the previous round, pull the working yarn through] 4 times, slightly lengthen the loops, draw the working yarn through all 9 loops on the hook at once
	Dc4tog-in-1: 4 double crochets into the same stitch and crocheted together
	Dc5tog-in-1: 5 double crochets into the same stitch and crocheted together

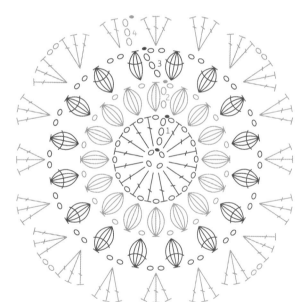

437 LATTICE CROSS

Begin the square by working an adjustable magic ring plus 1 beginning chain, and then work in rounds, following the chart. Work Rounds 1–7 once.

From Round 3 on, work the double crochet 2 stitches together, triple crochet 2 stitches together, and 3 double crochets into the same stitch and crocheted together in the chain space of the previous round, around the chain.

Chart Key

◯   1 adjustable magic ring

○   Chain 1

●   1 slip stitch

✕   1 single crochet

┬   1 double crochet

⑂   Dc2tog: Double crochet 2 stitches together

⑂   Dc3tog: Double crochet 3 stitches together

⑂   Dc3tog-in-1: 3 double crochets into the same stitch and crocheted together

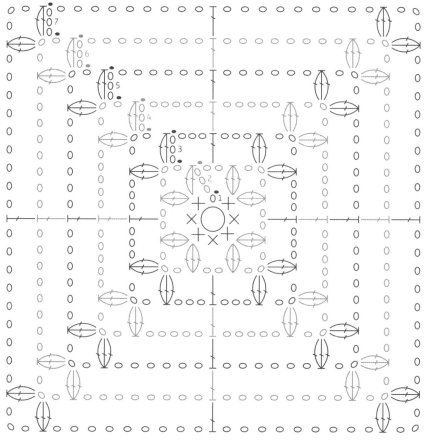

438 FOUR-LEAF CLOVER

Begin the square with a chain ring plus 3 beginning chains. To make the chain ring, begin with a chain of 10 and join into the round with a slip stitch. Work in rounds, following the chart. Work Rounds 1–4 once.

In Round 1, work the double crochets in the chain space of the chain ring, around the chain.

Chart Key

◯	Chain 1
●	1 slip stitch
✕	1 single crochet
⊤	1 double crochet
⋁	Dc2-in-1: 2 double crochets into the same stitch
⋀	Dc5tog: Double crochet 5 stitches together
⋀	Dc6-tog: Double crochet 6 stitches together
⋁◯◯	[1 double crochet, chain 2, 1 double crochet] into the same stitch

439 WINDMILL SQUARE

Begin the square by working an adjustable magic ring plus 3 beginning chains, and then work in rounds, following the chart. Work Rounds 1–5 once.

Instead of joining Rounds 3, 4, and 5 as usual with a slip stitch, work 1 double crochet into the top chain of the beginning chain.

In Rounds 4 and 5, work the first double crochet around the last double crochet of the previous round (= the double crochet at the end of the round).

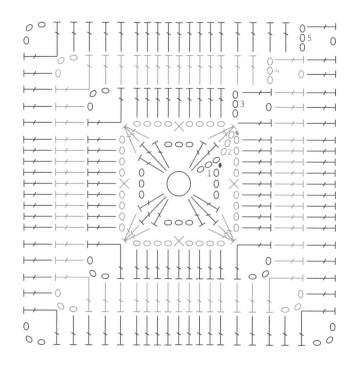

Chart Key

◯	1 adjustable magic ring
◦	Chain 1
●	1 slip stitch
✕	1 single crochet
†	1 double crochet
⋀	Dc2tog: Double crochet 2 stitches together
⋀	Dc3tog: Double crochet 3 stitches together
◦◦◦	[1 double crochet, chain 3, 1 double crochet] into the same stitch

440 STAR FLOWER

Begin by working an adjustable magic ring plus 3 beginning chains, and then work in rounds, following the chart. Work Rounds 1–3 once, changing colors after every round.

Always work the double crochets in the chain space of the previous round, around the chain.

Chart Key

⭕ 1 adjustable magic ring

◯ Chain 1
● 1 slip stitch

⏉ 1 double crochet

Dc2tog: Double crochet 2 stitches together

Dc3tog: Double crochet 3 stitches together

◀ The arrow indicates where to join the working yarn: After Rounds 1, 2, and 3, the end of the round and the color change are no longer in the same spot; the working yarn is joined in a new spot with a slip stitch.

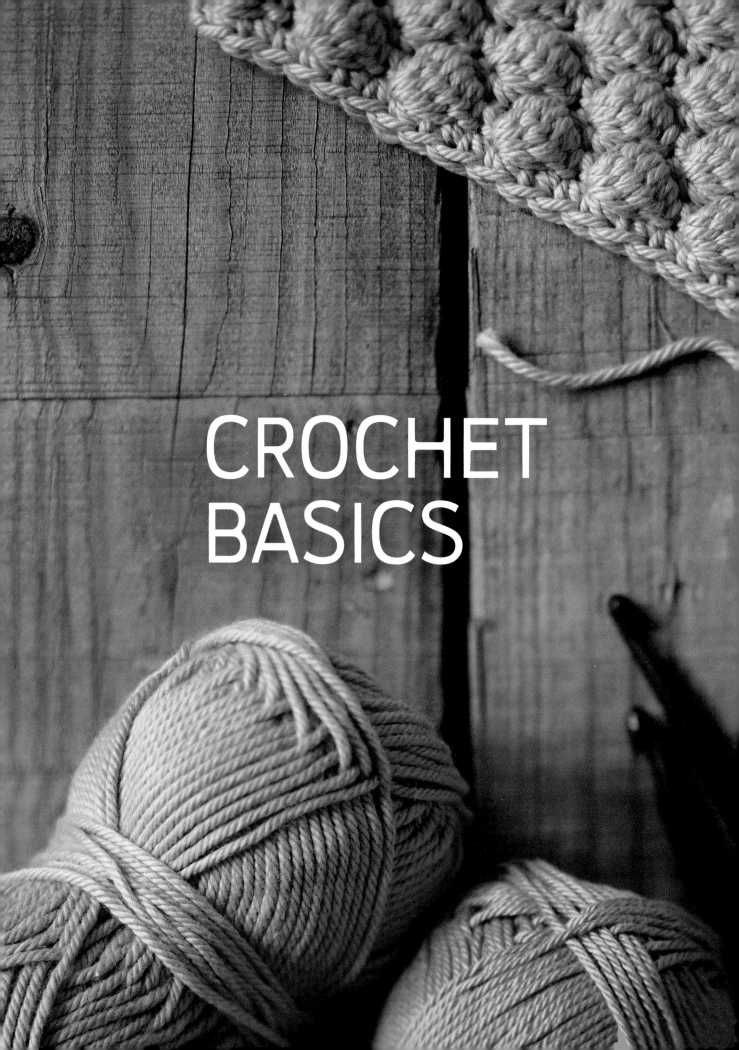

CROCHET BASICS

ABBREVIATIONS

Beg-ch: beginning chain of a row/round for height adjustment
Bel: below
Blo: back loop only
Bp: back post
Ch: chain
Dc: double crochet
Flo: front loop only
Fp: front post
Hdc: half double crochet
RS: right side
Sl st: slip stitch
St ct: stitch count
St(s): stitch(es)
Tog: together
Tr: treble crochet
WS: wrong side

SYMBOLS

➥ Stitch pattern is worked in the round

+1➚ For this stitch pattern, it is recommended to use a hook 1 mm larger than for other stitch patterns worked in the same yarn. This will prevent the crocheted fabric from turning out too dense, and it is also much easier to insert the crochet hook into stitches that are not too tight.

ABOUT THE FOUNDATION CHAIN

At the beginning of most stitch patterns, numbers needed for calculating the length of the foundation chain are listed within square brackets. Most crocheted pieces start with this chain—the first pattern row will be worked into it.

If there are two or three numbers, the first number shows the width of the pattern repeat, which has to be repeated widthwise to continue the stitch pattern over the whole row. If a second number is listed, it states any additonal stitches needed, for instance, to divide a stitch pattern for working mirror-inverted. The last number is the number of chains needed to reach the height of the first stitch in the first row or in the first round. For example, [multiple of 3 + 1 beg-ch] means the number of chains in the foundation chain has to be a multiple of 3, plus 1 additional chain for height adjustment. The example [multiple of 4 + 1 ch + 3 beg-ch] means the number of chains has to be a multiple of 4, plus 1 additional chain for the stitch pattern, plus 3 additional chains for height adjustment.

The specific chain into which the first stitch at the beginning of the first row has to be worked is marked in the crochet chart.

For motifs or pattern panels, the number of chains for the whole width is given.

HOW TO READ THE WRITTEN INSTRUCTIONS

Square brackets within a stitch pattern description or Chart Key either contain a group of stitches, all to be worked into the same stitch, or show a sequence consisting of several stitches that has to be repeated multiple times.

THE CROCHET CHART

A crochet chart represents the graphic expression of a stitch pattern. Every stitch in the pattern is assigned a specific symbol. It can show either rows or rounds, which are numbered at the sides or at the beginning of the round. How the symbols are arranged in relation to each other shows into which specific stitch another stitch has to be worked. Stitches are worked into the stitch of the previous row atop which they are shown in the chart (or into stitches in rows below as indicated in stitch key). If stitches are to be worked in the chain space of single chains or chain arcs (around the chain), the instructions will specifically mention this.

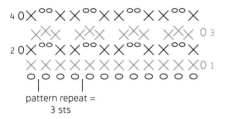

pattern repeat =
3 sts

HOW TO READ CROCHET CHARTS

Right-side (RS) rows are always read from right to left, wrong-side (WS) rows from left to right. Chart symbols are explained in the order in which they appear in the chart.

Arrows may be used to show the direction of work, or mark the spot in which the hook has to be inserted. Other special meanings will always be explained within either the written instructions or the Chart Key.

Two or more consecutive chains within the stitch pattern are called a "chain arc" in the pattern.

CROCHET CHART SYMBOLS

As a basic rule, if symbols converge at the bottom, all of these stitches will be worked into the same stitch or spot (have a shared base). If symbols converge at the top, all these stitches are crocheted together (have a shared top). A symbol's shape—straight or curved—does not have different meanings, it just resembles the appearance of the stitch in the crocheted fabric; the symbol meaning and order of working steps are explained in the Chart Key.

For easier visualization, rows or rounds are shown in alternating black and gray so that the row flow can be easily followed; this is especially useful for patterns that feature intertwined or interlocking stitches. For some of the stitch patterns, actual color changes are shown in the chart, too.

Furthermore, stitch combinations within the same row or round also are shown in two colors to make them easier to read and apply to the actual crocheted piece.

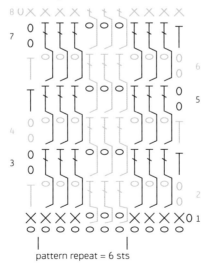

pattern repeat = 6 sts

THE GAUGE SWATCH

Before starting any crochet project, work a gauge swatch. This is necessary to find out whether the chosen hook size matches the yarn and to evaluate how the crocheted fabric feels to the touch. A gauge swatch is essential for calculating stitch and row counts for an actual item.

BASIC STITCH PATTERNS

ALLOVER TEXTURE
[odd st ct + 3 beg-ch] **18**

BLOCK MESH
[multiple of 3 + 1 beg-ch] **19**

BOSNIAN CROCHET STITCH
➡ [any st ct] **33**

BOW PATTERN
[odd st ct + 1 beg-ch] **27**

BROAD HORIZONTAL RIDGES
[any st ct + 2 beg-ch] **23**

BROAD SLIP STITCH RIDGES
+1 ➡ [any st ct + 1 beg-ch] **11**

BUD PATTERN
[even or odd st ct + 1 beg-ch] **24**

COMBINED STRIPES
[any st ct + 3 beg-ch] **14**

COMPACT TRIANGLES
[multiple of 4 + 1 ch + 4 beg-ch] **32**

CORD-LOOK TEXTURE
+1 ➡ [any st ct + 1 beg-ch] **11**

CURLY STRIPES
[odd st ct + 1 beg-ch] **12**

DOUBLE CROCHET DUO
[odd st ct + 3 beg-ch] **28**

DOUBLE CROCHET TRIO
[multiple of 4 + 1 ch + 1 beg-ch] **20**

DOUBLE CROCHET VS
[multiple of 3 + 1 ch + 3 beg-ch] **31**

FISH SCALE PATTERN
[even st ct + 1 beg-ch] **21**

FLAT SINGLE CROCHETS
+1 ➡ [any st ct + 2 beg-ch] **11**

GRITTY ALLOVER PATTERN
[odd st ct + 1 beg-ch] **16**

HERRINGBONE PATTERN
[any st ct + 2 beg-ch] **17**

HORIZONTAL RIDGES WITH
EYELETS
[odd st ct + 3 beg-ch] **25**

HORIZONTAL V-STITCH RIDGES
[any st ct + 1 beg-ch] **13**

JOINED DOUBLE CROCHETS
[odd st ct + 3 beg-ch] **25**

KNIT-LOOK GARTER STITCH
+1 ➡ [any st ct + 1 beg-ch] **10**

KNIT-LOOK STOCKINETTE
+1 ➡ [any st ct] **35**

KNOT PATTERN
[odd st ct + 2 beg-ch] **28**

KNOT STITCH IN ROWS
[any st ct + 1 beg-ch] **14**

KNOT STITCH IN THE ROUND
➡ [any st ct] **34**

KNOTTED DOUBLE CROCHET
[any st ct + 2 beg-ch] **14**

KNOTTED HALF DOUBLE CROCHET
[any st ct + 1 beg-ch] **15**

LITTLE BELLS
[even st ct + 1 beg-ch] **30**

LITTLE COMBS
[odd st ct + 1 beg-ch] **18**

LITTLE LATTICE
[odd st ct + 1 beg-ch] **23**

LITTLE TREE PATTERN
[odd st ct + 3 beg-ch] **29**

MESH TREE PATTERN
➡ [multiple of 3] **34**

NARROW TEXTURED RIDGES
➡ [any st ct] **33**

PLAIT STITCH
➡ [any st ct] **35**

PEARL EYELETS
[odd st ct + 1 beg-ch] **18**

PIXEL PATTERN
➡ [even st ct] **35**

RIDGED LINES
[any st ct + 1 beg-ch] **12**

RIDGES AND BANDS
[multiple of 6 + 3 beg-ch] **19**

RIDGES WITH HALF DOUBLE
CROCHETS
[any st ct + 2 beg-ch] **13**

SEPARATED BOXES
[multiple of 4 + 1 ch + 2 beg-ch] **26**

SHALLOW NUPP PATTERN
[multiple of 4 + 3 ch + 1 beg-ch] **22**

SIMPLE TEXTURED PATTERN
[even st ct + 1 beg-ch] **20**

SINGLE CROCHET RIDGES
[any st ct + 1 beg-ch] **12**

SINGLE CROCHETS
➡ [any st ct] **33**

SLING RIDGES
[any st ct + 1 beg-ch] **24**

SLING ROOFTOPS
[odd st ct + 1 beg-ch] **27**

SLIP STITCH RIDGES
+1 ➡ [any st ct + 1 beg-ch] **10**

SHELL AND FAN PATTERNS

CLUSTERS, POPCORNS, BOBBLES, PUFFS, AND NUPPS

SPIKE STITCH PATTERNS

RAISED STITCH PATTERNS

MESH AND TRELLIS PATTERNS

CROSSED AND INTERLOCKING STITCHES, CABLES

RIPPLE AND CHEVRON PATTERNS

EDGINGS AND BORDERS

GRANNY SQUARES

ABOUT THE AUTHORS

Nele Braas studied graphic design and photography at the Folkwang University of the Arts in Essen, Germany. After graduating, she held editorial positions in the photography departments of different magazines, including many years at *GEO*. Later she worked as a freelance photographer in the areas of architecture, interior design, garden, and people for several lifestyle magazines. Crocheting and knitting, started in childhood, have fascinated her to this day. Her greatest pleasure has always been creating her own designs and implementing them into useful objects.

Eveline Hetty-Burkart works as freelance editor and author for magazine and book publishers. Her area of expertise includes a wide array of craft techniques, spanning from the initial design idea and creative implementation to pattern writing. Crochet is her favorite. She lives with her husband and son near Hamburg, Germany.